01 14

RADICAL
UNLEARNING

RADICAL
UNLEARNING

THE ART AND SCIENCE
OF CREATING
CHANGE FROM WITHIN

LEWIS RAVEN WALLACE

BEACON PRESS, BOSTON

BEACON PRESS
Boston, Massachusetts
www.beacon.org

Beacon Press books
are published under the auspices of
the Unitarian Universalist Association of Congregations.

28 27 26 25   8 7 6 5 4 3 2 1

This book is printed on acid-free paper that meets the uncoated paper
ANSI/NISO specifications for permanence as revised in 1992.

Text design and composition by Kim Arney

*Library of Congress Cataloguing-in-Publication
Data is available for this title.*
Hardcover ISBN: 978-0-8070-1488-2
E-book ISBN: 978-0-8070-1489-9
Audiobook: 978-0-8070-2226-9

The authorized representative in the EU for product safety and
compliance is Easy Access System Europe 16879218, Mustamäe tee 50,
10621 Tallinn, Estonia: http://beacon.org/eu-contact

This book is dedicated to my mother,
Raven McCrory, for teaching me how to think
and giving me the courage to keep unlearning,
even when it hurts. Her quiet and fierce love
and intellect are powerful forces.

CONTENTS

Introduction ix

CHAPTER 1   Desire Lines: The Science of Unlearning 1

CHAPTER 2   Love 19

Questions for People You Love 36

CHAPTER 3   Cognitive Dissonance 39

CHAPTER 4   Community 53

Writing out of Normalcy: An Unlearning Opener 69

CHAPTER 5   Confrontation 71

INTERLUDE: *On Stories and Unlearning* 88

*Retelling Our Own Stories: A Few Questions
for Reflection* 95

CHAPTER 6   Questions 97

Unlearning Interviews: A Template 112

CHAPTER 7   Somatics 115

INTERLUDE: *"Coming out of the Fog" and
Embodiment Through Drag* 134

CHAPTER 8   Practice 141

CHAPTER 9   Poetry and Surrealism 159

What Is It Like to Be a Boat? A Reverse Presentation 179

CHAPTER 10 Immersion 183

CHAPTER 11 Accessibility 197

INTERLUDE: *Children's Minds, Adults' Limits,
and Unlearning as a Disruptive Pivot*. 206

Questions for Ongoing Reflection 212

CONCLUSION Desire, Yearning, and the Unknown 213

Acknowledgments 221

Notes 225

INTRODUCTION

My grandmother Sarah was raised to believe that Black people were safe enough to clean her home, but not clean enough to share her shower. She believed that my grandfather would rule the house with his cool eyes and strong hands, that homosexuals were perverts, that sex was never to be spoken of, that gender was a natural, biological, and binary divide. She saw no wrong in Confederate monuments and no lie in the southern culture of forced hospitality that created her. Her father was a powerful lawyer who once stood on the floor of the South Carolina General Assembly condemning desegregation.

Sometime in the 1960s, Sarah began to change. Something pulled her away from how she was raised, a force akin to a sliver in her foot. This discomfort required her attention. She began to pick away and dig into the biases and fallacies of South Carolina's white culture, clinging to keen observation and faith as she struggled to unlearn the racism, sexism, and homophobia of her upbringing. She began the painful process of debunking the ideologies of oppression that surrounded her, like the idea that white people were biologically superior to or inherently safer than Black people, and that men were smarter than women, these long shadows of the nineteenth century. By the time I came along, in the 1980s, she was both deeply racist and deeply anti-racist in her beliefs and practices. She had participated in anti-racism work in her Episcopal church for many years and advocated for openly gay leadership. And, as with many wealthy white women in South Carolina, Black people worked for and tended to her, and all her life she saw the twisted power dynamics that made that so. She challenged these in some ways, but she never fully rejected them.

I visited her in her retirement community when she was ninety-six and I was thirty-three. She remained eagle-eyed and opaque. To me, she was a mystery, as I was to her. Sitting alert in her leather chair, she was heavy with doubt, squaring off against beliefs that separated her from her values but remained deeply internalized.

"I hate that you're a boy," she said, "and I hate that I hate it."

My grandmother was harsh, but she also wanted to love me as I was, not in spite of how I was, to love my tattoos and my ambiguous gender and the people I brought home. Did she "succeed" in that love? I know that she tried, as she took me in with glittering eyes and spoke honestly about what still challenged her.

When Sarah died after a long battle with her own strong will, my mother pried my grandmother's silver wedding ring from her finger and gave it to me—*me*, the one of the thirteen grandchildren least likely to get married and have children, the one who'd just been fired from his job in journalism, the one who was living out of a borrowed pickup truck and writing a book about historical rabble-rousers. The one whom my grandmother struggled to love, but maybe saw something of herself in—she had always been a struggler, in her own way. Clasping this emblem of familiar contradiction, I'm entering a journey to explore my grandmother's unfinished work in the world. She tried, but did not always succeed, at unlearning. In a time of ever-increasing political turmoil and a resurgence of the very kinds of bigotry Sarah worked to change in herself, I became fascinated with how we uproot deeply ingrained beliefs and ideologies and replace them with new ways of living in the world. I call this process "radical unlearning"—a reeducation that gets to the roots of what we believe, and why we recreate systems of dominance and harm.

"What would convince them?" people ask about their political opponents. "How can they be so immune to facts?"

In February 2017, I read an article by Elizabeth Kolbert, "Why Facts Don't Change Our Minds," which affirmed a suspicion I'd been carrying about the limits of reasoning with others. "Providing people with accurate information doesn't seem to help; they simply discount it," she wrote, citing three recent books on the topic.[1]

I'd worked in public radio journalism for years, and the operating unspoken theory in that environment was that accurate information in itself was a driver of social change. If we reported "just the facts," and we were objective and therefore trustworthy, people would absorb the information and reason out the right answers to big social questions, then show their beliefs, mainly through the ballot box. Good policy and good government would emerge naturally from the educated masses; democratic, pro-capitalist liberalism was the assumed positive outcome, though no one said that explicitly. But this "objective" system of information and governance had always excluded and harmed people, beginning with our country's foundations built on colonization and slavery. "Objective facts with just outcomes" is a story with a lot of holes in it.

Those holes got bigger and bigger during the time when I worked as a news reporter, from 2012 to 2020. The fabric of perceived consensus in the US and globally was unraveling. Not only were the most basic facts up for debate, but so were the most basic principles. In early 2017, I was fired from my job in public radio for arguing on my personal blog that objectivity was not the right frame for journalists to face down "alternative facts" and Trumpian logic—I believed that those who sought justice needed conviction and moral clarity on our side, too, and that journalism might benefit from more transparency about journalists' values and goals. But, among the centrist media establishment, people clung to the belief that information stewarded efficiently would lead to positive political and social outcomes. Trump's win in the 2016 presidential election had come as a massive surprise to these same thinkers. How could so many people ignore the facts, the liberal editors and reporters behind the stories pondered, and "vote against their own self-interest?"

I toured the country in 2017, talking about my critique of "objectivity" and the false frame of both-sidesism in journalism. At nearly every stop, someone would ask me, "But how do we talk to people who don't care about facts?" I had no easy answers, except that maybe we start by listening, by trying to understand rather than convince—at a minimum, I knew, we cannot condescend to someone and then expect them to listen to us. Even though I found it slightly arrogant, the sincerity and desperation of the question nagged at me. I looked for answers in my interviews with my grandmother, in my stories about trans people and our allies, in my reporting on conservative activism, and only found more ambiguity. I began to ask my audiences a question: When *you* have let go of a deeply held belief, what made that possible? Why did you do it? What made you change your own mind?

Belief, as it turns out, isn't made of rational, scientific stuff—even when we think our views are based solely in fact, emotion, connection, and community all play huge roles in determining humans' opinions. Additionally, self-interest isn't easy for an outsider to judge—who's to say what is in someone else's best interest? Our beliefs emerge from a murky zone of emotion and spirit, a zone that was poorly understood by the run-of-the-mill journalist in 2017. And beliefs are shaped in community, through culture; hammering angry, alienated people with fact-checks and scientific studies didn't even come close to creating the mass community-based movement needed to battle Trumpism and its itinerant conspiracy theories.

During the years of the first Trump administration, it occurred to me that journalism's entire theory of change was wrong. The smooth voices on National Public Radio were powerless against Trump's emotional rhetoric. He drizzled consistent, expert propaganda to the shrinking white majority, justifying the festering open wound of systemic racism by encouraging white folks to blame the victims. By the time my book critiquing "objectivity" came out in 2019, it was clear to more and more people that "just the facts" had not been enough. People were as trusting of bots as they were of journalists.

It was also clear that unlearning deeply internalized beliefs that are shared by a community and reinforced by propaganda requires conditions that aren't offered by newspaper articles and algorithmically curated social media feeds. Unlearning and looking at the root causes of systems is tough work—it can be liberating, but it can also be harrowing.

The research agrees: once an ideology or set of facts has set in and calcified, disruption is required before we can adopt new ways of seeing, and some of us will cling to our old ways even at our own peril.

So, what actually happens to us during those windows of possibility when our belief systems might be disrupted, when we might choose to change? Nobody unlearns without at some point making a choice. But I wanted to know what makes that choice settle into our bones. If facts don't change our minds, what does?

Some of the most thorough study of unlearning is in the fields of business management and corporate leadership. Discovering this was disconcerting: the capitalists have figured out that unlearning is a necessary skill to adapting to an ever-changing future, and they are studying and optimizing it as we speak, with the goal of increasing the profits and efficiencies of global workforces and developing leaders who evoke trust and commitment from their workers. They are also teaching artificial intelligence programs and robots to learn as we learn; I would not be surprised if unlearning is mastered by an algorithm before it is thoroughly studied in humans. Experts in business management want us to unlearn old technologies in order to be more efficient users of the new and unlearn old habits in order to be more productive in a changing world. Corporate and political leaders, for the most part, do not want us to unlearn racism, colonialism, or transphobia—unless these seismic shifts can in some way benefit them at the bank or the voting booth. They certainly do not want us to unlearn the internalized values that keep people operating as obedient workers and passive consumers.

But while corporate leaders work to perfect unlearning as a kind of mind control, activists and pontificators across the political spectrum often depict unlearning as nothing but a ghost—attacking one another for our beliefs rather than acting on the assumption that how we see the world can and does change. Many camps would have us believe that once someone has adopted a given viewpoint, the possibility of change is nil, and that believing in mind change is for fools and naifs. This is the unfortunate logic behind aspects of cancel culture on both the right and the left—but what if the assumption that people cannot change and do not unlearn is itself an instrument of oppression?

Unlearning with the goal of exploitation is better understood and possibly more widely pursued than unlearning with the goal of liberation. It disturbs me that corporations have such an apparent leg up over social change agents in understanding what motivates individuals to transform. But we should also be careful not to imitate corporate approaches to unlearning. The unlearning that is a counterpoint to capitalist, authoritarian, and totalitarian thought can't be about optimizing the perfect activist. First, there is no such thing, and second (and maybe even more important), *any* ideological frame can become a trap. The rethinking I am hungering for has to be about freeing ourselves and each other no matter the contradictions of our attempts.

I am a materialist thinker, and I believe in social change through action, often disruptive action. But I also know we can't have a revolution without changing minds—if how we think did not matter, it would surely not be such a focus for those who wish to exercise power over others. In order to fight fascism and racism and create just global societies, we must embrace unlearning as a collective practice available to all of us. We must be willing to be unsettled, and eager to help others rethink. We must pursue and make real the hope that transformative unlearning is possible. The stakes are as high as they've ever been, but so are the opportunities to learn and unlearn as global communication systems put many of us in constant contact with new information. We have the tools to unlearn, we have the words and texts and even the pedagogies, but we need to understand the conditions that will make it likely for this unlearning to take root and transform not just our thoughts but our habits, relationships, and actions.

When I tell my parents' friends, generally white liberals, that I am working on a book about unlearning, they almost invariably nod their heads in approval. Over wine or antipasti, or over the nose of a protective face mask, they say, "That's good. A lot of people need that."

The more interested among them begin to wax political: "Yes, we need these Trump people to unlearn! People are so disappointing. It's unbelievable, the ignorance. How can we teach them? What would get through to them?"

I had an enormous crush on my piano teacher Michelle growing up, because she had giant frizzy auburn hair like Ariel from *The Little Mermaid*, and skinny clever fingers, and she flew around the room like a trapped fly. She grabbed my hands and screamed, "Slow! Slow!" or "Don't arch your wrist," or she'd thrust my elbow into the air as I played, posturing me just so because she wanted excellence. I was nine or ten years old, and I loved Bach, Beethoven, and discipline. I admired and feared this woman for whom nothing seemed more important than reverence for the ways music was meant to be played.

I saw her after an almost thirty-year interval recently—I am gray but sprightly, and she is sprightlier still. I was back home for a weekend, and we walked to the car together in my mom's driveway after a strong hug.

"Are you writing! What are you writing! Tell me what you're working on!" Michelle said. I got that immediate shyness that I used to feel when she was my teacher and I was a gangly little girl with big ears.

"My book is about radical unlearning?" I began.

"Wow!" she exclaimed, looking right at me, her eyeballs huge and cartoonish behind her eyeglasses. "I wish I'd had more of that! We need that." She sighed and nodded, gesturing toward herself with exasperated humility. "It's harder at my age."

I remembered why I didn't just admire but adored Michelle: she was *intense*, and within that intensity lived a hunger to learn that rooted down into some emotional place, a gut place. I was so moved that she didn't assume that unlearning was a job for others but something she immediately recognized as a job for herself.

"I'm sorry I was such a tough piano teacher," she said, and I said, "Not at all."

It is Michelle's spirit of enthusiastic openness that I hope you will carry into this book. Not because I want to deny you your rigor, your expertise, your lived experience—but because the subject of this book is *not* how to persuade others, or to turn around someone else's ignorant views. It is about creating the conditions for unlearning within ourselves, and in our communities, in such a way that we both model and invite unlearning in others. This project does not have room for the condescension of assuming you already know more than someone and trying to make them unlearn as you think they should. It is about unlearning as a way of living, creating a culture of unlearning that is not fueled by arbitrary deference but by true curiosity. What might change in me, if the conditions were right? How might I create those same conditions for others?

The premise of this project is that it is possible to recognize and transform the ideologies we've been handed as children. My question is: What makes these changes likely? This is an invitation for you to ask the questions with me. What are you striving to unlearn? How will you do it? Who around you is unlearning? What created the conditions for them to do it?

A bit of framing about what radical unlearning is and is not: I understand *un*learning as a form of learning, of building new knowledge and skills that we can put to use in the world. But it is a form of learning that requires us to disrupt and go against the grain of what we have learned before, whether consciously or unconsciously. That disruption has an emotional quality to it—it can be wondrous or discomfiting, liberating or life-shattering, or sometimes all of these at once.

Radical unlearning happens when we begin to reach the roots of thought, belief, and action, when we see ourselves, either suddenly or over time, as vulnerable creatures whose ideological frames and tacit assumptions might be leading us to complicity in systems and worlds we don't want to build. While my grandmother's unlearning focused on her whiteness and anti-trans beliefs, unlearning is not only for and about people with privilege; I have observed again and again that radical unlearning is often most vigorously pursued by people who have a self-interest in breaking down systems of oppression, in stopping war and violence, in freeing themselves. It is not a prescribed pathway but a skill, a way of being critical and open and ever-changing in the name of liberation. One of my interviewees, kai lumumba barrow, redubbed radical unlearning as simply "self-determination."

Radical unlearning is "radical" because it seeks the roots of belief. It seeks to root out mental paradigms that are grounded in or reinforce systems of exploitation and harm in the world. Determining what these paradigms are, of course, is context-specific. For example, people might be deeply engaged in unlearning India's ancient system of caste, or unlearning binary gender, or unlearning Christian hegemony or the teachings of a particular sect that no longer serves them. Radical unlearning also recognizes that hegemony and socialization often show up inside us in subtle ways, in our silences and quick reactions, not just in our sweeping statements and political views. That means we can challenge big ideas like racism, but we might also be challenging internalized habits, like needing to be in control, or unlearning deep internal barriers like trauma responses. Over time, we might find that these are all intertwined. Radical unlearning serves as a counter to both corporate unlearning and to simple unlearning, the kind that might be hard but does not necessarily implicate power structures or lead us to try to transform our societies.

Radical unlearning is not persuasion. We might succeed occasionally at changing someone's mind on a discrete, single issue, but the belief that we can sleight-of-hand, nudge, or pressure people into deep and rigorous personal and ideological transformation is misguided (and there are plenty of other books to read about nudging, persuading, and convincing).[2] As interviewee Adrianne Black—a former white nationalist who became an anti-racist activist—said, when we try to persuade someone to change their mind about something they care about deeply, our first question should be, "Who am I to you?" What is the relationship, the connective tissue, the context in which we are hoping to create change together? Radical unlearning rejects the popular contemporary tomes on persuasion and decision-making that teach us how to trick or coax or even pressure people into believing us. Radical unlearning seeks instead a restoration of the conditions that we know can keep us open, mentally flexible, and loving enough to pursue self-determination for ourselves and others. I describe this as a restoration of conditions, because children are often intuitively skilled at mental self-determination, following their curiosity and desire wherever they lead. We all have the impulse to learn and change alive inside of us; radical unlearning appreciates and makes space for that impulse, which goes against the ways many children are educated today.

Unlearning is a skill that in itself can be taught, learned, practiced, and protected. Rather than orienting toward how we sway others to "right" beliefs, *Radical Unlearning* proposes thinking about how we create communities, organizations, and spaces that allow for curious dissection of tough questions and that encourage compassionate rethinking. We might be thinking about how we cultivate the conditions for unlearning in ourselves, and where that unlearning might translate into changes in our actions. We might be seeking out new information in areas where we have an inkling that we missed something, whether because we've been "called out" or challenged, or because our cognitive dissonance has become unbearable.

Please don't read this book because you hope for a gospel of unlearning, where I (or you!) are the presumed preacher and others are our flock. I start with the assumption that even the most sincere and informed moral and factual certainty deserves a periodic dress-down—my own certainties included. Know-it-all-ism is toxic to the culture of unlearning, as much as it is celebrated in many professional, social, and virtual/digital contexts.[3] Please continue with me if you're willing to succumb to the vulnerability of wondering what you don't know; what you've missed; what you may now believe that is false, misguided, or pointing your gut in the wrong direction. And, of course, please challenge me on what you feel I have missed, misused, or misunderstood.

Here are some of the questions I've been asking myself throughout this process:

What is radical unlearning?

Does it require definition, or can it simply be observed as a phenomenon, something people attest to experiencing?

What conditions make unlearning possible, likely, and desirable?

How is unlearning different from indoctrination and propaganda?

Is there such a thing as being endlessly open-minded, and is that even what we're going for?

How can I share vulnerably about my own unlearning in ways that open up conversation, without inadvertently universalizing my experience?

How much "proof" and "evidence" should I provide for my theories of unlearning versus letting them exist as collections of ideas, developed in community?

Is there a science of unlearning?

Is there an art of unlearning?

Can people unlearn who do not want to?

I seek answers from my own viewpoint and without the assumption that there's a panacea for the various ailments of narrowmindedness, including my own. My exploration is inherently personal and subjective, open to contradiction and unsureness. After all, I can only assume as I write that I have much more to unlearn than I will be able to accomplish in the process of writing. As my grandmother Sarah once said, "All white people are racist, because we were born into a racist society." Holding on to her silver wedding ring, my hope isn't to solve or fully answer any question, or to absolve myself of complicity in harmful systems that I continue to benefit from. I only hope to grow old still asking the vulnerable questions she asked on her deathbed, still striving to align my actions with my desire for a more liberated world.

The examples I'll explore here are not intended as a blueprint for what it means to "be radical"—radicalism demands that we constantly seek the root causes behind harm and exploitation, improve our skills at change and transformation, and take action in the world. That pathway from transformation to action reveals a paradox at the heart of radical unlearning: unlearning often requires melting the boundaries of perception, blurring lines, and releasing judgment about "right" and "wrong." But changing our belief systems to resist dominant ideology requires us to make choices and ultimately to take action, to become not just different thinkers but different people. Radicalism requires action and urgency while unlearning requires patience and openness—and often we see that paradox resolved in favor of one or the other, radical certainty and action without room for unlearning, or unlearning that happens internally without transforming our actions. How do we hold close both active choice and inner uncertainty? How do we surrender ego and identity, yet continue to struggle and work to change material conditions making use of our selves and our bodies?

Radical Unlearning is a collection of stories, theories, and studies across multiple disciplines: psychology, neurobiology, social science, and literary and social history all hold nuggets of wisdom for creating the conditions for deep changes of mind and habit. Neuroscience in the last few decades has been revolutionized with insights about the brain's ability to change, as has the study of somatics and embodied transformation, increasingly popular in social movements and very important to the journey of this book. With the help of new research and expertise and informed by ancient traditions, *Radical Unlearning* searches for echoes down the hallways of human minds, including my own and those of people around me. It is not a definitive study but a single journalist's path through a winding, but surprisingly cohesive, set of wisdoms.

On this path, I came across a number of conditions that can clearly support unlearning—conditions that make unlearning more likely to take place. After the first chapter about the science of neuroplasticity, each chapter focuses on a way of creating conditions for unlearning that arose in my research. I chose to focus on conditions we can cultivate and, to some extent, control—for example, many people have named crisis and emergencies as a potential condition for unlearning, but I am not proposing crises as a condition here because they are not something we want to cultivate in the world, per se. Drug trips were also mentioned at multiple points, but typically these are short-lived and they may prompt or accelerate unlearning but they don't guarantee it; I looked for conditions that can be cultivated in a somewhat ongoing and intentional way. Here I am proposing love, cognitive dissonance, community, confrontation, questions, somatics, practice, poetry and surrealism, immersion, and accessibility as ways to create the conditions for unlearning. Finally, my inquiries forced me to deal with desire, and the erotic unknown that often draws us into unlearning—this is the one condition explored in this book that I am not sure we can cultivate in the world, but I remain curious and open. None of these conditions are a silver bullet, and certainly there are more ways into unlearning than what I explore here, but I do believe all of them can help, especially when their powers are combined. In between the sections on conditions, you will find activities and conversations that supported and enriched my own unlearning along the way, and encouragement to practice having unlearning conversations in your own life. I hope this exploration will be useful to other activists, educators, organizers, writers, artists, faith leaders, journalists, therapists, healers, abolitionists, and anyone else trying to connect individual and collective transformation.

When I asked my grandmother Sarah what allowed her to transform after her childhood, her memories were blurry, nonsequential.

"I saw Bull Connor pointin' hoses at those children on the TV," she drawled, recalling the '60s, then the '50s, and then the '70s, when she joined a lunch club in her hometown of Columbia, where Black and white civic leaders dined together—a rare occurrence in her rigidly segregated upbringing. In 1996, after a lifetime of avoiding the thought of "homosexuals," Sarah sat me down at a restaurant and spit it out:

"Your mother tells me you're identifyin' as a bisexual" (but more like *a bah-sick-shuwul*). I was terrified.

"Yes? I am?" I said. She looked me in the eye, unflinching.

"Well, you know I'm gonna love you no matter what."

She was five feet tall, sharp, and tough-minded. Still, I mostly saw the tough side: Sarah (whom we always called Sarah) scared me as a child, and the whole world of South Carolina, of supper with the family silver, a parlor with a grandfather clock, loomed over me. I would show up on her front step and she'd open the door and exclaim upon seeing me, "Are you *tryin'* to look ugly?"

I took after my mother, Raven: I was a self-righteous teenager, and spent my twenties doing activism, fighting with my family about privilege and identity, queen of the "call-out." It wasn't until I became a journalist, a professional question-asker in my thirties, that I started to really see my grandmother. On visits to South Carolina, I interviewed her for hours about her life, her earliest memories and her personal transformations. My mom and my aunt and I sat with her in the parlor and talked to her about gender-neutral pronouns. I laughed through her scowls and resistance and then, minutes later, quietly glowed as she tried out calling me "they" for the first time.

"Surely God knew what she was doing when . . ." She trailed off, not seeming to notice that she had just called God by "she" pronouns. "I don't know. This is kind of painful talking about all this stuff. But I know that . . . it's right for you to be who you are." She was visibly uncomfortable, but she faced me, striving even near her death bed to cross the chasm between what she'd learned when she was young and what she could see now, embodied in her own soft-spoken, androgynous grandchild.

In the months before she died, in the ironically named Still Hopes retirement community (maybe they meant "still" as in continuing, but the still water of the duck ponds and the stillness of the muggy South Carolina air lent Still Hopes an eerie vibe), Sarah was still fighting. One day during that summer of 2017, she had such a heated debate about welfare with a man in the Still Hopes cafeteria that he threatened to stab her in the stomach—he thought it was a handout, she thought that was malarkey.

Later that year, my brother joked while giving her eulogy: "Sarah loved everyone, except Clemson grads and Republicans." The white-haired room, easily one-third Clemson grads and Republicans, gave off a muffled cackle of recognition of the loving, judgmental woman she had been.

After she was gone, Sarah's silver ring, dangling from a chain against my heart, became a symbol of a path I hope to walk: the path of holding on and letting go at the same time, of embracing contradiction with practiced faith. It's a faith that allows me to unlearn, to make mistakes, and to continue to ask questions, that allows me to be tough as I face my own inner paradoxes, asking more of myself while accepting that I'm only human. I expect incompletion.

My grandmother died still doing battle with herself.

"I don't under*stand* poetry," she once said to me, with her signature scowl. But she adored what poetry attempted: that embrace of ambiguity. In her hospital bed, she dreamed she was preaching, giving a sermon, but couldn't remember those clear wisdoms when she awoke. That was one of the only times I saw Sarah with her silver hair down, looking vulnerable, trying to remember what she'd preached. She shook her head and mumbled to me: "We do not have adequate language to cover everything we need to say."

AUTHOR'S NOTE

I come from a community of unlearners. Trans people of my generation, as a tiny minority, have spent a lot of time unlearning our own assumptions about gender and the body, explaining ourselves, and disabusing others of assumptions about us. It's a challenge that has toughened me and made me interested in how we can all be tougher—not in the sense of holding hard to our beliefs, but in the sense of being confident enough to question them. I have sought my own unlearning in anti-racism workshops and prisoner-letter-writing groups and an endless study of history, media, and folklore. Most importantly, I have sought it through relating, talking to people whose experiences are close and far from mine and attempting to understand and be understood.

Radical unlearning in the sense that I explore in this book has roots in the popular education practices of Paulo Freire's *Pedagogy of the*

Oppressed, Augusto Boal's Theater of the Oppressed, and liberation movements globally. It also has roots in Indigenous thought systems and restorative and transformative justice practices as taught to me by my friend and mentor Mariame Kaba and Project Nia, in academic decolonial studies like the work of Gayatri Spivak and Edward Said, in anti-racist popular education like that of the Anne Braden Anti-Racist Organizer Training Program and the Catalyst Project (and its predecessor, the Challenging White Supremacy Workshop, where I was first trained as an organizer), and in Black feminist radical thought from Kimberlé Crenshaw and Angela Davis to bell hooks, Robin D. G. Kelley, adrienne maree brown, and Autumn Brown, a beloved friend who has directly shaped my own unlearning in many ways.

My unlearning is also rooted in the trans liberation movements that have always used popular education and grassroots communication to build community and collectively change minds, honoring traditions of trans movement leaders like Leslie Feinberg, Riki Anne Wilkins, Julia Serrano, Janetta Johnson, Miss Major, and Sandy Stone. I have radically unlearned for two decades alongside trans movement artist Micah Bazant; artist-educators Jesa Rae, Billy Dee, and Gabrielle Civil; and equine healing facilitator Janada Halbisen-Gibbs. I've spent much of the last decade learning from and with a quiet, remarkable leader in popular education, Mia Henry, a former director of the Chicago Freedom School who helps people unlearn in part by teaching social justice and civil rights history. My more recent unlearning is in deep conversation with abolitionist artists Catherine Edgerton, Kai Lumumba Barrow, and Jazz Franklin of Gallery of the Streets; activist media-makers including Roxana Bendezù, Steven Thrasher, Rae Garringer, Danielle Purifoy, and Tina Vasquez; and a creative collective called the Durham SeaRealists. Finally, radical unlearning is practiced by fiction writers and poets all the time—some of my teachers have been Octavia Butler, Ursula K. LeGuin, Joy Harjo, Leslie Marmon Silko, Louise Erdrich, N. K. Jemisin, Muriel Rukeyser, James Baldwin, and Alexis Pauline Gumbs.

In this text, I have chosen to tell the stories of people I am in relationship with. As you'll notice, many of the conversations for this book took place in person in North Carolina, where I live. Some also took place during a trip to Brazil with a group of fellows associated with the Ford Global Fellowship, which I joined in 2021, focused on challenging the root causes of inequality. Where I didn't know someone already, exploring unlearning with them meant that we entered into a warm intellectual relationship; the people who started as strangers or acquaintances became involved in my inquiry as I asked them questions and invited them to ask questions of me. I started with relationships because I wanted to unlearn the ideology of "expertise" in which I've been steeped in my own education—seeking, instead of academic or formal experts, the expertise of lived experience, in this case often combined with expertise gained through activism and advocacy. I also wanted to demonstrate that unlearning is an everyday act, something that people do all the time who are not specialists or exceptions. Finally, I have been on a journey for years now of unlearning the "objective" framework of journalism in which I was trained. Focusing my research on the subjective journey of inquiry, and being transparent about the process, felt like a step in embodying that change. The process of receiving feedback on what I wrote about others, and seeking their consent to publish their stories and ideas, was humbling and radicalizing.

Much of my thinking about this relationship-based approach has been inspired by reading about Indigenous research and Indigenous knowledges from Shawn Wilson, Leanne Betasamosake Simpson, and Linda Tuhiwai Smith. As Wilson writes in *Research as Ceremony: Indigenous Research Methods*, "Knowledge cannot be owned or discovered but is merely a set of relationships that may be given a visible form."[4] I recognize that their work tending the fires of resistance to the colonial cult of individualism is what makes this work possible, and I do not take lightly the ways that dominant knowledge systems have silenced and excluded Indigenous thinkers specifically. I am not Indigenous, and in the process of trying to unlearn the ideas I've internalized from dominant US culture about knowledge and ownership, I risk being treated as an overnight "expert" where I am just a learner with a platform. My own unlearning demands that I undermine these colonial ideals of expertise and mastery and also challenge the ongoing occupation of Indigenous lands here and elsewhere. As Simpson explains in depth in her beautiful book, *As We Have Always Done,* Indigenous knowledge for her people, the Anishnaabeg, is inherently and relationally tied to their lands, the lands where I was born and raised around the Great Lakes.[5] I am in debt, both literal and figurative, to these lands and peoples and the ideas they have cogenerated, and humbly aware that these ideas were not generated for me.

Two and a half decades as a transgender activist focused on anti-racism and abolition has me surrounded by people who practice unlearning to the ends of social transformation, mostly because our lives have necessitated it, but also because our communities have cultivated these skills. In choosing to focus on relationship-based research and interviews, I found that my world is rich with people practicing unlearning in their lives, from my late grandmother Sarah McCrory and my mother, Raven McCrory, unlearning transphobia; to my once-editor Adrienne Johnson Martin on unlearning through love; to my friend Gabriel Wer unlearning homophobia and becoming an anti-corruption activist in his home country of Guatemala whose story appears in the chapter on community; to Tashiena Combs-Holbrook unlearning from inside prison walls in Michigan and calling to tell me about it.

When I did reach out to strangers, it was in part to fill gaps in the kinds of unlearning or diversity of experience I saw around me. For example, some people's unlearning comes at a higher social and personal cost than others—both Adrianne Black and Micha Kurz were people that I reached out to because their journey was documented publicly and had cost them family, identity, and sense of place. Their stories— Adrianne of leaving the white nationalist movement in the US, Micha of turning away from the Israeli occupation of Palestine after serving in the Israeli army—were more "extreme" than most of the ones that my family and friends told me, and their wisdom about the conditions that make radical unlearning possible was deep and wide in part because of how much they had personally sacrificed. Adrianne inspired me to focus on community, while Micha inspired me about the importance of discomfort and cognitive dissonance. Additionally, some seemingly key conditions of unlearning simply didn't come up from the people in my circles, which is how I came to Cherokee writer Daniel Heath Justice, whose interview on stories and unlearning is an interlude in the book; Down Home North Carolina's Bonnie Dobson on questions and deep canvassing; and Liberation Spring's Anjali Nath Upadhyay on accessibility. Community leader Denise Perry of Black Organizing for Leadership and Dignity taught me about unlearning perfectionism and about somatic "practice," which shaped a whole chapter of the book. Roxy Manning, author of *How to Have Antiracist Conversations*, generously shared a story on practice that also became part of that chapter.

Every person is an expert on their own life, but I also sought out the additional expertise that arises from specific forms of experience, study, and practice. I wanted to talk to people who knew enough about unlearning that they could analyze their own, so that I wouldn't end up in the potentially awkward and unethical position of applying my analysis of unlearning to them after the fact, psychoanalyzing or projecting onto their stories. I strove to let people explain their reasons for unlearning in their own words and theorize with me about the conditions that made it possible. The result is a document of my subjective journey through unlearning, populated by remarkable and inspiring people who have fully consented to the process of sharing their story and contributed to the arguments I make.

These interviews asked a lot from the interviewees, and one way in which the voices in the book are not at all diverse is that every single person featured is someone who was willing to vulnerably explore their own reasons for changing, in addition to sharing their story of change. Somatic practitioners Yashna Padamsee and Eliana Rubin show up as both expert somatic coaches and personal friends and storytellers; art curator and magic-maker Chantal Wong and theater artist Hashem Adnan share their expertise on immersive practices and their own international and internal journeys; Lebanese LGBTQ advocate and conflict transformer Tarek Zeidan brings key expertise to the question of generative confrontation; Kai Barrow and Catherine Edgerton are living archives of surrealism and collage as portals to unlearning. My close friends Tori Grace Nichols and Jesa Rae Richards both accompanied me on the journey; their words appear as interludes that could not be contained by a particular category or condition. Finally, in between several of the chapters you will find interview questions, writing exercises, and a curriculum for an unlearning workshop I call a "reverse presentation"—a presentation that begins with the Q&A and asks participants to imagine a world without the things they are trying to unlearn.

As uneasy as unlearning can be, I experience a sharp edge of pleasure in knowing how many people truly want to change. Like my grandmother, we don't want to be as we were, because we don't want the next generation to suffer our foolishness, or because we have identified dominant knowledge as a source of ongoing psychic or physical pain and premature death—our own and other people's. We want to be free, to know a future without all this gunk currently clogging up our minds and interrupting our attempts at liberatory relationships. Unlearning belongs to us, the people who crave belonging, curiosity, and a path away from dystopias, present and future.

I want unlearning to be a cultural value, and a skill that we can embrace, embody, and lead. Throughout this book, you will find a few guided activities and conversations that you can bring into your own life or community to explore. I also encourage you to open yourself up to the questions that arise in you. When have you changed your own mind? What made that possible for you? What can *you* build that will make unlearning more likely within and around you?

RADICAL
UNLEARNING

CHAPTER 1

DESIRE LINES

The Science of Unlearning

Y ou're standing at the street corner, its sidewalks chipped and tattered, looking across an empty lot which is just a square of crabgrass. The grass is dark with early fall, ready to brown and regenerate. You are faced with a choice: walk along this sidewalk, turn right at the next corner, and continue down the paved walkway. Or you could walk across the empty lot, cutting a diagonal toward your destination. Your choice is made easier by a simple fact: every day for months you have walked this way, and probably others have, too, and now slicing diagonally across the dusty green grass is a stark brown pathway to the next corner. Every day you choose this shortcut across the grass, and every day you wear a slightly deeper rut into the path before making your way down the walk. You will go the same way today that you did yesterday.

Urban planners call these "desire lines," or "desire paths." I first learned about them in Detroit, where the preponderance of empty lots and the large numbers of people who walk to get places means the city has its own, human-made map—a cartography that shows where people *actually* go and want to go, often very different from the official map of streets and pedestrian crossings. The more people walk along a desire line, the more other people do, too. Well-worn pathways are made this way, so much so that they show up clearly in aerial photographs of the city. Urban planners and landscape architects are interested in desire lines because they show how people move given the choice, in reality. As a lifelong walker of footpaths, I have seen desire lines that take you up a slope and over the train tracks, a better way through brambles, or around a fallen tree. As a teenager I created desire lines across my hometown, pathways to the places we would go away from school bells and parents.

These unofficial pathways are a good metaphor for the events that take place in our minds as we learn and unlearn. Forming a track across a field of green requires revisiting the same path over and over, and the more we walk a given path, the easier it becomes to return to. Our minds are like this, deepening desire lines.

Unlearning might be thought of as carving out a new desire line, abandoning the paved sidewalks and modern grids of oppressive teachings and learnings. It is a form of learning, but learning that requires us to redirect old patterns—to recognize that we have been following a rigid pathway and choose another way. It's learning against the grain of dominant ideology and paradigms, learning to recognize and follow pathways that reflect where we want to go rather than what we've been told or pressured into, or what we have absorbed by osmosis. As this chapter will explain, the architecture of the brain is a series of connections between neurons, and the routes our brains use to make those connections are shaped by the society around us. The ideas we absorb and the environments we participate in forge our neural pathways. Dominant ideas and ideologies—the ones we intake the most, both explicitly and implicitly—turn into the paved walkways that our brains find easiest or most automatic to traverse. Unlearning is a disruption that relies on our inherent neuroplasticity and on recognizing the desire to walk a new path.

It also might be thought of as a return to playfulness, to the possibilities of the mind in childhood. We create millions of intuitive pathways in the first few years of life, maps that allow us to speak, to move, and to process the world—and our minds are open to a great many ways of being, our ruts and paved walkways are not yet deep or wide. We also leave behind literally billions of open fields, paths untaken, different ways we could have thought, spoken, and learned. You can see this in the eyes of young children: anything is possible, and every input matters. Through play and school and language and immersion in the culture and physical environments around us, we begin to follow the pathways most practical for thriving in our immediate world, often following the sidewalks of hegemony and dominant culture. Unlearning is the form of learning that emerges when we realize some of those pathways we have learned aren't serving us anymore.

The dominant learnings that this book tries to help us unlearn might be thought of as sidewalks—the city grid—the hegemonic narratives, familiar inheritances, and unchecked habits that we're not sure if we learned out of desire or out of obligation. The high level of flexibility and plasticity in our brains when we are young children and adolescents paradoxically means that the neural pathways that form in that stage can become very ingrained, particularly the implicit forms of knowledge and memory that form the backdrop of *how* we think and react.

All unlearning is a kind of learning—but some learning is more rigid and easier to default to, or more rigidly required by our surroundings. The people and structures around us have invested so much time and energy in paving those pathways, or sometimes even fenced off the spaces in between. So unlearning might require going a new way, but first it requires noticing that a new way is possible—as my friend and education expert Jesa Rae Richards says, "Unlearning is learning with a disruptive pivot." It can be terrifying and intimidating or pleasurable and exciting, or all of the above. And it might require a machete to chop our way through the tangled brush between us and where we truly want to go.

In order to become the person that I am, I had to unlearn binary gender. This colossal unlearning started when I was a teenager, in the late 1990s, and the mood I remember was self-righteous and solitary, hours in an upstairs bedroom suffering from insomnia and hating my body. But the reality—or at least what I wrote down and have since pieced together—is that I was surrounded by people, influences, and opportunities to ask questions. I remember the scenes with my mother: her in the kitchen, tense and asking me where I am going with this "transgender" thing.

My anger and storming back up to my room. My parents fighting about my freedoms downstairs, surrounded by wood walls and built-in book-shelves, floor-to-ceiling windows through which the pair of them would bond over bird-watching. My mom, Raven, a Southern debutante who'd left her hometown to become a teacher and engineer, cried when she once got to shake Bill Clinton's hand. My dad, Bruce, a lanky nerd from the Rust Belt suburbs, drove a pickup truck and had a cabin upstate where he fished and drank Bloody Marys on weekends. They were a professor and a lawyer raising us up in a lush green college town in southeast Michigan, on the path of the intellectually elite and upwardly mobile.

I hid in my angular pale blue bedroom as a wide apple tree watched me from two windows through the seasons. The room was strewn with letters, acrylic paints, collections of rocks and trinkets, scrap cloth and magazine cutouts dangling from the walls, beaded curtains, stacks of journals. I wrote volumes and volumes of words as a teenager, and I went back in search of evidence of how I became myself, how I unlearned gender. I was raised as a girl by a strong second-wave feminist—Raven was a Smith College graduate who let me forgo shaving my legs and armpits and discouraged me from Barbie dolls and Britney Spears. But even with that flexibility, I remember feeling trapped, lying awake, calling my friends on the landline. I had a cutout of skinny white '90s model Kate Moss on my wall for years, which my mom disapproved of. But what if I wanted to *do* Kate Moss, not be her?

The summer I was sixteen, I had a job as a host at a popular down-town brunch place. I learned to smile and look around and overestimate the wait. "It'll be an hour," I told rich Ann Arborites through my shaggy blue hair and acne, wearing colorful skirts. That same summer, I wan-dered home through downtown every day after work, dropping in on my friends at their jobs selling falafel or espresso drinks, sitting outside with other young punks who would play guitars and card games.

I'd gotten off work one summer Saturday and was meandering home on my bike when I saw a girl with a guitar giving a show at the corner of Liberty and Washington streets. There were wide brick steps up to an old bank there, and a few people stopped on the steps to listen. I stopped, too, tired from serving a stream of angry yuppies since 8 a.m. But I stayed, captivated, not by the music, but by another person a few steps down: five foot three, thick and stocky, masculine, with clean-cut sandy hair and angular nerdy glasses. I drew a picture of them in purple marker in my journal, and we made eye contact, briefly. I got back on my bike and sped off to the wood-paneled garden paradise where I'd been sheltered throughout my childhood, where my parents were midway through a ten-year standoff with one another, and I had lots of room to grow on my own.

That summer I saw Jason, the sandy-blond butch, everywhere. And it turned out that Jason would be the first trans person I would actually meet. He was a grad student in geology, a twenty-three-year-old with dad humor ("Geology rocks!") and seemingly seasoned life experience. He partied at goth clubs on the weekends and had a best friend with a zillion piercings and a split tongue like a snake. Jason and I fell in together; it was easy, as he liked attention and I liked giving it, and I wanted to be him, or to fuck him, and even though he was seven years older and I was a high school junior he managed to charm my parents and got along great with my friends. We cavorted around town together on his green tandem bike, joking and talking shit, and he taught me about class ("I didn't come up with parents who were gonna pay my way to college and cover my rent. I haven't had jack shit given to me," he'd say pointedly), and he taught me that there was such a thing as trans fags. He liked dudes—a revelation. I liked dudes, too, but not in a straight way.

The crush lasted for years. What he taught me that summer and fall was that I wanted to have sex with trans guys, and that this was possible. I had assumed I had to be a dyke because I'd started dating girls when I was twelve. But watching him butch out and then go limp-wristed, listening to him describe in great detail the big men and pretty boys he fucked, I got to thinking I could do the same. It became a mission, to get close enough to one of those young-looking trans boys I suddenly knew existed, to crawl into their skin.

There was not one moment that I realized or knew I was trans. I hardly knew what "trans" was when the question arose in me about whether I fit with the gender I'd been given. Whether that questioning was "innate" or whether it came to me through desire, context, and choice, I will never know for sure.

How would I draw, depict, give shape to the process of unlearning binary gender and coming into my transness? Being a girl was not a bad fit for me. I was a tomboy, a smart girl. I got called a "bitch" for the first time when I was nine. I had girl best friends who I adored with a singular focus, doted on and pretended to marry. Boys ignored me because I was ugly and tall, or because I was always up in a tree writing poetry. I hit puberty and couldn't bring myself to care about push-up bras or having a body, and so I hid in baggy punk clothes, or did it up in purple lipstick and cheetah pattern dresses, platform boots like a drag queen. Ears still pierced, hair still short, looking like Tank Girl with teenage zits.

Years went by. I always had crushes, constant crushes. I would later learn a phrase, BUFU (Be you? Fuck you?) that was how I felt about every gender-nonconforming person I met. I obsessed over femme men and butch women. To be with one or become one—I would take whatever I could get.

In the fall of the year I met Jason, I went to Chicago on a scholarship to attend the national conference of GLSEN, the Gay Lesbian Straight Education Network, with the permission of my strange and remarkable parents. They had no idea what they were getting into, but they allowed me to explore a world they themselves knew almost nothing about.

The conference was crawling with sharp, angry queer kids. People asked me my pronouns, and I think it was then that I first tried on something that wasn't "she." I attended workshops about transgender and intersex people, sat through nighttime hotel room conversations about race and power, and met a small cadre of kids from Oakland who called themselves "genderqueer." I was embarrassed and thrilled and drew pictures in my journal, pen drawings of me in my little fedora and suspenders, eyes wide. Suddenly, without much ado, I was one of them. I quipped in my notebook about how activists like to talk about "space" and referred to speaking as "taking up space." But, on a more serious note, I wrote, I'm going to come home and tell everyone about "safe space." And about "genderqueer."

Within months, my friends Billy, Blue, and I had all changed our names and pronouns, to our parents' confusion, and my parents had me going to see some kind of gender specialist therapist, the details of which I've completely blocked out. Our whole little crew ran youth groups at the local teen center, where queer kids would come from the exurbs and small towns, escaping violence and abuse for snippets of light and laughter as we sat on couches and talked about our lives, with no adults listening in.

I was facing a previously unseen desire line: Gender was still a binary all around me. No one had heard of "genderqueer." But I was free, we were free. My journals from that time are a litany of new relationships, trips to the Fleetwood Diner to write, full nights talking to my friends, with the occasional mention of finishing up high school and making decisions about what was next. I was derisive of my upper-middle-class family and their attachments to capitalism, but I was also loving and loved—I had safety, nurture, and education, all the things I assume a person would want in order to become themself. I never had a doubt in my mind that my family would support me.

Something propelled me that seemed to begin and end somewhere outside of my environment. Describing my own new style of dress and self-presentation, and how much better I was beginning to feel, I wrote, "I have never seen someone like me." And this was true; I hadn't. I had Jason as a primary influence—but he was a trans man, where I have never identified as a man or tried to be one. And I had the kids from the GLSEN conference, who gave me the word "genderqueer" and went back to Oakland. My friends and I scrounged up zines, including zines by trans luminaries Micah Bazant and Dean Spade. Kate Bornstein's *My Gender Workbook* made its way into our hands, and we facilitated workshops about gender with the Gay Straight Alliance.

But there were no existing desire lines to follow that I could see. Jason was on hormones, headed toward surgeries, and strongly "man" identified. I was something else, and I didn't really have any examples of what I was trying to become—there were no models, no media representations, no distant mentions of a family member, no TV characters. In the '90s, Brandon Teena had been raped and murdered and depicted terribly, both in the news and in the film *Boys Don't Cry*, and when I told my mom I was trans, her first thought was that this could happen to me. She was so scared.

On November 8, 2000, I scribbled in my journal: "Maybe what I just can't seem to get is how I can be true, be this, live in my realness, and also exist in reality. My reality tells me there's no space. Not in my body, not in my family, not in my brain, not in my life, and what if my real is sliding away now, right now?"

I was experiencing the body as a trap. "Which body, what to love?" I wrote next to chicken scratch self-portraits, my face and torso disconnected from one another. I wanted to escape, and much later I would discover that I could escape without leaving, that the body could be a home. But before I could settle into that, I experienced years of constant strain, a constant desire to get out, without knowing exactly what I was escaping. I wrote about dark matter, the "missing matter" that scientists were looking for, and said with confidence, "I know what it is."

I had accessed some space in between the galaxies, within my body and my spirit which was still so free at sixteen, and I knew it was the antimatter the scientists were looking for and trying to explain through years of study. I could *feel* it. My gender was much the same way. Even if it couldn't be observed or described, I could *feel* it.

"I feel so unrealistic, like I'm imaginary," I wrote. And I imagined what I might become, dressed up in boy clothes, bound my breasts even though I'd barely heard of that. Later I learned words like "faggy" and "nelly" and "fey" from friends and reading zines. But in those early years, it was just a wordless series of motions, loss of identity with nothing clear to replace it. I processed it through frantic writing that focused on outer space, other people, elsewhere. Anything but how it felt to have taken shape in a pale, soft, female body in the 1990s in southeast Michigan. Anything but girlhood.

In this story, I see traces of all the ways I've begun to understand unlearning through study: there is love, community, poetry, and immersion. There is also youth—our powers to change and adapt at age sixteen are often stronger than they are at thirty-five. And there is desire, straining against hegemonic beliefs because of some ineffable sense that what I

truly want is over there, that person on the street whose body is magnetic to me, those people at the conference who have words I want to
live inside of. I never felt right on the paved pathways of binary gender,
and desire propelled me toward a new path.

The human mind, for neuroscientists, is more like the ocean than it is
like an aerial map of a city landscape: they've got a vague image of its
regions, but most of its depths remain unknown. Therefore, theories of
the mind should be taken as just that—theories that describe and explain the experimental results and observations neuroscience has made
thus far. Neuroscientists can now look at what lights up in the brain
in response to certain stimuli, study neurological changes following
brain damage, and theorize how learning occurs based on increasingly
complex brain imaging technology and controlled studies.[1] While much
of what they "see" is still shrouded in mystery, recent changes in the
study of the brain have brought Western science closer to a science of
unlearning—after hundreds of years of relative darkness.

Less than a hundred years ago, academia in the US and Europe was
confident in the idea of a bounded brain—that after childhood, the
brain is set in its ways. The belief was that we grow a bunch of cells
in the earliest years of life, get those big Homo sapiens brains into our
adult skulls, and then lock 'em in and make use of them until our cells
eventually "die off" with age.[2] Much of the thinking that accompanied
this was also racist: many scientists in the European tradition believed
in measuring the size of adult brains as a reflection of intelligence, and
argued for race-based differences in brain size (a now-defunct field called
phrenology). A finite and racialized brain was expected, and that is what
the phrenologists "found" in their studies—which were later thoroughly
debunked. Still, the mythology of finite human brains persisted—I grew
up in the 1980s and '90s in a haze of beliefs about dead brain cells and
the dangers of drug use: *This is your brain*, the TV man droned over
a picture of an egg between two white fingers. *This is your brain on
drugs*, he said, and the egg was cracked into a frying pan and sputtered.
Even in the early '90s, the model of the adult brain was still that of the

unbroken egg, in line with many of the cultural binaries of the Western twentieth century—people were smart or dumb, good or bad. Brains were big or small, broken or whole.[3]

In the new millennium, the stubborn assumption that adult minds can't change has been upturned by developments in neuroscience. Scientists in this tradition now acknowledge neuroplasticity, or the idea that the brain changes over time in both structure and function, and that the brain can change with specific kinds of training and inputs.

"Far from being fixed," writes Moheb Costandi in his 2016 primer on neuroplasticity, "the brain is a highly dynamic structure, which undergoes significant change not only as it develops but also throughout the entire lifespan."[4] Neuroplasticity encompasses all of the processes that change our brains' structures, allowing us to respond to our environments, adapt to new constraints or stimuli, and learn and unlearn throughout life. The neuroplastic brain is capable of creating new connections, eliminating old ways of thinking, replacing "broken" functions with similar functions carried out by another part of the mind, and growing whole new brain cells in certain areas.[5] Our brains remap themselves, at a physical level that has relatively recently become measurable through new technologies in microscopy and brain scanning.

Neuroplasticity describes the fundamental malleability and changeability of brain functions—not just our ability to learn new tasks or process new information (although that is a part of it), but our ability to rearrange the circuitry guiding certain activities and reactions in our minds. Of course, these Western academic traditions of biological and medical science are just a series of ever-changing theories, and frequently these theories come full circle and collide with theories of health and medicine that have existed in other parts of the globe for thousands of years. Whole-body healing, somatics, meditation, yoga, and therapies involving pressure points, touch, ritual, and light: all of these work with human neuroplasticity and the ability to train and retrain our minds. So in that sense, neuroplasticity is not a "discovery" at all, just a different way into something people have known about for millennia.

A few brain basics can help us get a picture of the mechanics: neuro-science now understands the brain as an interconnected web of nerves that extends throughout the entire body. The part of the mind that lives in our skull and brain stem is where the most of these cells, our neurons, live and grow, but the network extends everywhere that has a nerve ending, down to the tips of our toes. Each neuron has inputs and outputs capable of carrying electrical impulses from one neuron to the next; the spaces in between the neurons, through which these impulses pass, are called "synapses."[6] When a neuron receives enough excitatory signals, it sends its own signal through the outputs to transmit through the synapse.[7] The chemicals that carry these transmissions are called "neurotransmitters," and the whole system of connections is often referred to as our brain's "wiring." These messages shoot off constantly, both voluntarily and involuntarily, and with each use of a certain set of connections, the synapses strengthen.

"When we say that neurons 'rewire' themselves, we mean that alter-ations occur at the synapse, strengthening and increasing, or weakening and decreasing, the number of connections between the neurons," explains neuroscientist Norman Doidge in his book on neuroplasticity, *The Brain That Changes Itself.*[8] But this plasticity is competitive; one habit, skill, or way of thinking competes with another to use the same limited circuitry connecting our minds to our actions. This is why unlearning "bad" habits can be harder than simply learning new ideas or facts, before a habit has been formed in that area of our brain circuitry. "It's best to get it right early, before the 'bad habit' gets a competitive advantage," Doidge says.[9]

Over time, our base of learned knowledge and memories becomes an extremely complex network comprising literally billions of neurons and around a quadrillion potential synapses—the equivalent of ten thousand times the number of stars in the Milky Way.[10] Every time we think, feel, or do anything, some series of connections lights up across the network in milliseconds. The brain maps (and remaps) itself according to which functions are most closely related. "Since the thumb and index finger often touch at almost the same time, sending their signals to the brain almost simultaneously, the thumb map and the index finger map tend to form close together in the brain," Doidge explains by way of example.[11]

It is at the junctions, the synapses, where learning and thus unlearning occur: we are capable of "rewiring" our brains, creating stronger
connections at the synapses or weakening and even eliminating those
connections through neglect, in addition to having the capability of
growing new neurons altogether in certain parts of the brain.[12]

How we learn and retain knowledge, conscious or otherwise, is also
intricately linked to memory. We might understand remembering, in its
simplest form, as the ability to return to neural connections we've made
in the past. Explicit memories are the kinds of memories we are aware
that we have—the knowledge base we use when we fill out a crossword
puzzle or take a multiple-choice test.[13] Our networks of neurons and synapses created by use and repetition return us to these explicit memories,
and the network system is the reason why we can feel like we "know"
something, but we can't remember it; maybe the pathway through our
neurons has not been used often enough to fire off automatically, or
the pathway has gotten muddled up on its way and landed us at some
other factoid stored nearby. This is why an elder might call you by your
sister's or mother's name, for example, or why you might feel like you
"know" that word in French but can only remember a different word
for a related thing.

Implicit memory, on the other hand, is all the things we know without
knowing *how* we know them, and therefore the hardest kind of knowledge to unlearn. Implicit memory is prominent in the human ability to
learn languages, particularly complex underlying syntax and grammar
structures—as a native English speaker, I know these structures without
being conscious of them, just as I know how to walk and play music. I
"know" English, but I couldn't explain it to you (unless I revisited my
linguistics notes from college), nor could I list off all its rules, vocabulary,
and grammar. Implicit memories arise as skills, muscle memory, ideological framing, and sometimes also as emotional triggers, as when a smell or
a look on someone's face sends us spinning off into uncontrolled emotion
not directly tied to the moment. Implicit memory is responsible for large
parts of communication, for how we love, and for many of our emotional
reactions and deepest convictions; it also encompasses countless cultural
assumptions and understandings of signs and symbols.[14]

Much of what we internalize from the dominant ideologies of our surroundings sets in as implicit memory. This phenomenon has been studied extensively in the form of unconscious bias, which triggers re-actions of racism and sexism that are seemingly out of our conscious control, as well as in the form of trauma response, especially complex trauma caused over the long term, which triggers fear and fight-or-flight responses that can circumvent conscious, rational thought long after the trauma has ceased. Language learning and much of the learning we do in school teaches us a particular worldview that becomes ingrained as a series of feelings and assumptions beyond conscious thought. These pathways paved into our minds from living and surviving within harmful social structures can be hard to see, because they are so ingrained—they simply seem like the natural, or normal, or safe way to go, even when they are hurting us or making our lives, or other people's, unnecessarily hard.

The good news is, neuroplasticity affirms that both explicit and implicit forms of knowledge can be changed—implicit learnings are more likely changed not through conscious thought and memorization, but through experience and practice, as when we relearn a physical capability through physical therapy after a stroke, or learn to play a new instrument by repetition. It is this subtle undercurrent of change, and the ability to tap into such change, that is the neurological fabric of unlearning. Unlearning is complex neuroplasticity in action.[15]

Over time, some of our neural connections will strengthen with re-peated use and stimulation, while others will weaken or combine with existing connections—as neuroscientists like to say, "Neurons that fire together, wire together."[16] Our brain maps enlarge in areas that we use or train extensively, and then hone back down to the most efficient use of neurons as we improve and become accustomed to that skill or activity. Individual neurons also become more precise and fine-tuned in response to training, and neurons can be trained to fire faster.[17]

The strengthening process is helped along by neurotransmitters, those chemicals that "excite" or "inhibit" certain kinds of connections or modulate the effects of other neurotransmitters.[18] Serotonin is one of the better-known inhibitory neurotransmitters, helping to regulate everything from mood and sleep to sexuality and appetite. Dopamine is another much-discussed neurotransmitter that controls our body's "reward system," making certain kinds of neural connections feel delightful and helping to regulate attention and learning (sometimes to a detriment, as in the example of social media use, which provides small dopamine rewards for the experience of constant distraction).[19] Oxytocin, the so-called love hormone, is a neurotransmitter involved in the experience of physical touch and parental bonding as well as sexual bonding (a lot of it is emitted, for example, when we have orgasms).[20] While there are at least one hundred known neurotransmitters, these chemicals are still only vaguely understood, and there are likely many unknown transmitters with unknown purposes.[21]

While our youthful experiences provide us with durable wiring that helps us navigate our environment, the gift of neuroplasticity is that we can still change, regardless of age. Therapies based in this newer science engage motion, light, and mindfulness to address long-term issues of addiction, pain, and trauma—hearkening to ancient Eastern traditions that have long understood the mind as malleable and integrated with the body. Not surprisingly, scientists have also found that such rewiring of our brains only results from doing tasks that we are paying close attention to[22]—the neurological understructure of adrienne maree brown's wisdom, "What we pay attention to grows."[23]

For adults to unlearn beliefs and habits that engulf our implicit memories and unconscious responses, we must rewire our brains through attention, practice, and patient repetition. This process starts with noticing that the patterns our brains create are not the ones we want—whether because they cause pain or disconnection, or because, as with many forms of addiction, the pleasure isn't worth the cost. But even once we have noticed what we need to unlearn, we can't simply think our way out of our own habits of mind. We need help: we need relationships, experiences, and practices that engage with our brains' natural plasticity and support a shift in focus. Redirecting our attention takes time, and often uncomfortable changes of environment, relationships, and sense of belonging.

When I told my friend Tashiena Combs-Holbrook that I was working on a book about unlearning, she responded with an immediate, inspired idea.

"Unlearning?" she wrote to me in a JPay message. "There should be a whole institution of Higher Unlearning. Don't you think? We need to unlearn what it means to be human. Boy/Girl. Good/Bad. Right/Wrong. Black/White. Nothing is as simple as any two categories can convey. So nuanced and complicated we are. Us Humans. Unlearning that we know anything for sure is definitely paramount. A growth mindset. One that allows room for other explanations. Other views to point to for reasoning. Accepting nothing as conclusive. Only one small piece to a never ending puzzle."

Tashiena has a daily practice of unlearning, of choosing neural pathways against the grain of dominant ideology, that she's had to establish while incarcerated in the state of Michigan. She's been locked up since she was twenty-three years old, and now, at forty-nine, she lives in Women's Huron Valley Correctional Facility, just miles from where I was born and used to run around as a teen. The streets she grew up on in Pontiac (exurban Detroit) were very different from mine—while I learned and unlearned in a context of relative safety and comfort, she came of age in a place and time where fear and violence were the baseline for how to protect yourself. We connected in 2023 as part of a writing cohort I facilitated, and I became friends with her and her wife, Natalie, who both live spitting distance from the rivers and strip malls and late-night diners of my teenagehood.

Tashiena remembered her impulse to resist binary gender as a kid, to resist the teachings of public school and parents much the same way I did.

"Even though there is some really serious bullshit detectors which reside in me," she wrote, "I still went through the same socialization processes as everyone else so I have experienced a brainwashing which still requires me to challenge my own biases and prejudices." Like me, she absorbed parts of it even as she rejected others, and, like all of us, she has to constantly choose to challenge dominant ideas, especially because she lives in an environment where everything is constrained, regulated, and controlled. In prison, the messages about how the world is and what is expected of people are particularly rigid and encompassing.

On the phone a few days after her email, I asked Tashiena how she does it—what does she do to actually choose the new desire lines, create the new neural pathways, the question I had started asking everyone. She gave the example of the impulse to call "the authorities" when there's a conflict between people, especially if it gets escalated—she and so many women are behind bars because problems in their communities were being dealt with through a vicious cycle of violence and criminalization.

"Your whole body, your whole being has been conditioned to respond in a particular way," she said. "You can learn all these new words, and language, all these different things. But until you start practicing new practices, your body will want to respond the same way it always has. . . . You don't adopt a new catchphrase and you've changed. . . . You start living into new ways of being."

For her, this unlearning takes the form of a daily practice.

"It had gotten to the point with my mother where we would get into this broken record conversation, she starts talking about everything I did when I was thirteen years old," Tashiena said. She realized that to stop arguing with her mom about the past, she would have to unlearn her habituated role in the argument. "I recognized that this was a broken record conversation, and I didn't repeat my part in the pattern. I was able to step back and say, 'You're right. That was then. But what are we doing today?'"

Now that ability to choose a different way of reacting extends to her life inside—recently, someone was talking negatively about her, and in the past, she said, she would have jumped to her own defense, engaged with the person.

"There was a time when I would have gone and confronted her. Unlearning means doing stuff different and recognizing in yourself that you're engaged in the same cycle of whatever it was, abuse or harm" and stopping.

In Tashiena's stories, and in many of the stories I've encountered, there's no deadline for unlearning—it's never too late to start.

But it also doesn't happen overnight. It's a deliberate retracking of neural pathways, a deliberate choice to begin to act and react in a new way. Desire lines appear faint, as mere suggestions or fantasies in the woods or field. We choose the path and begin to wear it in.

The desire lines of the mind reflect a mysterious combination of automatic behavior and personal agency. What allows us to choose a path— call it desire, or consciousness—is outside the purview of neuroscience, remaining one of its thrilling mysteries. We humans might be purely biological networks of actions and reactions, or we might have a soul, and, for our purposes, these are basically the same: in either case, there is more mystery than there is "fact."

Perhaps the greatest proof of neuroplasticity is simply that we know we can change our minds, when we want to and when we try. We don't need a scientific explanation of desire lines to feel them, and to notice that doing as we have done before might feel easy even when it's causing us pain. Unlearning wears down a new desire line where the older one has become automatic. Unlearning takes us on a less-worn path that becomes easier to travel with use.

These neuroscience theories are just one framework, but they resonate with what nearly everyone says when I speak to them about unlearning, even random people on the street. Unlearning is hard, but possible. It requires choosing new ways while addressing old habits, and it takes time and practice and rigor. Here's Tashiena, responding to my questions about how she unlearns in the context of her daily life in prison: "The unlearning can only come by doing something different, and doing that just as often, or more, than what has been conditioned into us. And that has to be a community effort." She told me she was unlearning everything from how she relates to her family, to how she responds to and resolves conflict, to how she understands race and gender and oppression. She was unlearning the way she was raised to turn to violence as a response, the fighting tendencies that arose from a challenging childhood where she often felt defenseless and afraid. Now she's married and nearly fifty years old—unlearning is a constant, that also requires her to sometimes go against her family, and certainly requires her to resist the ideology of her surroundings at Women's Huron Valley Correctional Facility.

"When I made choices and decisions that I want to live differently in community with people, share differently, create differently," she said, "the journey that I went on . . . it's difficult."

Sometimes, in prison, she feels alone in her unlearning. "It's like being a lit flame on a single candle in a room where a bunch of people are blowing in your direction—it's difficult to stay lit. You need a community of people who are willing to do what's necessary, to not operate the way that we always have."

The foundation of that support system, as we'll explore in the next chapter, is love itself.

CHAPTER 2

LOVE

"I'm into reimagining everything," Adrienne Johnson Martin said, smiling across my kitchen table. As we talked, her with her cat-eye glasses and gap-toothed smile, me with my clunky microphone and big headphones, Adrienne was enthusiastic, casual, unintimidated by the hard work of changing herself. She laughed a lot. We made easy eye contact and shared deep breaths (this would become typical of my conversations about unlearning—they were often revelatory and relaxing).

She told me about her path through journalism: she'd worked for over a decade at the *Raleigh News and Observer* before the constant staffing cuts and the sense of being on a sinking ship sent her packing for a more secure job at Duke University. She spent eight years at Duke before the pandemic and the uprisings of 2020 over police killings urged her back into journalism. The video of George Floyd calling for his mother did something to her, she said, and journalism had changed in the time she'd been gone. When she found there was a place for her in a new kind of justice-driven news outlet, she took it. When we talked, Adrienne was the relatively new executive editor of MLK50: Justice Through Journalism, a Memphis news outlet founded and run by Black women and dedicated to the legacy of Martin Luther King Jr.

But Adrienne's penchant for reimagining started much earlier than the death of George Floyd. Adrienne has a son, and when he was two years old, she learned he had autism.

"After my son was diagnosed, I probably spent a solid two weeks crying every day," she said. "And then one day, we were out walking and he sort of toddled onto someone's lawn and there were some flowers there. He sat there and kinda looked at them and was playing with them. And I looked at him and thought, 'If that's what autism looks like . . . what [am I] so upset about?' That shifted me into a place of 'What can I do to help him?'"

Raising her son has been an exercise in constant unlearning for Adrienne: First, unlearning her expectations about what kind of child he would be, and unpacking her preconceptions about autism. Then, more unlearning as she saw the way systems of schooling and care treated her son—as if he was the problem, rather than the institutions' lack of accommodations.

"As he's gotten older, I have had to shift in a lot of ways to really get to a place where I'm not trying to fix him, and just accept who he is, and teach him how to be in the world as that. Because a lot of what's done for kids with special needs is trying to make them like typical kids," she said. "I've learned to see how exhausting that is for him to try to be like everyone else."

She credits her son with starting her on the path to questioning her own worldview, both because of how different his world is from hers and because she saw how the world treated him—"how it won't yield to you, allow you in, and the damage that comes from that." It was loving her son that taught Adrienne she could unlearn anything.

I first met Adrienne Johnson Martin when she showed up in a tiny Zoom box one day—I was in my apartment in Durham, North Carolina, she was in hers in Raleigh. Three years deep into the COVID-19 pandemic, I was holding virtual "office hours" for journalists interested in abolition and contending with police propaganda through my job at Interrupting Criminalization. Without knowing I was researching the topic, she came to office hours to talk to me about unlearning.

Adrienne shared that her immediate bout of unlearning started with the cascade of pain that marked 2020 in the US: "During the beginning of the pandemic, after the George Floyd murder, I was thinking about my relationship with police, and it led me to this kid Randy Evans. I never forgot his name. I think he was the first police killing that I remember."

She was twelve years old, living in the Bronx, New York, and Randy Evans was living in Brooklyn. Someone called the police, he was on the street with his friends, and a cop shot him point blank in the head. Those are the details she remembered; further research reveals that Evans was a fifteen-year-old ninth grader, unarmed, and cops were responding to calls about "a man with a gun." The shooter, Robert Tornsey, was acquitted after pleading insanity.[1]

"I never forgot that story," said Adrienne when we talked at my house a few months later. She was wearing a black T-shirt and soft black pants, and we hugged as we met in real life for the first time, then relaxed into interview mode, leaning our elbows on the lacquered blue tabletop. Neither of us were interested in small talk. She called Randy Evans "her first," and said when Minneapolis police killed George Floyd, the memories about Evans flowed back. "That made me think about other people's firsts. I talked to my mother and she talked about [Abner] Louima. My grandmother's first would be Emmett Till. My son remembered Trayvon Martin. I started thinking about the muscle memory . . . "

For Adrienne, that muscle memory was the gut feeling, the familiarity, of seeing another unarmed Black person unjustly killed, of feeling the fear and weight of it. Now she was asking why, after all these years as a Black woman in the United States, it had taken her until recently to question the existence and purpose of police. She had always assumed that police were occasionally violent, but that having them around was necessary; she had been an advocate of reform, not anti-police altogether. But now she was grappling with the limits of reform, as the lead editor of a community-driven news outlet that covered so-called crime and policing. She wanted to rethink the idea of live-tweeting police press conferences, to rethink her own weekly columns on reform, and to begin talking about abolition—the idea that police are not a viable "solution" to violence, but instead a part of the problem, and that to address violence and harm we need to get rid of police and prisons and focus instead on root causes. She had read Derecka Purnell's *Becoming Abolitionists* and she was curious.

The beginning of the pandemic and the uprisings that took place in 2020 in the US had been a catalyst for her, as they were for a lot of people. After George Floyd, after the conversations with her mother and friends, after holding close Randy Evans and Abner Louima and Emmett Till and Trayvon Martin and questioning what their lives meant to hers, she'd quit her job at an elite university alumni magazine and started working for MLK50. "Once the world, in this heavy way, shifted me, that broke the dam open," she said. "I felt this urgency that I was not in the business of actively trying to make the world better. It was a betrayal of me raising a son and feeling like the world he is inheriting is pretty lousy, and what had I done to try to make it better?"

In February 2023, Memphis police killed a young Black man named Tyre Nichols by beating him to death. He was unarmed, and official police videos show his assault in graphic detail. Notably, the officers who killed him were also Black. Adrienne's weekly column for MLK50 traces her change of heart about the role of police and the possibility of reform:

> I've spent a lot of my working life trying to change systems from within. I've joined all the committees and lived through all the phrases—tolerance, multiculturalism, diversity, diversity and inclusion, diversity, inclusion and equity, belonging and equity.
>
> For every half step I celebrated as proof of the organization moving forward, I soon felt the sting of them taking four steps back. Sometimes the resistance was deliberate; sometimes it was inadvertent.
>
> I know now that there was no way they were going to truly change. They were built to be exclusive or exclusionary. They were built without people like me in mind.
>
> And that's why I don't believe policing can be reformed. Yes, there are people with good intentions in policing, people who wouldn't have beaten Tyre Nichols to death, people who are horrified by those who did, people who signed up with service to the community in their hearts.
>
> But I'm not talking about individuals. I'm talking about the institution. Institutions are borne from the idea of control and shaped by

political choices. To reform an institution like policing means holding
fast to its basic idea and tweaking it.

That doesn't lead to the fundamental change that's necessary.

I was struck by Adrienne's openness, her ease with the language of
change. When I asked her why she is so unintimidated by unlearning
she hesitated, only briefly, and said, "Probably because of my son."

In exploring the conditions for unlearning, I've come to believe that
loving and being loved are the headwaters, the source from which the
rest of the possibilities of the mind flow. "Love takes off the masks that
we fear we cannot live without and know we cannot live within," writes
James Baldwin in his classic essay "The Fire Next Time."[2] (If you haven't
read this seminal text for unlearning white supremacy, please abandon
ship! Go read it and come back!) "I use the word 'love' here not merely
in the personal sense but as a state of being, or a state of grace—not in
the infantile American sense of being made happy but in the tough and
universal sense of quest and daring and growth."

Baldwin writes in "The Fire Next Time" about what would be possible if white people in this country were ready to actually look at ourselves, to love ourselves and other people enough to take off the masks
of dominance and superiority and face up to history and the present.
Through love, he argues, we can arrive in a shared reality beyond superficial power structures and see one another clearly. But white people
specifically will have to let go of supremacy and distance and denial,
which are incompatible with the kind of love he is talking about. States
of grace don't allow for mediocre lies like racism to thrive. Baldwin
implored the country to be honest with itself and openly grieved the
consequences of the ongoing collective dishonesty of the United States.
He was tough-minded, and love was what he came to as a solution.

A related way of looking at love comes from scientists. In the 2007
book *A General Theory of Love,* a psychologist, a psychiatrist, and a neu-
robiologist pool their knowledge to lay out a physiological explanation

of love. They describe love as a series of neural reactions and responses, an emotion drawn up through the action of human contact and resonance between the limbic systems of our brains—the parts of our minds that control how we relate to others, emotion, and memory. By their accounting, love is an action with a deep evolutionary source and purpose: it is the force that makes us want to care for one another, that gives us the resources to do so even under duress, that creates desire lines around acts of cooperation. As a neurological presence, it is also almost a spiritual one: an omnipresent, invisible force driving everything. *A General Theory of Love* also argues that, even at a mechanical biological level, love extends beyond the bounds of individuals and allows us to coregulate our nervous systems, to connect with those around us by feeling what they feel—much as Adrienne Johnson Martin did with her young son as she learned to support him in his disability.[3] This process starts with the youngest children as they receive soothing eye contact or touch from caregivers as a way to calm them down; those who don't receive this kind of support and mutual attunement often struggle with self-regulation later in life.

"From birth to death, love is not just the focus of human experience, but also the life force of the mind, determining our moods, stabilizing our bodily rhythms, and changing the structure of our brains," write authors Thomas Lewis, Fari Amini, and Richard Lannon. "Love makes us who we are, and who we can become."[4]

Being loved—the purview of parents, children, friends, partners, community members—means being seen in light of what is possible within us. It means attuned, intimate interaction. It means a relaxation of the senses and, with all of that, an increased likelihood that we will be able to change. To cognitively connect with our creativity and our ability to unlearn, we cannot be in a constant state of terror, alarm, or even hypervigilance. We must feel safe enough to let down our guard. That safety may happen alone, but it is most likely to happen when we are receiving and giving love.

———————

Nearly every story I have encountered about unlearning revolves, in some way, around a relationship. The growing science of neuroplasticity supports this: underlying each new theory and discovery lies a suggestion that what we feel as we interact with others is key to neurological rewiring. James Baldwin already knew, but based on this "new" neuroscience, it's arguable that love is a key driver in brain change. The connections we make with other people, from birth until death, change our hormones, our immune systems, our breathing, our physical and mental growth, and our memories. And our design as humans, an inherently interdependent species, is to be able to change and be changed in relationships, to enable the kinds of closeness and dependency that define human health and well-being. Loving and being loved are key motivators that have the power to create ongoing conditions for unlearning.

All this attunement pitter-patter emanates from the limbic system, the parts of our brains that tend to emotions, memory, and connectedness. Mammalian limbic systems aren't isolated islands. They're sensitive to one another—they reach beyond the individual boundaries of humans and allow us to shape one another's thoughts and feelings. That's why other people can make our palms sweat, make us tired, or make us feel safe.

"Emotionality enables a mammal to sense the inner states and the motives of the mammals around him," Lewis, Amini, and Fannon write.[5] "Limbic resonance" is the phenomenon we feel when we connect deeply with tiny babies, share sleep patterns, hug or touch one another and find ourselves syncing up breath and emotions, or delve deep into a long conversation full of eye contact. We have what the authors call an "open loop arrangement," "a symphony of mutual exchange and internal adaptation whereby two mammals become attuned to each other's inner states." Through this ability to resonate, we can also pass feelings along—anxiety and calm, anticipation and satisfaction, heartbeats and breaths. The effect is real among pairs and even in relatively large groups. As they put it, "Limbic resonance is the door to communal connection."[6]

These resonances are helped along by hormones, which can act as supportive neurotransmitters as we open up new desire lines in our minds. Oxytocin is a particularly potent force at moments of major relational change: birthing parents experience high oxytocin levels around birth and postpartum, teenagers gush with it during crushes and first loves, and adults catch a dose when we begin to bond with new partners and form attachments.[7] It's often called the "cuddling hormone," but it also shows up in sex, breast-feeding, and even sustained conversation. It makes us want to bond and softens us to change. We're shaken up in these hormonal moments, and there's a fluidity and openness of thought and learning. Recent studies show the hormones literally make us more open-minded, and they also help consolidate neural changes.[8] They turn us toward new desire lines and can even make them pleasurable to explore.

Dopamine helps, too: the reward hormone runs thick through our minds when we are young, when we learn new things or explore curiosities, and when we are anticipating the excitement of romantic love. As Norman Doidge writes in *The Brain That Changes Itself*, dopamine reinforces plastic change, which means that the experience of falling in love can be a time of great transformation, where we see things anew and develop habits and pathways in our minds that form into lasting changes. Dopamine gets an extra kick out of new experiences, which is part of why the initial high of love and of learning has a tendency to wear off.[9]

Doidge relates the neurological phenomena of falling in love specifically to unlearning. "Love creates a generous state of mind," he writes. "Because love allows us to experience as pleasure situations or physical features that we otherwise might not, it also allows us to unlearn negative associations, another plastic phenomenon."[10] A certain open-mindedness and putting up with things is necessary to bond closely with another person, to commitment and attachment—basically, we become mentally flexible so that we can allow ourselves to depend on others. Dopamine and oxytocin lend a hand, and this unlearning becomes a process of pleasure and reward.

This chemical influence of love has been most clear to me when I have bonded with my friends' and sibling's newborn babies. Even though the baby wasn't mine, I felt that weird druggy feeling babies give some people: the baby's breath synchronizes with yours, the baby's funky little smell is somehow sweet, and you become the super-protective bear-parent who will jump in front of a Mack truck to protect this helpless being. It feels like the baby is dosing me, making me soft and pliant so that when it cries and screams, instead of thinking, "God, this is revolting," I feel love and concern. I am drawn toward the sound of the tiny screaming.

This effect that babies have on many adults isn't just parental "instinct" that kicks in when the kid is plopped into your arms. It's also a neuroplastic *change* that can happen to people who parent. These days, scientists think that part of the bond that forms between adult humans and babies is hormonal, driven by the "love hormones": dopamine, oxytocin, and vasopressin.[11] The same hormones that get us to fall in love with adults help us fall in love with babies. And when that love requires us to change our sleep schedules, our lifestyles and priorities, our preferences and relationships—well, it's helpful if we can tap into an open and nonjudgmental state of mind and stay focused on the pleasure of the bond between us. Raising children requires rewiring, and at a hormonal level, love isn't just a motivator but a facilitator of this change. This relationship between children and parents provides one explanation for why we are so good at unlearning: humans evolved to *need* one another, and that need drives us to change, to be better caregivers of children and to be better partners, cohabitators, and members of teams.

"Life now involves ongoing cooperation that requires a plastic reorganization of the brain centers that deal with emotions, sexuality, and the self," writes Doidge. "Millions of neural networks have to be obliterated and replaced with new ones—one reason that falling in love feels, for so many people, like a loss of identity."[12]

A lack of love and attunement can also make us more closed off to change. This phenomenon is explored by Dr. Bruce Perry in his book with Oprah Winfrey about childhood trauma, *What Happened to You?* As Perry explains, sensory input moves sequentially through our brains. As a matter of practicality and safety, the things we see, hear, and experience are processed first by the parts of our brains that control reflexes and fight or flight impulses—what some refer to as the "lizard brain." Processing things first through our most basic control centers is practical because if we are facing a life-or-death threat, we may not have time to think in the conscious sense. The part of our psyche that makes us automatically fight back, run away, freeze, sweat, and pulsate gets first dibs on our reactions; only after that do outside inputs hit the limbic system and the cortex, where they can translate into conscious feelings and thoughts. What we call "dysregulation" happens when an external input triggers our fight, flight, or freeze responses—sending us into fear and reactivity regardless of what we consciously "think" is happening.[13] (We will explore the science of these dysregulated states further in the chapter on somatics.)

When we are in a dysregulated state, we are preparing for disaster. Our physiology is telling us we are going to need to take quick action, and our cortex (thinking brain) and limbic system go into partial shutdown to make way for the reactive capacities we need to stay safe. That partial shutdown means we often can't even remember events that happened in that state, or words we said. Conscious memory, moral reasoning, ethics and values, creative ideas, and understanding of others are formed in the cortex, supported by calm breath and states of connection and ease. None of this can happen when we're going miles a minute in a state of unbridled fear. People experiencing intense dysregulation literally cannot think or reason.[14]

And, quite simply, dysregulation is what happens to children and adults who are experiencing abuse and neglect, who do not have sufficient access to love and attunement, or who are under intolerable stress. It's also what happens when we're transported back into emotional memories of violence or neglect, even if that's not what is happening anymore. Without addressing our fundamental needs for love and attunement and healing the harms of childhood abuse and neglect, it can be difficult to calm our brains enough to engage openly.

This is a huge factor in why facts alone don't change our minds: a fact that lands on a dysregulated system is a big nothing-burger, return to sender. Only through a sense of safety and connection can we properly "think" about anything at all, and nothing is more effective for calming us down than positive relationships with other people. "Being connected is the most efficient and effective way to get information up to the cortex," writes Dr. Perry.[15] But he is conscious that modern neuroscience has only just "discovered" what cultures that value connection and collectivity have known all along: we need to be together, in loving and safe connections, in order to deeply learn or unlearn.

The importance of love and attunement is also a factor in how cults and autocratic leaders are effective in their recruitment and propaganda: they often focus on people who are traumatized and dysregulated, encouraging and amplifying fear and reactivity over mental flexibility. Mental flexibility is not a matter of education (many educated people are remarkably closed-minded), but an emotional skill, and these leaders understand very well how to manipulate the collective lack of that skill.

Talking with Adrienne Martin for hours took me back to my own family—my mother and grandmother, who, like Adrienne with her son, were willing to be changed by me. But my people were often opaque about how and why that had happened.

Late in my grandmother Sarah's life we had dinner at the farm, the aged off-white wood slats cutting lines behind her, tiny and birdlike at the head of the table, long shadows from black oaks falling over the floor. I made a black bean soup that was too spicy and watched my grandmother and mother pick at it, eating mostly bread and butter for supper. That extra jalapeno was another little failure on my part to conform that added to my usual self-consciousness around them.

Suppers with my South Carolina family were always awkward. There was more silence than noise. No one drank—too many recovered alcoholics—and it was rare for people to cackle with laughter, to fall apart. The silence became a symbol that penetrated the walls of the farmhouse, went down below the foundations, whispered about what built this place: slavery, complicity, a certain kind of womanhood. Until she died, Sarah held court, with her always carefully pinned gray-and-white bun, quietly judging me and my partner as she sniffed at my soup and sipped her iced tea.

The last time we met like this at the farm, the subject came up of Sarah's years working as a legal clerk for my great-uncle Gus. He did the lawyering, but Sarah, who was one of the first women to get a law degree at the University of South Carolina, spent years in the office with her brother, applying her smarts to research.

"There were some stories, oooooh my!" she recalled with a sly smile. "Things I had *never* thought to think of." Her strong southern belle drawl emphasized the scandalous nature of what Gus's clients possibly used to do, be, or talk about. A classic Sarah line came out: "I can't repeat *any* of that here."

The younger people at the table closed-mouth-smiled, overjoyed. This was the closest my grandmother ever came to talking about sex in our presence.

Even when there is love, unlearning can be hard or feel impossible. My grandmother loved me, but she was up against a lifetime of conditioning: she could never talk easily about sex or gender, and she still never fully believed that I am trans, that trans exists. The ruts of "woman and man" / "he and she" ran deep through her neurological channels, as did the synapses linking transsexualism to fear, androgyny to shame, queerness to danger. My mother Raven, a feminist raised in the 1950s when girls at college were still "coeds," also struggled to accept me. The unlearning would be long, maybe even unending.

But over time they faced their fears, unlocked from shame, and unlearned their initial sense that having these conversations was dangerous. It started when I was a kid in the '90s, a grungy hippie, which was discouraged, but permitted; I wore beaded necklaces and fairy wings and tailored my own clothes. When I was twelve I got platform shoes and neckties at thrift stores and went out wearing things that gave Raven a conniption. "You look like a streetwalker!" she once said to me. I was wearing purple lipstick. Not long after that, I started trying out suits and fedoras.

"At the time I just thought a girl was a girl and a boy was a boy," Raven said to me in an interview decades later. "So it didn't occur to me that you wouldn't be a girl."

When I came out as genderqueer and trans, she was shaken.

"The first thing I remember was when you started wrapping your breasts. What I remember most about it was how scary it was," she said. Her concerns for me were not moral, but practical. All she knew about trans people was that it wasn't safe to be one—the high rates of suicide, the murders. "I was just scared for you, that something awful was going to happen to you."

Those fears translated to me as disappointment, as the words of a mother who couldn't accept a reality that was at the core of my being. I wasn't ever a very masculine person; I didn't fit the clinical description of a transsexual at the time. The words I was saying—"transgender umbrella," "genderqueer"—were young people's garble that made no sense to her.

"I was puzzled and confused," she said. She had heard about transsexuals and crossdressers, but only as distant whispers about sexual perverts or psych cases. She had a lot to unlearn. To their credit, my parents, still married at the time, got *True Selves: Understanding Transsexualism* from the bookstore in the year 2000 and went to work.

I can only guess at why it was easier for my father. He wasn't attached to my womanhood, the way my mother's second-wave feminism inclined her to be. And somehow, intuitively, he understood me. When I announced at age nineteen that I would be having top surgery the following year, my dad said he got it—that I was trying to align my body with how I saw myself, that I wasn't doing it for anyone but me. He flew out to Texas to care for me after the operation, taking me and my partner out to eat at the Cheesecake Factory, especially careful with his dad-ly shoulder pats as I walked around in the 100-degree heat, bandaged and delicate.

My mom couldn't process it. She was disappointed and terrified, convinced that I was too young, and that I didn't make sense as "a man"; I was too feminine. She believed I was rejecting my womanhood because I'd internalized some deep misogyny from my father, and she was hurt that I didn't want to grow up to be like her. In her mind, she was grieving the loss of a daughter—and she stayed long in the denial phase of that grief. A month before my surgery I stopped talking to her, so that I could take care of myself without the divisive distress of arguing with my mother about whether I was making a mistake. We spent several years with a chasm between us over this.

My mother will probably never be a PFLAG parent or a bleeding heart—not her style. She'll probably never hug me over and over and say, "I love you so much," the way I have seen some people's moms do in the airport or at graduation. That's just not how she was raised; the WASP-y repression of expressive love runs too deep. But we love each other by showing up, sitting at the table quietly with the iced tea clinking in tall sweaty cups, bringing each other biscuits or cakes, talking on the phone about our days. The years went by, and she started calling me by my pronouns, started loving the people I brought home—genderqueers and high femmes, trans boys and brilliantly trashy girls, all the people who made me possible. By the time I was in my thirties and we were eating spicy soup at that quiet table with Sarah, I was Lewis to her, and she could more or less see me as I was. Somehow along the way, Raven had unlearned binary gender.

I interviewed her in 2018 about what happened in between. We sat in her office, the wall-to-wall books and Persian rug soaking up the echo, my niece and nephew flitting in and out of the room trying to get my attention. South Carolina still felt alien to me, but it had also shifted to a place where I felt intricately acknowledged—by these kids who were constantly curious and called me "Uncle Lewis," by my grandmother's smart gaze before she passed, and even by my mom. Raven couldn't really explain why she had changed. But, she said, over time, she came to believe that my gender transition was not a threat to who I was, that it was a way of getting closer to myself. And—important for my particular story—she came to see that my relationship to gender was one of resistance, of inherent tension. I was not a "man"; for nearly two decades now I'd insisted that something else was possible, and around us the world had started to change, to see nonbinary people like me. Not entirely, not safely. But still.

"You are making a very strong statement about life and reality in the way that you live, and that's really important," she said to me. "You are living the life that you think it's important to live in the face of pressures that would have you live in a different way."

She surprised me with how proud she seemed of my decision to live as myself. Her love for me had opened her mind to more possibilities of what my gender identity meant, disentangling it from her fears, attaching it to my freedom.

Unfortunately for so many trans and queer children, fear is sometimes stronger than love, and fear is a constant product of our culture. If we don't fear trans people directly, we are taught to fear becoming them, or fear that it will happen to our children. Dominant culture associates trans people with tragedy and a life that is somehow less; some versions of Christian culture also reject transitioning as sinful, unnatural, and dangerous. In this fear, some parents never change, letting cultural preconceptions and narratives about "detransition" and "mutilation" and "nature" supersede the love even of their own kids. The fears that we are taught by dominant society—and the subsequent evolutionary reaction of dysregulation—make it harder for love to do its work on our minds.

Love in action changes us, whether it is parental love, sibling love, friend or community love, or romantic love. It reorganizes our synapses. It makes us braver, because we know we have secure relationships to fall back on. This love is not syrupy or simple—nothing about my mother and my grandmother's versions of love are that way, and neither, frankly, is mine. When we love someone we struggle to understand, love motivates us to try. When we are faced with a challenge, being loved makes it safer to imagine that we can meet that challenge.

When people detach and detox from supremacies, from cults, from learned patterns of abuse, they do it in part by loving and being loved, attuning and being attuned to. And conversely, the state of emotional dysregulation that makes unlearning feel threatening is unfortunately deeply common in US culture. Expressing that dysregulation with anger, defensiveness, and attacks is misinterpreted as a form of strength, and it is encouraged by what we see on TV and even what we learn in school. For an everyday example, we need not look any further than the spectacle of televised presidential debates to find the defensive posturing, eye-rolling, and interrupting that characterize people who not only are *not* engulfed in love, but who are proudly unwilling to change. Disconnection reads in their faces and their body language, and afterward pundits celebrate their resolve, trading notes on who more firmly stood their ground.

To live outside of and against this "stand-your-ground" culture in the US is to risk being unmasked, being vulnerable in exactly the way James Baldwin demands.

Adrienne Martin exemplified that for me: an unmasked person. We watched the panes of light move across the wall in the North Carolina afternoon.

"I feel like really everything is on the table. I really do," she said at my kitchen table, flashing that disarming smile. "I question everything."

And it's true: it wasn't just systems of schooling, care, and policing that she was rethinking. It was everything. Since she left her university job, the #MeToo movement happened, and she says she felt "unburdened." The young people at her new job were talking about sexual harassment, and racism, and mental health, and work-life balance. "That made me think about all of the ways that my generation . . . just allowed things to happen, or just excused it, or navigated around it and didn't challenge it," she said. "So I'm rethinking that. When I hear some people say, 'Oh, these kids are so sensitive, I think, 'No, they're right!'"

I wanted to know what made this relaxed response to social change so straightforward for Adrienne. "Why didn't this feel threatening to you?" I asked her. She thought for a minute. "The only thing I can think is that my parents . . . they allowed us the space to think differently, be creative, have a sense of ourselves and be confident in it. I didn't really grow up with this sort of sum zero idea. A lot of Black people talk about that idea of 'You have to be twice as good.' My dad told me that most people are going to be pretty mediocre, so you just do what you need to do and you will be fine. I never felt like I had to earn a place. So maybe that's why I can be open."

Adrienne was changed by the love she felt for her son—but perhaps she was prepared for this change by the love she received from her own parents. They gave her the feeling that she could be what she wanted, be curious and open. In a world full of the message that she would need to prove herself as a Black woman, they told her over and over that she was enough. That lack of fear has been with her ever since.

"I love a startup," Adrienne said, "I love the idea of something beginning, new. It appeals to me. We've burned something down, now what do we do? I find it very exciting. I'm not afraid of change, I'm not afraid of newness. I understand it can be uncomfortable, but I think I've learned that discomfort is the beginning of something. And you know, discomfort is not the worst thing in the world. Feeling a little on edge, that's not bad either. It makes me really happy to be in this process. And maybe it makes me feel young, too."

The human mind is made for changing, for following desire toward learning and adaptability. Octavia Butler wrote that "God is Change"— and her fictional work *Parable of the Sower* explores the power that people can find by embracing change and transformation as something that we have the ability to shape and influence. I might also propose that *we* are change: our very biology, our internal interconnected systems are set up to learn, unlearn, adapt and evolve, to allow us to face multiple complex conditions and participate in collective efforts. Our minds are literally connected to one another and to our environments in an elaborate ecology designed for social adaptation. The synapses that connect us, the mycelial threads and limbic resonances, are made and strengthened through love.

Love, a core condition for unlearning, isn't about forgiveness, absolution, "going easy" on someone, or politeness. Love is about trust and a deep interest in and curiosity about the other person's reality. Other people can offer that to us, but we can also offer compassionate curiosity to ourselves. We might ask: Why do I think this way? What am I afraid of? Who taught me this? What are the stakes? What parts of me want to let go? What parts of me want to hold on? We can be our own guides in unlearning. But love, even self-love, isn't necessarily gentle: love is what makes discomfort tolerable, what makes us able to swim in contradiction.

These are questions to guide personal self-reflection or conversations with people in your life about unlearning. They are intentionally general—start anywhere, and a meaningful conversation will likely ensue!

I suggest approaching these questions in a context of love, or at least, of openness—if you are asking them of yourself, and you feel shame or self-deprecation arising, that's okay! If you are asking them of someone else, and you find yourself getting tense or judgmental about their answers, that's also okay! But pause, take a breath—and come back into the conversation when you can be really present.

Unlearning systems of oppression that surround us, or unlearning aspects of our own identities or lived experience, can be painful and scary. Notice the tension, write about the tension, or speak about it in these loving conversations, but don't let it stop you from exploring.

1. What are you unlearning? [*Usually, the word "unlearning" resonates with people and they offer examples readily. But if they are confused by the idea, you can prompt them—say, unlearning means trying to let go of a belief or way of looking at things you were taught growing up.*]
2. Where did this idea or framework [that you are unlearning] come from?
3. How did you come to believe this was important to unlearn?
4. How is it going?
5. What feelings come up for you when you try to confront the unlearning you need to do?
6. What are your practices for digesting and moving through those feelings?

7. What are you having to let go of that you find yourself still clinging to? What purpose does that thing you are clinging to serve in your life? How has it helped or protected you in the past?
8. How can I support your unlearning?
9. Who or what supports your unlearning?
10. What are you confused about or struggling with?
11. What is a practice you might commit to, to keep yourself focused on this unlearning?

CHAPTER 3

COGNITIVE DISSONANCE

"I wanted to be Israeli," said Micha Kurz. Growing up, his deepest desire was to fit into his own nascent society.

His childhood was defined by this yearning. His parents had emigrated to what was then known as Israel in the late 1960s—his mom driven by her experience of antisemitism growing up in Canada; his father driven by his political commitments cultivated in LA. Micha's father was an activist and ally of the Black Panthers and Brown Berets, and he came to Jerusalem to help build what he hoped would be a socialist utopia. This was how Israel/Palestine had been described to them both. His parents were hippies, activists, and "peaceniks," he said. Finally, after generations of persecution and fear, they sought to live safely and create something good in the world. Micha was born and raised in Jerusalem.

Being Israeli, to him, meant conforming—learning the cultural mores of directness and intensity (so different from the white Canadian and Californian standards of polite company and "niceness"), celebrating the holidays, joining the military. Every year a series of holidays taught him and everyone around him about Israeli national identity: Passover was followed by Holocaust Memorial Day, then National Memorial Day, then Israeli Independence Day, then Jerusalem Day. Each one identifying threats to his people, the Jewish people, each one with sirens and military parades and increasing fanfare.

In this way, he internalized the idea that being an Israeli Jew also meant being under constant threat: "From religious to spiritual, familial,

39

like national identity are all interwoven into a massive collective psychology of everybody's out there to annihilate us," he said. If it wasn't Hitler, they were led to believe, it was Palestinians.

But growing up, Micha had never heard the word "Palestinian."

"The term that was used, if at all, was Arabs. We were in a sea of Arabs in the Middle East, was what we were taught." Within the borders of what was called Israel, they attended segregated schools, had segregated public transportation, and "the Arabs" were people who worked in construction, cleaned the streets, and lived out of sight. He had no idea that, in the 1980s, the Israeli government offered incentives to Palestinian farmers to leave their lands and come work in construction jobs, building the Israeli settlements. He had no idea that what Israelis referred to as the Arab-Israeli war of 1948, Palestinians called the "Nakba," or catastrophe—that the establishment of his country had come at the cost of the self-determination of theirs.

He remembers how much he loved being a scout as a young boy, participating in the youth movement and then in the '90s peace movement, advocating for peace accords and new borders between Israel and Palestine. He was a self-identified peacenik, following in his parents' footsteps. He wanted a homeland, but he wanted it to be utopic and not at war. Even so, he said, "I was still really gung-ho to go serve my country and join the military as a combat soldier."

When he joined the military—as all Israelis are required to do when they turn eighteen—this worldview began to fall apart.

It was the year 2000 when Micha Kurz was deployed into the Israeli Defense Forces (IDF), a conscript military that was formed in 1948 to expand the Zionist project in occupied Palestine. Since the 1967 Arab-Israeli war, which expanded the parts of Palestine that Israel occupies and controls, the US has been a constant supporter of the IDF and its efforts to restrict freedom of movement for millions of Palestinians, providing hundreds of billions of dollars in military aid, weapons, and direct training and support.[1]

"I joined the combat unit. Combat? Turns out it wasn't really combat. We were there to control a civilian population," Micha said. He was sent to Hebron, known in Palestine as Al-Khalil, a city in the occupied West Bank where Israeli settlers have been notoriously aggressive and violent toward locals.[2] When he went, he thought he was going to a battlefield, to a line where the Israeli military was fighting with the Arabs—the image in his mind was of the front lines of a war like in the movies.

When he arrived, he saw the winding roads of an ancient city, full of people and history, mosques and markets. And the IDF's job there was not to fight terrorists, as he had been told. "It's not two like platoons, two armies against one another," he said. "It's the Israeli military apparatus controlling the Palestinian civilian population."

A few hundred Israeli settlers had come into the center of this historic Palestinian city of about 150,000.[3] They were armed, and they were nothing like what he expected—nothing like the hippie, peacenik Israelis he had grown up around.

"The Israelis, the Jewish supremacists, were the most volatile, violent, vile group of people, who would at any opportunity attack Palestinians. Old folks, women, children, it didn't matter," Micha said. "The goal was for them to expand and they would say blatantly, 'Our job is to transfer, is to get rid of the Palestinians, to make sure they're not here anymore, ethnically cleanse them out of town.' And my job was to protect those guys."

His vision, the beliefs he had grown up with, of the whole world against the Israelis, the assault on the Israelis, the victimhood of Israelis, the Arab threat—it all began to blur. It was his first time encountering Palestinians in a place that was still labeled "Palestine," in their own homes and neighborhoods. And they were mostly just people, living in this ancient place, shopping at an open-air market where the Tomb of the Patriarchs is. The settlers, who were essentially armed far-right militants, were there threatening them, dumping trash and urine on their heads from the apartments they'd occupied above the marketplace, and calling on the Israeli army to bully and harangue Palestinians. None of what he saw fit with what he'd been told.

"The cognitive dissonance got harder, got more heavy," he said, "thicker to move through, to work with." Still, here he was in basic training—witnessing abuses and atrocities, but loyal to his platoon, to the men around him, to the identity he'd spent a lifetime working to construct.

When we feel certain about something, it can seem immovable even in the face of contradictory information. That's because certainty is not rational. Certainty is like sadness, anger, or love—it's a feeling. We believe that we are right not because we can prove it, but because we sense it. These feelings can come off as innate and natural, but often they are also learned, in the realm of implicit memory—rituals like the nationalist military holidays Micha grew up with create associations that strengthen and deepen with repetition. Subtler rituals—learning language, for example, or learning how to fight or debate—also become forms of certainty as we repeat them. These certainties (this word means that; this symbol means this; these people are safe and these are not; and so on) begin to feel like facts no matter what their basis is in shared reality.

"Certainty and similar states of 'knowing what we know' arise out of involuntary brain mechanisms that, like love or anger, function independently of reason," writes Robert A. Burton in *On Being Certain: Believing You Are Right Even When You're Not*.[4] He's a neuroscientist and a doctor, and his work aims to dispel the myth that knowledge is arrived at through studious and reasoned processes, and show that the "feeling of knowing" instead emerges from a layer of the mind that we give input into, but do not control.

"The concept of neural networks . . . helps explain why established habits, beliefs, and judgments are so difficult to change," writes Burton. "Imagine the gradual formation of a riverbed. The initial flow of water might be completely random—there are no preferred routes in the beginning. But once a creek has been formed, water is more likely to follow this newly created path of least resistance. As the water continues, the creek deepens and a river develops."[5]

This is the flip side of our neuroplasticity and penchant for being curious, the part where we get to enjoy *not* changing our minds. All facts, all views of the world, all perceptions that we experience and replay, flow through neural networks, repeating themselves until they become a certainty. The more certain, the deeper the riverbed. The deeper the riverbed, the harder it can be to reroute. These pathways aren't impossible to change, but simply being presented with a new bit of information won't do the trick. "To expect well-reasoned arguments to easily alter personal expressions of purpose is to misunderstand the biology of belief," writes Burton.[6]

By design, Burton argues, it feels good to know, to sense a truth settling into our minds. "The feeling of knowing, the reward for both proven and unproven thoughts, is learning's best friend, and mental flexibility's worst enemy," he writes.[7] We need this feeling in order to stabilize aspects of our identities and relationships: feeling certain allows for communication with common languages and assumptions, for example. It allows for the development of bodies of knowledge, the study of history. Feeling certain also allows for nationalism and groupthink—at a mass level where this is enforced through violence, this rewarding feeling can very easily go too far.

But why hold on to a fact or belief, once we have witnessed evidence that it may be misguided, or straight-up wrong? What is the self-interest in deluding ourselves? Western psychologists and neuroscientists grapple with this question and are admittedly uncertain: The neuroscientists like Burton theorize that we hold on because neural pathways are like ruts in the road, and the more we drive down them, the deeper they get. The psychologists theorize that we hold on because of our intolerance for the experience of cognitive dissonance.

Cognitive dissonance is what happens when we're deep in one of those ruts, and something or someone informs us that there's another pathway we could—or should—be choosing. Social psychologists Carol Tavris and Elliot Aronson are two of the leading researchers on cognitive dissonance and uncertainty. As they write in *Mistakes Were Made, but Not by Me*, "Cognitive dissonance is a state of tension that occurs when a person holds two cognitions (ideas, attitudes, beliefs, opinions) that are psychologically inconsistent with each other . . . Dissonance produces mental discomfort that ranges from minor pangs to deep anguish; people don't rest easy until they find a way to reduce it."[8]

Tavris and Aronson present studies that give credence to the theory of dissonance as discomfort: for example, some show that reading contradictory information not only reinforces people's preexisting beliefs, but in many cases makes those beliefs stronger, as people search for ways to justify what they already thought.[9] In the work of journalism we see this (and fret about it) all the time: People prefer news that reinforces their worldview, and when they encounter news that challenges it, they become acrobatic in their arguments against the validity of that news. There is no neutral reader, and it seems that many people are in love with the ideas and frameworks they already have. This is part of why right-wing cries of "liberal bias" work so well—the trip from certainty to denying someone else's reality is short and easy.

Even reading a "both sides" argument will tend to produce this outcome; we read with an eye to how well our side is doing, rather than considering both arguments rationally. As a result, journalism that presents issues as a polarized "both sides" debate runs the risk of reinforcing preconceived assumptions just as much as one-sided journalism—essentially, presenting an issue as a binary causes people to view it in increasingly binary terms. (This phenomenon, called "binary bias," is explored in another accessible text about mind change, Adam Grant's *Think Again*.)[10]

Tavris and Aronson argue that cognitive dissonance can be resolved, either by releasing one of the beliefs that creates contradiction, or by defending the contradiction.[11] And here is where the experience of uncertainty, the moment of dissonance when what you knew and what you see collide and contradict, is deeply important to unlearning. Cognitive dissonance might cause us to dig our heels in and turn away from unlearning—but it can also create a fertile plain, a place where we begin to see that we are lost and begin to look for another path, another creek bed. It's rare that such dissonance is immediately resolvable. But tolerating and becoming curious about contradicting realities is at the core of unlearning, a key condition and skill.

Defending the contradiction isn't always an option. In these situations, unlearning becomes a necessity.

For Micha Kurz, exploring the dissonance of being an Israeli soldier was a years-long process, full of loss, grief, and alienation; he didn't so much resolve the dissonance as learn, over time, to live with it. The first stage, while he was still in the army, was seeing just how heinous the justifications and acts of the IDF were—acts that he was witnessing, that his comrades were committing, in the name of the country he'd grown up so desperately trying to be a part of.

"Literally, we would get away with murder," he told me when we talked in 2022. He was in the military through the second Palestinian Intifada, a period of resistance that lasted from 2000 to 2005 and led to intense backlash from the Israelis: they built walls, they built new checkpoints, and they killed nearly five thousand Palestinians.[12]

"We did whatever we wanted," he said. "We crossed all kinds of moral and ethical red lines. There were numerous war crimes that we were part of and witnessed."

Finally, the cognitive dissonance overwhelmed his patriotism. In 2004, he and two other members of his former battalion founded Breaking the Silence, an influential Israeli organization that called out abuses in the Israeli Defense Forces. Even then, Kurz says, he wasn't unlearning his fear and hatred of Palestinians—he was just trying to rehumanize himself and the Israelis. "We got to talk about this," he and his comrades thought, "not about what we're doing to Palestinians, but what happens to us, what it means to be controlling a civilian population. . . . We've turned into monsters."

No one wants to be a monster, to see ourselves as wrong or corrupt. Kurz was then faced with a new set of questions about Israel itself—now that he knew about occupied Palestine. The story of "a land without a people for a people without a land" was so clearly untrue. Did his parents know? He asked them.

"It's hard for me to think of my parents as folks who would make evil choices. I don't think they were hoping to displace Palestinians, but

I think they were hoping for a better future for themselves," he said. "In hindsight, I ask them a lot about, like, 'Did you not know about the Palestinian catastrophe, about the Nakba? Did you not understand that Israel was an apartheid state?'"

A year out of the military, Micha was beyond lost. "Being Israeli was everything growing up. All I wanted to be was Israeli. And then suddenly I was like, 'Wow, what is it? This isn't true. This isn't real.'"

He met someone who told him about enlightenment, about Buddhism, and left Israel for a spiritual tour—Australia, New Zealand, India. He did embarrassing white dude stuff like taking ayahuasca and growing dreadlocks. He went far, far away from where he'd started. "All of it was a journey into integrity," he said. He began the painful process of rejecting the beliefs that were causing him dissonance: rejecting nationalism, Jewish supremacy, and Israeli exceptionalism. Rejecting the foundational belief that Palestinians were not a real people. But in rejecting all of that, he found himself without an identity. A few years later, he returned to Jerusalem, where the far-right Arizona governor and future US presidential candidate Mike Huckabee was visiting to shill for illegal Israeli settlements in East Jerusalem.[13]

"Mike Huckabee was in town cutting the ribbon to a new settlement in Sheikh Jarrah. I went to the protest and lost my shit and screamed at the top of my lungs. This isn't Jewish! . . . This isn't even human! How dare you? What are you doing in this? And I came home that night and my skin broke out in hives. I got a terrible fever. My body couldn't handle the dissonance."

On that same trip, Kurz returned to Bethlehem, the city in occupied Palestine where he had been a part of placing the Nativity Church under siege during the Second Intifada. He thought he was ready, that he had enlightenment enough to visit Bethlehem as a new man.

"I had done enough ayahuasca for, like, five lifetimes. It was going to be enough. And I thought, *Sure, this is going to be a walk in the park.* But my body, once we drove through the checkpoint, went right back to, like, a nineteen-year-old soldier. I just was gonna pee my pants because I was scared silly that everyone was a terrorist around me."

He had resolved the dissonance in his mind, but not his body.

"My Palestinian friends put their hands on my shoulder and said, 'You can calm the fuck down. Have some tea, eat something. You're fine, you fucking occupying son of a bitch.'"

Bethlehem had changed in his mind: it was no longer a zone that harbored terrorists, or a place to control. It was a city, with people baking bread and biking to work and walking up steep terraced hills. It was a city in which his new friends, Palestinians, had full, complicated lives. And even though he was scared coming back, he knew in his mind there was no danger to him there—*he* had been the dangerous one, the occupying force.

"And I broke, it broke me," he said. "Once a thread, like a loose end happens . . . and you start pulling on that thread and you pull and pull until it all unravels, realize that it's all based on a pile of lies, which is essentially really, really heartbreaking because it also means that all the adults and all of my counselors and leader development in the scouts and the teachers at school and the commanders in the military and anybody I'd ever, ever looked up to was either willfully ignorant or lying. It's a really heartbreaking moment."

After that first return to Palestine—what he previously called "Israel"—Micha left again, continuing his quest. He still couldn't reconcile his former self with the person he was becoming. The dissonance drove him deeper into unlearning.

"I only wanted to be Israeli," he said of his young self. "All I ever wanted was to be accepted and normal. But it's obscene. . . . You can't stand in the middle of Hebron and not be like, 'This is obscene.' And I don't know how they live with themselves. I live up in a cabin in the Rockies as far away as I possibly can get at this point. And I still have a hard time living with myself."

I contacted Micha Kurz on a hunch: I'd heard him speaking on a podcast about his process of reckoning with masculinity and whiteness. He mentioned his history as a member of the IDF, and I tracked him down through mutual friends and got on a call. He was noisy and energetic and loose. When I started by asking him about unlearning, he demurred.

"I wouldn't be able to say I've been there, done that, I get it," he said. "I know better than to say that at this point."

As the unlearning expanded within him, he also found he had much to learn:

"In Jerusalem alone, there are forty-five different Palestinian communities that have been there for anywhere between 150 and 3,000 years," he told me. By the time he moved back to Jerusalem again, he'd learned about Indigenous sovereignty movements, about anti-Blackness, about patriarchy. Then his unlearning meant he could see a place he had never known before. "All of this right under my nose. And I've been living on this treasure. Fucking decades of my life, not even recognizing . . . You know, when you drive around the mountains of Jerusalem, they're all terraced. . . . I thought that's how mountains grew."

The terraces are ancient Palestinian structures to allow the hills to be farmed and irrigated. They are a sign of a land that was intimately known, intimately peopled, before the current occupation. In 2011 he cofounded another organization, Grassroots Jerusalem (or Grassroots Al-Quds), which creates Palestinian maps and tours of Jerusalem, helping people unlearn through re-narrating the landscape. And then he left again—increasingly aware that his role as an Israeli man was taking the focus away from the Palestinian women who now run the organization.

When I traveled to Palestine in 2018, I got a tour from Fairouz Zarqawi of Grassroots Al-Quds and saw the maps that bring back the Indigenous place names for what are now Israeli neighborhoods, strip malls, airports, factories, and walls. We visited a Palestinian village that is now part of a public park in Jerusalem, its homes emptied out and presented as ancient ruins, light-skinned Israeli kids playing in the swimming holes. One of the Palestinian women we were traveling with, Nadya, said, "This is where my grandparents were displaced from in the Nakba. This is my village."

When I came home from Palestine, I was heavy with my own unlearning, and my own wish: that I hadn't been born in a settler colony. The cognitive dissonance that is laid bare as I look at the situation of the Israelis is also a part of my daily reality. I was born on Anishinaabeg land, in a place where the rivers and lakes carried the names of the Indigenous people and the towns carried the names of the colonizers who pushed them out—the Huron River, Ann Arbor, Detroit. Like Micha, I was in a sense conscripted: mine would be a white body, taking space and resources and ownership in a place that had once had enough, now defined by deprivation. That is what Israel was making of Palestine's ancient markets and thousand-year-old neighborhoods; that is what my own ancestors had made of Cherokee languages, Seminole grave sites, Anishnaabe waterways and meeting places.

Whiteness and colonialism, when you are not trapped in the denial made possible by privilege or power, provoke a constant cognitive dissonance. I see shopping malls and highways and a million iPhones as a kind of grand cover for colonialism's cardinal sins, slavery and the robbery of land, maps redrawn and villages and pathways disappeared. Now we have maps to where and how to drink and forget, never maps to how to grieve. Even those of us who are privileged by it, whose family names appear on these new maps, are suffering a loss—because we don't know where we belong, we don't know how to live with ourselves. I remember one night at a campsite somewhere in the South, listening to the cicadas hum and drinking whiskey with my partner until I was in tears. I cried about the lost cities, the places—it was a feeling I wasn't sure how to tie up, so I vomited into the ferns instead. The cognitive dissonance, I believe, lives in all settlers' bodies and makes it hard to live with ourselves. Because our temporary sense of belonging comes at such a steep and unfathomable cost.

The year after I interviewed Micha Kurz, I found myself in tears again over a lost place. This time it was Gaza: we watched in horror as the Israeli military assaulted, gunned down, bulldozed, and razed the place. I thought about Palestine and its fabrics and bright contours, its ancient terracing and warm people offering tea and a seat. Gaza City became a place that now nobody, anywhere, can go back to, at least not how it was—a place whose ancient stories are being erased by bombs and drowned in blood. I thought about the millions of traumatized families, children who will spend their lives unlearning the visceral fear of loud noises and fire, if they survive at all. Through the internet, the world watched families, doctors, teachers, journalists, babies buried in the rubble. No amount of disentangling could ever be enough.

But witnessing Micha's unlearning, and the unlearning of so many Jewish Americans and Israelis who had been lied to about Palestine, was a balm. Jewish Voice for Peace, an anti-Zionist Jewish organization, staged walkouts and sit-ins in solidarity with Palestinians; in December 2023, the organization had more followers on social media than the Israeli government's propaganda accounts. Many of my friends and the people I organized and got arrested with were deep in dinner-table debates with their families, confronting the dissonance of Zionism as it revealed itself to us through an unfolding nightmare in Gaza. The settler violence that Micha had seen in Al-Khalil in the year 2000 could now be seen on TV and on Instagram.

The leadership of the US stood by, claiming to want peace but funding war. Our role in building a protest movement was to create constant cognitive dissonance around that choice. We showed up at congresspeople's offices, at Capitol Hill, at Grand Central Station, on highway overpasses during the holidays, at the farmer's market with balloons and songs. How can you shop, play, pass budget bills, and scroll past an unfolding genocide? We created discomfort because we know that it's a portal, that at least some people will find it intolerable to accept war crimes in our names.

Micha didn't unlearn by being comfortable, or sure. It was painful, a constant breaking, an inability to ever go back. Unlearning requires us to be vulnerable to having no idea who we are, vulnerable to having no map and vulnerable to loss. "The folks that I love working with the most are veterans," Micha said, "who are, for the most part, heartbroken. I don't know too many veterans who are not heartbroken, that didn't leave the service and realize, 'Oh, I bought into something that was a lie. My nation lied to me, my parents, my teachers, everyone.' The grief, the heartbreak, is real."

Through the lostness and dissonance, we start to see new desire lines.

"You think you know what's going on here?" he asked, excited by the possibilities of unlearning. "You have no idea. I have no idea. The veil is so thin."

On the other side of the veil, maybe, is the sense that we are part of a larger whole.

CHAPTER 4

COMMUNITY

In the opening scene of *The Great Muppet Caper*, Kermit the Frog and Fozzie the Bear, playing identical twins, get fired from their job in journalism for missing a big story about a jewel thief. The pair decide to fly to England, together with their photographer Gonzo, and report the story anyway. Upon landing, they ask the first person they see for a hotel recommendation—something cheap or, better yet, free. The trio are sent along to the Happiness Hotel via a red double-decker sightseeing bus.

When they walk into the slumping hotel, the wallpaper is peeling, the front desk man is snoring, and when Kermit says, "We'd like a room," the old man, also a Muppet of some renown, responds enthusiastically. "Really?!" And he calls out to the gallery of residents, "Somebody's checking in!"

Cue the banjo music, tap-dancing rats, full Muppet jazz band, and a chaotic musical performance sung by clowns, hippies, and bears. The multigenre dance number ends with a cracked lightbulb as Kermit retires to try to get some sleep in a bouncy Murphy bed. This sequence introduces the ensemble, the eclectic group of Muppetistas who will help Kermit, Fozzie, and Gonzo in their quest to find the truth about the missing jewel. Outside the Happiness Hotel sits a two-story bus with a spiral staircase, and when the group travels, the full band plays from the top of the careening vehicle, dubbed the "Happiness Hotel Courtesy Car."

I still struggle to accept that the Happiness Hotel isn't everyone's dream, Murphy bed and all. For me, the Muppet dream abides. As a five- or seven-year-old, I was completely absorbed by the vision of a free place to stay, full of musicians and scientists and other noisy coconspirators. They support each other's escapades and have their own bus! For small me, the Happiness Hotel was a glimpse into possibility, into a collective future that was more scrappy and rundown than the crisp main streets and shopping malls of the midwestern US. But it wasn't just aesthetic appeal: it was the ensemble, the Muppets and how they related to one another. Wherever they went they were full of light, laughter, connection; they supported each other without question; they celebrated one another's skills and strangeness. I craved an environment like that, and, as I came of age, I gravitated toward those kinds of places—underground and warm and weird. I think a lot of queer people do.

Gabriel Wer's first encounter with a Happiness Hotel didn't come until he left his home country of Guatemala. "I moved to Spain suddenly when I was twenty years old, because I couldn't see a way through."

That year, he went out into the streets of Madrid on the day of Gay Pride.

"It's cliché, I know," he told me. "I'm suddenly walking in the streets and then seeing this massive amount of people just walking with flags and happy, all different types of bodies and everything . . . and I was scared to participate. I was just standing there." It was thrilling.

"Oh, my God . . . am I allowed to do this? Is this okay? Am I part of this? Is this who I am? I just jumped in and I just started marching with everyone. And I felt something that I didn't feel before, which is just that I was part of something bigger than myself and that I was connected to all these strangers by our experience in this world."

Gabriel had known he was gay for a while, but he'd been hiding it from everyone around him. He grew up in a mostly conservative family, a descendant of coffee farmers and oligarchs in Guatemala City. They were Catholic, traditional, and had proximity to people in power. Everything around him told him that it was wrong or shameful to be queer. But when he saw all those people cutting a rug on the streets of Madrid, he said, "That was a really big moment where I thought, *Okay, I have to embrace this rather than keep fighting it.*"

There was another, more intimate experience that propelled him into unlearning his fear of coming out—another one that reminds me of the Muppet hotel.

"My roommate started dating this guy, and they were having a Sunday lunch type of thing, late lunch," he said, describing a Spanish kind of scene of a long, leisurely meal in someone's living room. "I was just looking at this group of people, they were eating, cooking together, having wine, chatting and everyone was so different. But at the same time they were also connected. I cannot explain, but I was like, I want this, you know. . . . This is what I need, or this is something that everyone should have. And why don't I have it, why is it not possible?"

This glimpse into community was simple, but profound. Before then, he'd known he was queer, but he thought being queer just meant being an outsider, going to bars to try to hook up, living in solitude, or attending drunken parties—nothing he thought was wrong, but he struggled to see himself in these images, so he had stayed largely isolated. Here was a third way, "just seeing that there are other ways that you can feel at home with people that are not necessarily your family," Gabriel said. Instead, people were sharing stories, laughter—and they were comfortable with the ways they had been deemed different. "I didn't know this existed."

By the time we met, as members of a fellowship program, Gabriel had gone from being a tentative unlearner to a lifelong one. He'd stayed in Europe for many years, exploring his identity and living far from his family of origin.

"The more I got comfortable with my own sexuality, the more I was able just to open up to the world," he said. It affected everything all the way down to the way he carried himself. He became comfortable listening to his body—he stopped slumping his shoulders, hiding himself. "My posture when I sit, when I stand, how I walk, how I approach people. When my body feels relaxed and comfortable or happy, or excited, or just feels good—it means that that's something to continue exploring."

He carried himself with this centered, present calm. He was big, tall, and beautiful, smiling openly, hugging and laughing easily; a head shorter than him, I greeted him for our interview by nuzzling into his shoulder. We sat on a porch together in Rio de Janeiro for our interview as a rainstorm brought down sweet sounds on a tin roof over us, thick jungle trees all around. We were giggling, talking with our hands, connected. Together, we created another little Happiness Hotel, the manifestation of this sense of togetherness that we each yearned for as kids.

But when we connected, Gabriel was also a political exile—living not in Spain, or in his home country of Guatemala, but in Mexico City, where he'd fled to after being targeted for his work facilitating unlearning.

Here we are. The heart of unlearning. The heart, perhaps, of everything that matters: being together, in community and connection, which is both a birthright and an experience that dominant capitalist cultures deny or destroy access to. The feeling of the Happiness Hotel is so much like the feeling of a blues band playing on a street corner, which is so much like the feeling of an open-air market in Palestine, which is so much like the feeling of Gay Pride in Madrid. There's connection, safety in numbers, life taken to the brass tacks: music, bodies, laughter, food. And yet these are essential ingredients, essential conditions for letting go of preconceived notions, whether it's so that we can become who we are or so that we can act differently in solidarity with others. As my friend and collaborator Mia Henry likes to say, "Everything important we do is done with other people." Unlearning is no exception, and simply entering a community where we feel belonging can suddenly make impossible changes within us feel possible, or even joyful.

A lot of the social science research into why people take up or express certain views focuses on a particular framing, one that might be summarized as "peer pressure." Countless studies show that people are social, that we do what others want us to do and believe what others around us seem to believe, and that we also gravitate toward others who seem to share our beliefs. Sometimes this is also described in the negative, as "mob mentality" or "group think."

On the one hand, the social scientists might lead us to conclude that people are natural conformists—which also means that authoritarian or bigoted views are easy to pull over on people. On the other hand, that research reveals a social, interconnected element to both learning and unlearning. One famous study conducted in the 1950s by social psychologist Solomon Asch shows just how much others' views can change ours. He asked people to compare the length of a single line on one card, with the lengths of three lines on another card—and choose the best match. It's not a trick and it's fairly easy to see which line matches. But then he let people see what others in the experiment were answering, and he introduced plants, fellow experiment subjects who seemed to be seeing a different match. The experiment could throw anywhere from one-third to one-half of a group to change their previously correct answer to an incorrect one, to literally see something different.[1]

The only consequence of choosing correctly was the implied social consequence of differing from the group. This isn't weak or wrong: it's human. Asch's experiments have been interpreted over and over again to show an innate human tendency toward groupthink. But, to me, an overlooked part of the experiment is the one-half to two-thirds of people who see others giving a different answer, and persist in their own. Another interpretation of the experiment might be that, in any given group, there are people whose instinct is to conform, and people who insist on seeing for themselves. Imagine how ripe a conversation might be among that group, especially if there was love and connection between them, if people identified with the group—imagine how possible learning and unlearning is, if we are so deeply able to influence one another. Often this is discussed disparagingly by Western researchers, as a sign of weakness or an embarrassment to the rugged individual. It is also discussed frequently in the context of identity development or "tribalism"; as these thinkers would have it, we identify with our in-group and need in-group spaces to develop new beliefs, and this is a bad thing that should be overcome by reason, logic, and individualism.[2]

I remember my own first experiences of community spaces that were rich with unlearning: rolling up to Camp Trans, a transgender protest camp in the woods of western Michigan, made up of nothing but a few tents and a few dozen people, was a homecoming. I was scared and delighted, urgently hungry to belong, suddenly eating under-salted chickpeas and starchy veggie dogs with people who were loose and wild and not obviously any one gender or age. I was only seventeen, and I was trying so hard to dislodge myself from my own gender, from girlhood. It was in this liminal space, this Muppet camp in the woods, that I found my own version of the community Gabriel found in Madrid. It wasn't *before* Camp Trans that I finally came out and started living into the body and identity I so desperately needed; it was after.

We want to be in community, and community depends on a degree of shared communication tools, behavior, and belief—which can mean that, even as we unlearn, we might succumb to a new pressure to conform. In theory, strong communities also have room for conflict, confrontation, and rancor, and our desire to share reality can be a strength, something we use to facilitate unlearning rather than pressure one another to conform. If you're gay and isolated in a place where no one accepts you, the dynamic of peer pressure and community inclusion or exclusion can be a nightmare. But if you're gay and have access to a welcoming community, the same reality—that we learn and unlearn in groups—becomes a dream come true. It follows that one of the key ways to create conditions for radical unlearning is to create communities around our visions for the world, to enact and invite people into them—to create experiences like the parade and the Sunday lunch for Gabriel, like Camp Trans for kids like me and the Happiness Hotel for the Muppets, and to make these commonplace.

Of course, even a community that facilitates unlearning some dominant ideology can also become a source of rigidity and scapegoating. At Camp Trans, people also recreated exclusionary dynamics of classism and racism and transmisogyny (even though the protest was about trans women's inclusion, trans women were underrepresented). And I know too well that sometimes that pressure to conform becomes even more intense in groups of people who are outcasts in their own families. I remember the vicious ways people spoke about each other at Camp Trans, the fears I carried of being rejected or pushed out, the terror I experienced after my first queer breakups, that I would lose this little space of community I had carved out. I unlearned so much, but I also tried hard to fit in, struggled daily against my own fear of becoming the scapegoat. Probably no community is immune to the rigid downsides of groupthink. The vulnerable edge of unlearning becomes possible in community, but, unfortunately, any community can also become a trap.

"I have come up with the essentializing, radical proposal that people only believe things because of community. I don't think anyone believes anything for any reason other than it serves their role in a human community," Adrianne Black said, adding with a chuckle that "white philosophers hate that idea."

Do communities trap us, or free us? Adrianne has known this question from a wide range of contexts. Her story is told in rigorous detail by journalist Eli Saslow in the book *Rising out of Hatred*. She was raised by key figures in the white nationalist movement; her godfather, David Duke, is a well-known neo-Nazi and leader of the modern Ku Klux Klan, and her father, Don Black, founded the website Stormfront. During the Obama era, Adrianne, a bright-eyed redhead, became a teenaged figurehead of the movement, cohosting a popular syndicated radio show with her father that laid the groundwork for the racist dog-whistling frenzy of Donald Trump's candidacy.

But when she went to school at the New College of Florida, where she graduated in 2010, something told her not to immediately "come out" as being part of the white nationalist movement. Before someone on campus found out and outed her, she made friends with Jewish people and people of color for the first time. After she was outed, there was an enormous and ongoing outcry on campus—people tried to have her removed, staged walkouts and tense debates. And some people also remained her friends and invited her to challenging discussions; a small group of Jewish students held regular shabbat dinners where they welcomed Adrianne and respectfully debated her neo-Nazi beliefs. Adrianne—who was living as a straight man still at the time—eventually fell in love with a girl who abhorred white nationalism, but agreed to meet Adrianne's family. Her girlfriend disagreed with her on every single point of white nationalist rhetoric, and engaged with her on each one. Not long after she graduated, Adrianne Black famously published a blog on the Southern Poverty Law Center website under the name she was then known by, renouncing her family's views and cutting all ties with the movement. A few years later, she came out publicly as trans.

Adrianne said she was moved to change not by the dispassionate presentation of facts, but by the relationships she cultivated and, most importantly, by her membership in a new community—the people who saw her fullness, who *liked* her, who were curious and chose to spend time in loving persuasion and disagreement rather than rejecting her all out. Her girlfriend, Allison Gornik, whom she ended up staying with and later marrying, was a key part of this gradual persuasion. It took three years, but, in many ways, that's actually a very fast conversion, compared to the twenty years of indoctrination that came before.

But she said it wasn't only the sense of safety and inclusion that made unlearning white nationalism possible for her. It was also the pressure, the confrontations, and the complaints of the people on the New College campus who feared and reviled her.

"In my own experience, the moment when I realized I needed to change was when my college community that I cared about was in so much pain because of me," she said. The process of change began in the emotional dissonance created by connection with people to whom Adrianne's views were harmful.

"I think I'm right, and I also know that they're not wrong, because I talk to them and I know them. My question was, where's the misunderstanding? That was a motivation to learn something new."

When we first talked, Adrianne was just a few years clear of the white nationalist movement. She'd lost most of her family when she publicly renounced them and was still sorting out her new identity—unsure of how much to speak publicly or engage with politics, gradually easing into liberal and radical spaces. White nationalism was still a fringe community based on principles of exclusion, but, for a long time, it had been all she knew, and she had received love and accolades and appreciation there. The adjustment was slow.

When we talked again a few years later, she had recently started coming out as trans, changing her pronouns, and presenting as feminine. Her natural red hair was layered, and her bright blue eyes were sharp and soft. I immediately recognized a kindred spirit. We sat in a hotel lobby in Baltimore, where she lives, and talked for hours, rapt by the growing threads of connection between our stories and beliefs, in spite of having grown up in ostensibly very different situations. Adrianne had a memoir coming out, and was grappling with how to talk about gender. Some of her ideas about white nationalism and community and unlearning had ripened into a strong clarity that few people have on the topic.

"You can only change somebody's mind because you start out from 'I care about you in some way,'" she said. "'I am connected to you, I understand you, I've taken the time to understand you. We have this shared reason that it matters if we are on the same page.'"

Even though her story of leaving white nationalism is often held up as an example of successful persuasion, she doesn't believe in persuasion in the sense of presenting reasons to change your mind.

"Persuasion is exactly the same thing as changing the community that you feel beholden to," she said. "People often think, at least in cultures I'm familiar with, that persuasion is, like, you encountered a better argument. But the reality is that persuasion is having a new group of people who you feel responsible for."

Unlearning for her came as a direct result of a shift in which community she felt accountable to—and included in. But I had to ask, as many people do: Why you? Was there something in Adrianne that made unlearning more likely for her, or made her more drawn to this new community than your average white nationalist? She's not sure, but she did hold a personal value, even as a young child, that came into direct conflict with staying in the white nationalist movement.

"I really hated the idea that I am a person who has closed off to other people, just as a rule," she said. Her parents had taught her to believe that white nationalism wasn't about "hate" or violence—but when she arrived at New College and learned about how others saw and understood the movement, she gradually became convinced that the movement *was* about hate and violence. And she thinks it's significant that she wasn't "out" as a white nationalist until after she had developed relationships—the longer she remained a part of that community, the greater the cognitive dissonance became. "How could it be that I am super close and want to be a great friend to people who are horrified, and terrified, and are saying, 'You are making my life so much worse'?" She said it can look naive in retrospect, but, in the moment, her confusion was very real: "'I care about you and I'm hurting you. I don't want to be hurting you. How do I reassess this? How do I act, if I care?'"

Another key part of her experience was that while it happened through strong relationships and community, it also required both cognitive dissonance and intense confrontation—the condition for unlearning the next chapter explores. For a long time, she confessed, she believed that the confrontational people on campus, especially the people who wanted to excise her from the community altogether, simply made unlearning harder for her. Later, she said, she saw their importance. "If those people hadn't existed, I would not have felt compelled to examine myself," she told me. A gentle invitation to unlearn was not the only push she needed. "I needed the people who were reaching out a hand so that I could feel like I was safe with somebody, but I wouldn't have done that had I not been confronted. . . . Both of those have the message of 'You are a part of something that I'm also a part of.'"

Being confronted, threatened with ostracization, obsessed and protested over—all of that to her now appears as "almost a form of care. It's almost a form of love. It's not saying, like, 'I've never heard of this person in my life. I don't give a damn.'" The message was that, in the broader community of New College, what this person believed and enacted mattered to people. It was the first time she had mattered to people outside of her family and the white nationalist movement, and the process of separation took years—but the toughness of the love, and the diversity of the community's views and tactics, made her unlearning more likely.

Adrianne's story is not full of pat, simple answers. One hard reality is that during her years in white nationalism, that *was* her community—and, like many of us, her firm and enduring feeling was that she ascribed to those beliefs because they were true and morally correct.

That feeling, however misguided it looks from the outside, is extremely hard to shake when your whole reality is at stake. The uncertainty and eventual unlearning arose primarily because she entered a new community and spent years being absorbed into it, challenged and invited. This one person's unlearning from such a rigid original set of beliefs took a large community, and came at an emotional cost for the people who were made uncomfortable or felt unsafe in her presence at New College. None of it was easy—and much of it would be difficult to replicate at scale. Adrianne herself cautioned me against speaking too lightly about the challenges of this kind of unlearning, the kind that requires undermining one's whole personal identity. For her, it was a terrifying precipice: "The feeling of 'I'm going to unlearn a thing that is fundamental to how other people see me' feels the same as, like, 'I might die,'" she said, looking me in the eye. "'I just don't know how I exist after that.' Like, 'If I fully change this, my disconnection from other people feels like it's going to be so complete that I don't know what exactly existence looks like after that.'"

Exclusion from a community is frightening for humans, by design; we were meant to live and thrive in complex communities, and we have an instinctive desire to be included. A new community might make new ways of thinking and acting possible—but I can't help but ponder the shadow side of belonging in a new community as a motivator for unlearning. What is the difference between closed-off and cult-like belief, and communities that facilitate and allow for ongoing unlearning? How can we cultivate uncertainty and questioning while still upholding some community standards and beliefs? Is my community that I think is so open-minded meaningfully different from someone else's that I find so closed?

In *The Great Muppet Caper*, when Kermit the Frog scores a date with Lady Holiday during their trip to London, his twin Fozzie the Bear is desperate to join him. At first, Kermit insists on going it alone—"It's *my* date, Fozzie, not *our* date." Fozzie is hurt. But finally he gives in. Fozzie exclaims in delight, "Oh, boy! Great news, gang, we can go!" and throws open the door of their Happiness Hotel room to reveal the entire rest of the crew, ready to join the date. I loved this, as a polyamory-inclined youngster—we're *all* going on the date! It's a community thing! And all the genders and tall and short and blue and yellow Muppets pile into the bus and go to meet Miss Piggy.

This is the kind of magical collective space that so many of us grew up without, but wanted. When we offer it to ourselves and each other now, we can make space to unlearn. Community, like love, both softens and toughens us to transform. But communities are not all the same: establishing flexible, adaptive, and loving community that strives to break down hierarchies is constantly undercut by dominant US culture. When someone harms us, instead of addressing it with those who love us both, we are encouraged to bottle it up or secretly "report it"; when we lose someone, instead of carving out space for collective grief, we are encouraged to power through, get back to work. When we feel lonely, we are encouraged to seek solace in the self, drinking, Netflix, or at best a single partner or nuclear family unit. But, in this atomized and confused society, there is no replacement for the safety of healthy togetherness.

The idea of community and relationship as a portal to rethinking is nothing new—as Māori academic Shawn Wilson writes in *Research Is Ceremony: Indigenous Research Methods,* the very concept of knowledge in Indigenous traditions exists only in community.

"The concepts or ideas are not as important as the relationships that went into forming them," he argues.[3] Knowledge systems encompass relationships between people, between people and ideas, between ideas and the cosmos. "Knowledge cannot be owned or discovered but is merely a set of relationships that may be given a visible form."[4] As Indigenous wisdoms from around the world will tell us, all learning and unlearning are a reflection of community presence and collective process.

Those of us who grew up without an experience of belonging in a community will face the challenge of unlearning individualism; we have probably internalized the idea that we must go it alone. There is no solo pathway out of narrow thought, just as there is no solo way to change the world—even the sterile Western social scientists acknowledge that people need groups in order to activate change. What's more, the systems of behavior we are trying to unlearn are almost always bolstered by individualism and broken down by collectivism. The simple act of doing things together to resist can shift the dynamics.

The problem of individualism is not incidental: it's part of the structure of a dominant culture that thrives on consumerism on the one end, and exploited labor on the other. What do collectives, or strong communities, do for capitalism—unless the community beliefs revolve around what we consume, where we work, or a God that tells us that the rich are blessed?

Kermit the Frog and Fozzie the Bear in *The Great Muppet Caper* act so very unlike many of the journalists I know, who are trained to compete for sources and scoops. When we do move collaboratively—thinking together, changing together, unlearning and reshaping reality together, bringing the whole gang along—we offer a form of resistance that challenges that dominant culture. Radical unlearning can never be an individual act, because its entire purpose is to get to the roots. The roots of trees are interdependent, communicating beyond words belowground. As human beings, so are we.

Getting to the roots for Gabriel meant that he had to go beyond his own personal liberation, and move toward something larger in his unlearning.

"The more I got comfortable with my own sexuality, the more I was able just to open up to the world," he said.

He returned to Guatemala in 2012, looking to revisit and resolve some relationships. "I felt like to be able to understand myself better, I needed to understand my family, my country, my society, the city where I grew up."

And, as a part of coming into this new self, he began to notice more.

"One of the things I was sort of unlearning was not being so afraid of expressing what I thought. . . . I was really working on being more open and really working on being more vulnerable."

He chuckled as he recounted that his first move toward overcoming this fear of being vulnerable was to start posting on Facebook. His posts asked questions about the Guatemalan government and the status quo and pointed out the corruption of the president at the time. "What are we gonna do about this?" he posted one day.

At that, someone invited him to organize his first protest, an anti-corruption demonstration at Guatemala City's main square. Unsatisfied with the confusing Facebook invite, to which thirty people had responded "Going," he rewrote it, renamed it, and gave it a snappy new graphic. People started sharing the protest invite; it went viral, and within twenty-four hours there were thirty thousand people saying they would be there. "It was crazy. It just exploded."

Just about a week later, he was in the streets of Guatemala City as a co-organizer of a historic anti-corruption protest, with tens of thousands of people present.

"We were very nervous that something might happen, but it went great," he said. "And then we did another one, and the vice president resigned, which was a big surprise and a big win for everyone. So we just kept going and going until the president resigned a few months later. And then suddenly I was in the middle of all that."

This was a defining moment for him: all the unlearning had materialized, connected him to something so much greater, and changed the trajectory of his life. "You see very clearly that you are in the right place, in the right moment and that you're supposed to be there. I felt a lot of that, in that period of my life."

For the last eight years, Gabriel's job has been organizing people around civil rights, political engagement, and corruption in Guatemala—first through the grassroots protest movement and an organization called Justicia Ya, then through a more formal community project, Instituto 25A, where he served as the director starting in 2019. He moved from unlearning his own fears and assumptions, to facilitating unlearning for others.

He learned quickly that, in order to create those spaces, they needed to help people tolerate discomfort.

"When you organize, when you start to be part of a collective group of people around a common issue . . . you're going to get uncomfortable at some point," he said. "You have to embrace feeling uncomfortable."

His organization began to experiment with how to help people stay in discomfort rather than avoid it. They used jokes, memes, theater, self-reflection, and collective sharing. Often the thing people are first unlearning is simply the idea that they don't have power over their own lives. "We ask them to write on pieces of paper what they thought about their everyday life that shouldn't be normal, but it feels normal." Often, people in the room would share similar or related things. "You can see in their eyes, like, realizing that their issue is not just their own issue, it's a community issue, it's a collective issue."

When I asked him what creates the conditions for unlearning, he went immediately to the role of community—specifically, collectives that strive for a less hierarchical, more countercultural way of relating. "I didn't do it by myself—it was in a collective setting, you know, and a few of us went through an important unlearning journey together."

But it's also a process rather than a moment, unlearning. It is moved forward by collective action, but it requires remaining in stages of discomfort and facing contradictions. "I think it might be a condition," he said, "to have that ability to be able to be with both thoughts in your mind and your body at the same time before letting go, before releasing."

And it helps immensely if people can see what's on the other side. "We're always trying to bring to the table an alternative or another way of seeing things that's enticing, that's fun, that's attractive, that's beautiful, that's moving."

After a series of enormous successes, the anti-corruption movement became the target of backlash: conservatives, evangelical churches, and corporate powers banded together and began a campaign of disinformation against them. The anti-corruption organizers were gay, they were pro-abortion, they were sinners and devils, they were committing acts of terror. A new president was elected on the force of talking points that echoed the popular movement, but soon after was revealed to be in the pockets of a corporate cabal; he managed to shut down the UN anti-corruption commission that Congress had established in 2007 after many years of work from civil society organizations in Guatemala. A new attorney general he appointed then began a witch hunt. "They started going after prosecutors, judges, journalists, activists, anyone that played an important part within the movement," Gabriel said.

In 2020, during a protest outside of Guatemala's Congress, someone started a fire inside the building; this act was blamed on protesters despite a lack of evidence. Later that year, Gabriel learned that he was among those likely to face charges of terrorism over the fire. In January 2021, someone put up a website with his name, face, and address, and the names and home addresses of his family members. Things escalated quickly, and by February he had left for Mexico City under a protection program for political activists. Initially, he only meant to be gone for three months, but, as the situation at home devolved, it made sense to stay. We met in 2022 in New York, where we had both flown to for a Ford Global Fellowship gathering. By the time we talked about unlearning in the fall of 2023, he had settled in Mexico City and started a new organization, this one a community center for Central American political exiles in Mexico.

Even as an exile, he believed in the power of collectives and community. He mused out loud, though, that he doesn't believe that people go easily into the unknown—it helps greatly when people who are unlearning already have something new to grasp onto, whether they realize it or not.

"I keep seeing the image in my head of the monkeys, you know, like the monkeys that are going through the jungle, that they don't release a branch until they have their hand on the next one," he said. "Until you feel a little bit of sense of safety in your new way of seeing things, your new way of feeling about the world, you won't completely let go of the previous one."

WRITING OUT OF NORMALCY: AN UNLEARNING OPENER

The totalitarian menace is one of intellectual foreclosure, ceasing to question—and creating obedience and unquestioning populations is an open strategy of leaders attempting to silence people across the world.

That means the art we are trying to practice and protect is that of asking questions.

My friend Jesa Rae taught me that everything has a curriculum—our surroundings, what we consider "normal," what we do and accept on a daily basis, the objects and maps and environments we move through, all of these are teaching us something. What is the curriculum of an iPhone? What is the curriculum of a highway? What is the curriculum of a relationship? Imagine that prison is curriculum, airport is curriculum, bathroom is curriculum, Instagram is curriculum, porn is curriculum, New Year's Eve is curriculum, the clinic is curriculum. What do you notice about what is being taught?

QUESTIONS FOR REFLECTION

1. What shapes your environment?
2. What languages, signs, and symbols do you interact with every day? Make a list, as long as you want.
3. What tools or physical objects do you routinely interact with? Think computers, phones, pitchforks, chopsticks, dishwashers, cars—whatever is around you that you regularly look at and use.
4. Who do you talk to?
5. Who do you listen to?
6. What do you spend most of your time doing?

7. Now go through each thing you listed—language, words, signs, symbols, tools, and objects. What are these languages, signs, and symbols teaching you? What is their "hidden curriculum"?

8. What do you notice about your life or surroundings that shouldn't be "normal"—but is? (Thanks to Gabriel Wer for this question.)

9. Why have you accepted this as normal?

CHAPTER 5

CONFRONTATION

We can't shift outside of what we know until we recognize at least a glimmer of what we don't know. Confrontation can be a necessary tool for unlearning: when it serves to crack something open, to manifest cognitive dissonance or doubt where before there was none.

Growing up in a mostly white liberal college town, I was taught to believe that racism was more or less a thing of the past. We learned about cultures from across the world, and we studied civil rights, celebrated Black History Month, and read Langston Hughes. We were not allowed to use racial slurs. Our classrooms—also mostly white—were racially diverse in part because of a complex public school busing system (making up for the reality that our neighborhoods were still segregated; southeast Michigan is to this day one of the most racially segregated landscapes in the country).[1] Racism was explained to us as a form of prejudice that was wrong and backward and mostly over; everyone was to be seen and treated as equals.

The first time I experienced what I then believed was racism was on the playground in second grade. During morning recess, I would hang around a group of three girls all of whom were Black, who lived in the same housing development and came to school via the school bus (the other white kids at the school and I walked or got dropped off by our parents). I was vaguely aware that they were Black and I was white, until the day we were swinging from the monkey bars, and two of the girls started mocking me, chanting, "You're white, you're white." I went home and told my parents—I'd finally seen it: racism! And I was the target! The biases I'd learned about as theoretical appeared to me, then, to be real—but reversed. As far as I remember, at the time, no adult could properly explain this to me. Why would people mock me for being white? Was reverse racism a thing? What was the difference between the stories I'd heard about civil rights and my mom growing up in the segregated South, and the playground moment where I felt, briefly, like a victim of racism myself?

I had always had a feeling that I was "missing something" about race—but I was rarely directly confronted with it. Mine was a world mired in mixed messages; racism was supposed to be over, but Black and white people still seemed to live in different worlds, and their world had far fewer material resources than ours. Occasionally it would be revealed, like it was on the playground that day, that Black people *saw* that gap between Black and white life, between the post-racial narrative and the lived reality. But white people never spoke of it. Thank God for James Baldwin: I read "The Fire Next Time," and he began to help me make sense of whiteness, of the probably universal white experience of actually missing the point.

"Something very sinister happens to the people of a country when they begin to distrust their own reactions as deeply as they do here, and become as joyless as they have become," Baldwin wrote, decades before I was born.

> It is this individual uncertainty on the part of white American men and women, this inability to renew themselves at the fountain of their own lives, that makes the discussion, let alone elucidation, of any conundrum—that is, any reality—so supremely difficult. The person who distrusts himself has no touchstone for reality. . . . Whatever white people do not know about Negroes reveals, precisely and inexorably, what they do not know about themselves.[2]

All these unexplained aspects of living in a racist society that claimed to be a colorblind one produced exactly this effect within me—I didn't trust myself, I didn't understand what I was encountering, and this was largely because I really did not know about Black life in the present day. Racism was supposed to be in the past, and that was confusing. It made honest conversations hard. Coming to terms with the present, as Baldwin implored white people to do, meant confronting a very uncomfortable set of facts, conversations, and emotions; it meant learning how racialized people actually experienced, felt about, and saw white people, and digesting what the historical legacies of colonialism and slavery actually look like today.

I was lucky. Anarchism, feminism, and being a queer youth activist took me into spaces where most people don't have the chance to go. At age eighteen, I was at a conference called "Against Patriarchy" in Eugene, Oregon, watching a white trans speaker talk about disability. He was wonderful, talking on a fluorescent stage with velvety chairs in front of a group of mostly white mostly anarchists on a college campus. I was alone and big-headed—encountering a zillion new ideas while milling around a world of sexy political Pacific Northwest queers. I had wide swimmy eyes and a blue "mohawk" haircut I'd sported for years, and I had just arrived on the west coast a month or two prior via Greyhound and hitchhiking, filthy and enthused. I sponged up every word, wondering how I'd got this far never having thought much about people with disabilities as a group (the answer, by the way, is that people with disabilities are systemically kept out of public space and discourse by inaccessibility and forced poverty).

During the Q&A after the talk, a person near my age with a shaved head stood up in the back, leaning on a cane. They talked fast, smart, and passionately. "Why didn't you talk about white privilege and colonization?" she asked the speaker. "Why are disabled Indigenous people like me invisible to you?"

Truthfully, I don't remember how the speaker responded from the stage—his defensiveness or lack thereof didn't make an impression. I just remember gravitating toward the person who spoke so forcefully and critically from the back. Her defiance and her fearlessness were magnetic. I approached her afterward: "I really liked what you said," I said, not even really knowing what she had meant, just knowing the feelings behind it mattered. She responded, long-winded, confrontational, continuing to crack open the conversation I'd been waiting for all these years to have. And, with little question or hesitation, I had a new friend.

I spent the next few weeks in the Northwest, meeting queer, Indigenous, and disabled activists and sitting quietly as long, exciting conversations took place around me. People were talking about cultural appropriation, disability, and mental health, ideas that suddenly moved from my periphery to my center. My new friend with the shaved head taught me about her daily experiences with people who claimed to want to "help" her when she went in public using a wheelchair. She taught me that to be disabled is often to be broke because the US enforces poverty for people on disability.

There was so much to know: I remember my friends' jaws dropping collectively when a couple of them were talking about buying things on layaway, and I asked, "What's layaway?" In all my eighteen years, I'd never had occasion to know the word. I'd been living without taking out loans, in a home where the next paycheck wasn't a constant concern, for my whole short life. I was traveling the country on little money but with my parents' credit card in my wallet, a constant safety net. In these moments of acute and sometimes embarrassing absorption, I faced my own limits: it was time to unlearn the assumptions of a wealthy childhood, and time to learn about the lives of people in legitimately impoverished situations, who were poor because of their context, or because they were born in a different location than me. I began to unlearn the innocence of wealth, too—the idea that my parents were rich because of something earned and deserved, rather than as a result of an unequal and exploitive system. Poor people work harder than anyone, but my whole life I'd been shown a different story.

My new friend turned the lens quickly on me. "Where are your people from?" she asked me the night we met, standing on someone's porch in Eugene in the streetlight shadows. I stumbled. Michigan? New York? South Carolina? I thought of myself as an American (although by that point it was in sort of an ironic way, like the Allen Ginsberg poem "America," which is all about addiction and queer outsiderness). But, still,

I vaguely believed I belonged here on this land; I was from this country, because where else would I be from?

But where are your *people* from? my friend pushed. I hesitated. I had never before defined myself in terms of European ancestry, but learning about colonization challenged the whole idea of being simply "from here." I called my parents (who were worried sick about me, generally) and asked questions, and slowly began a process of identification with a deeper ancestry: I was Irish, Scottish, English, Welsh, Dutch. I descended from people who'd come on the *Mayflower*, from people who'd enslaved people on the South Carolina Sea Islands, from sharecroppers in Mississippi, from capitalists in New York and North Carolina. My ancestry, like my class experience, became something to identify, investigate, and question.

This revelation, rather than discouraging me, helped me make sense of the nonsensical way that race had been explained to me: I learned that whiteness was a construct created to oppress and steal from Indigenous and Black people, that my ancestors had only become white when they came here. I was white only to the extent that whiteness continued to exist and persist as a structure of power; racial prejudice was just the tip of the iceberg, a surface expression of a glacial problem.

My new friends talked sharply about stolen land and white entitlement, and the rage was refreshing—I'd been traveling the country, wandering around in a vague guilt as I learned more about its history. I was excited by all this challenging stuff, by these new ways of relating: it almost seemed like my place could be *in the resistance*.

In an echo of that second-grade playground scene where my whiteness was first pointed out to me, people would joke: "You're, like, the whitest person in the world." I no longer perceived it as racism, or even as an insult—it was a jestful exploration of the real power differentials in the worlds we'd been born into and the assumptions that created our lives. They'd tell me white people had a debt to pay and I should be a part of paying it. I received all this with a mix of shame and enthusiasm, a blushy but anxious feeling. Naming these truths made them seem more possible to face.

But I wasn't ready for every part of the confrontation. Sitting on someone's living room floor in a Seattle punk house, covered in sticky cat hair, which I'm very allergic to, people explained in bitter tones how white people, my ancestors, had come to this land and pillaged and raped, exploited, and destroyed Indigenous cultures. Now people of European descent in this made-up country wanted to do a sweat lodge or sell a dream catcher or sport a "mohawk"? Mohawks are a people, the hairstyle a rip-off of those people's traditions. It was no small point, because European invaders not that long ago had made Indigenous religious practices illegal or impossible; they had forced Indigenous children to cut their traditional hairstyles. I blew my nose and felt defensive when I first heard this idea—after all, it's just a haircut!—and my blue "mohawk" stayed smushed under a baseball cap as I went deeper and deeper into these new relationships. I'd developed a huge crush on the girl from the back of the room and tagged around after her helplessly, hiding my hair.

My big ears went bright pink when I finally took the hat off. *You have a mohawk?* She said. I was ashamed, and with no real explanation. I guess I just . . . didn't know what it meant? I stumbled. My friends proposed we cut it off that very night and I agreed, so my last "mohawk" haircut (I now find the terminology itself offensive) was removed by giggling Cherokee queers in a bathtub in Seattle. Maybe my youth explains the quick turnaround, the seeming ease of absorbing something so new and so counter to my own sense of comfort. A couple weeks later we made fliers and printed them at Kinko's, and I started going around queer spaces giving white people with "mohawks" and dreadlocks a head's-up about why these hairstyles were hurtful. It was fascinating how defensive people were about their hair, how hard it was to let go of symbolic ownership over an idea.

Unlearning colonialism, and all the entitlement that comes with being on the settler side, isn't something that happens while drinking tea or inhaling cat hair one night in Seattle. There's no absolution in shaving off the offensive haircut, or distributing some fliers about appropriation. The damage of colonial ideology and violence is intergenerational, and it's a harm that's still underway, as corporations build mines on native land and education systems wipe out native history. It is ugly to see settlers pick freely through the remains of native culture and take what they will, and it is ugly to be one of those settlers. These moments were unlearning encounters, not necessarily deep commitments to solidarity, but, ideally, the one feeds into the other.

The beginning of unlearning in this story was confrontation, a brush with impassioned anger and also with my own guilt, that alerted me to my specific role, to a world of experiences I had overlooked, and to my own cognitive dissonance. The dissonance signaled a desire for deeper connection and understanding. The moments I described were not easy. But there was positive friction: magnetism, curiosity, friendship, heat. I was pulled further into unlearning by people who somewhat remarkably invested their time and energy in me, who taught me patiently—but not necessarily gently—how I had inadvertently carried on harm. To this day, I experience that opportunity as a radical act of generosity, one that my ancestors' own violent legacy works against. Colonialism does not want the colonizer to listen to the colonized—in fact, those kinds of authentic interactions are generally made structurally difficult or near impossible, and the person in the power position usually has the option to simply write someone off as ungrateful, angry, or delusional.

I feel obligated to my unlearning, because the people who have taken risks to confront me have done it in a world that would otherwise support me to completely ignore them, or even to subject their views and feelings to ridicule. White power is structured to mean that if I had stayed disinterested in Indigenous people's experiences, I could have lived my whole life unscathed. I could have worn the "mohawk" without consequence. I could have gone through life pretending this country belongs to me.

"When someone decides that they want to unlearn, to me the hard part's over," said Tarek Zeidan, a sexual and bodily rights activist from Lebanon who works for the rights and protection of LGBT communities in the Middle East and North Africa. Tarek and I talked by Zoom, he from a dimly lit office in Beirut, and I from a friend's trailer on a mountain in West Virginia. His salty beard and sharp eyes made me swoon me a little. But we were there to talk about conflict and confrontation—Tarek, now a scholar at Harvard University studying the risks of AI for global LGBT populations, had also studied human rights advocacy and adaptive leadership at Harvard's Kennedy School. He took a special interest in the cultivation of confrontation as a means to transformative change. I called him to ask him to elaborate on his views after a brief conversation we had in South Africa in 2022.

He started by clarifying that conflict and confrontation are not the same thing. Conflict begins and persists when we each stay stuck in our own worldview, unwilling to challenge the underlying assumptions of the conversation. A lot of people, when confronted with something difficult or uncomfortable that contradicts their beliefs, begin to defend their existing assumptions—a tendency sometimes described by neuroscientists as the "backfire effect," where individuals respond to intellectual threats as viscerally as they would to physical threats. And many of us tend, in moments of tension, to revert to the sympathetic nervous system, the one that tells us to avoid danger by fighting or running away. As we react and defend, rather than opening up a portal, we find ourselves in conflict.

"Unfortunately, conflict is a much easier, more seductive, more available method . . . than curiosity and compassion," said Tarek. Confrontation, on the other hand, serves to open up space, to ask questions rather than reinvest in staked out positions. It can manifest sufficient tension to push a person or group towards unlearning.

"There is a purpose behind confrontation," Tarek continued. "It's part of a plan to shift things, shift values, shift systems, manifest conditions, change. Conflict is a reaction. There is no purpose but to ensure the continuation of the status quo."

Tarek has seen the effect of confrontation on many occasions in his own work, as people who are uncomfortable with queerness or nonbinary gender lean into and learn from the tension created by queer movements worldwide. He's also seen the intractability of conflict—many times in our conversation, he mentioned the ongoing genocide in Palestine and the overly defended position of the Israelis.

He shared an anecdote about facilitating a multiracial group in the US that included white Europeans, white Americans, and Black Americans. The white Europeans were confounded by the amount of time spent talking about privilege and race, and, over time, a conflict emerged. Tarek came in as a facilitator. Instead of opening with an agenda, or even a real question, he simply asked the group to explain what was going on—to explain the nature of the conflict.

The tension built in the room, and for a minute, no one spoke. But then a German white man piped up—to explain that he didn't think any of it was a very big deal. "Why are we even still talking about this?" he asked. "Is everything about racial privilege all the time?"

Tarek intervened with a simple question: "Do you think it's a coincidence that you were the first person to speak?" There: the confrontation. He didn't name race, or accuse the German man of anything—but he did ask him to explain his analysis. Do you feel comfortable speaking first, and speaking for the group, for a particular reason? What might that reason be? Or, alternatively, are there aspects of your experience we might not be seeing that compelled you to speak first? Is it all a coincidence?

The way the man responded is unimportant—what mattered here was that the first question sparked a confrontation, a moment of tension, that broke open the room. Some were surely perceiving the moment as very racialized and gendered, while others were likely not thinking about it. After Tarek asked these questions, everyone chimed in to explain their point of view. The issue was no longer theoretical, but in an active state of collective challenge.

"Adults need to be shaken to learn something new," Tarek said. Tense confrontations—about racism, sexism, transphobia, any system of oppression and power—can break down certainty, and may be necessary to do so. The confrontation does not have to be one on one; it can also be in group contexts or even in the context of protest and uprising. Think, for example, of the confrontation created by the mass protests over police violence in 2020. Tarek explained that creating tension in order to prompt unlearning does require a measured approach: "The tension is in a sweet spot. Too much and they'll leave, or cancel you, or completely remove themselves, and nothing's happening. They'll still remain where they are. So, how do you calibrate that?"

Calibrating the tension requires genuine curiosity and compassion, he said. But a fear of confrontation will make it impossible to even start the conversations we need to have.

"You have to have the courage to step into danger because this is dangerous work," he said. "And you also have to give a shit about the person and the thing enough to do that."

But what about guilt and shame? Are they valid tools for transformation, or emotions to be avoided if we are to create a fertile ground for unlearning? We see this all the time in confrontations about white supremacy and white privilege: as white people learn about the consequences of white-dominant culture and behavior, it's not unusual that they fall apart into some combination of guilt and shame. I see the guilt and shame, too, when people mess up my pronouns or say something uninformed about trans people and then stumble, fuss, and over-apologize. It's unhelpful to descend into a spiral of efforts to be forgiven and absolved after we do or say something hurtful—and yet I've waded into that muck from both sides.

But I also recognize something authentic in the guilt and shame that arises after realizing hurtful mistakes or unearthing our complicity in systems of harm. A word, a name, or a haircut can also symbolize lives lost, stories erased, and daily patterns of exclusion and violence. And the violences of institutionalized oppression can never be redressed by individuals "doing better" or changing how we see—hence, the guilt and shame. When I first began to learn about racism and anti-racism, I had nightmares about it, insomnia about it. I would stay up worrying about my own missteps. I also verbally attacked other white people in my life, accusing them of being *even more racist* than me or razzing them for not doing enough, relishing the relief of finger pointing. I was afraid to say the wrong thing, and I was hungry to be a different person. And for me this desire to change, the realization of lack, has often started with a moment of guilt or even shame: a flash of paradox, when I realize that who I want to be is not who I truly am. I still have moments like this all the time, and I am still frequently tempted to guilt people to cover up my own shame at having thought, felt, or represented the exact same thing.

Researchers into the emotional experiences of guilt and shame describe them as "self-conscious" emotions, meaning that both require some degree of reflection on one's self in order for these emotions to come up at all.[3] They are also considered moral emotions, not because they are "right" to feel, but because they help instruct us about prosocial behaviors, behaviors that align us with the moral beliefs of our society or community. As such, some psychologists consider them helpful to upholding group conformity and shaping morality—basically, guilt and shame are internal rule-enforcers that help us follow social rules without even having to be told what they are.[4] But they can also cue us that something is wrong, guiding us to change our behavior or to reject the society that requires it.

Importantly, guilt and shame are also generally interpreted as meaningfully different emotional experiences from one another: guilt typically focuses on a specific action or event for which we feel we can take responsibility, while shame is a generalized sense of humiliation at who we are, or how we measure up to our own and others' expectations. Guilt is about something we did wrong; shame is the feeling that "I am wrong." And guilt tends to focus on the private and personal need to change, while shame tends to assume an audience (even if this audience is just an imagined person or group judging us).

Following this interpretation, guilt might help us ameliorate a situation by offering accountability and repair, while shame tends to send us into spirals of self-focus and might even make it hard to be empathetic or make us want to hide or deny rather than repair our behavior. Shame can turn easily into self-blame, or even hostility toward others, and may make it even harder and less likely to deeply unlearn and change behavior. So if we get confronted about something and we can identify and process through that guilt, maybe it can aid unlearning. If we face confrontation and descend into shame, the path forward can be harder to find. We may even become more defensive or more set in our ways.

And, yet, I know I've felt deep shame in moments when I've realized my own ignorance or learned that I have caused harm. Is feeling shame going to slam the door on all unlearning to follow? Not inevitably: researchers find that while guilt and shame are different experiences, *both* of these feelings can point us toward repair and transformation. They are feelings that were designed to help us survive in groups, to self-regulate away from destructive, harmful behavior. They can go too far or focus on the wrong things, but they are prosocial when they're used in ways that align with our desired collective values.[5] If we can greet our shame with self-love and forgiveness and assess its causes carefully, we may still be able to transform it into action—as many queer people know well, shame might also sometimes indicate that what we need to shift is our community, not our own beliefs, and it becomes a guide to finding acceptance.

Shame can be transformed into unlearning when we identify concrete opportunities for repair and forward motion, rather than stay focused on self-condemnation. So, if your starting point is shame, the goal is not so much to avoid that shame as to move through it toward something that still leaves space for you or your environment to change. Shame and guilt might not be avoidable—but the impetus is on us to turn them into transformation.

Unlearning white supremacy, then, means learning how to breathe through the knot in my throat to show up wholehearted, to not take myself too seriously even when everything feels heavy and my angry spirit wants redemption, fullness, to feel seen. White supremacy—not a sin, but a system from which I benefit—denies all of us humanity in unique ways. For white people, a part of that is in how we develop a tendency to defend, to respond to feedback with guilt and fragility, to avoid Black rage and look away from Black people's healing. Showing up whole means simply listening, not as some performative act of deference but as an embodiment of the recognition that I truly don't and can't know what it's like. Embodying curiosity, overriding shame, retracking my thoughts not so that I never "fuck up" again but so that I can be flexible in the face of feedback, not so that I "do better" but so that I contribute less to others' suffering and create new pathways through acts of resistance, forge desire lines towards collective liberation.

There's an important distinction to be made here, between embracing and moving through our own shame and guilt, and intentionally shaming *other* people as a strategy. While shame might be generated by a confrontation, Tarek said, it should absolutely not be the goal.

"Shame is so destructive," he said, but "you are not responsible for what others feel. I cannot make you feel ashamed. I ask the question. If you feel ashamed, then that is something that you need to question."

When I argue that the feeling of shame might be transformed into an opportunity to unlearn, it does not follow that shaming people creates the conditions for unlearning—more likely than not, it will end in defensiveness, defiance, or retreat. But calling out, calling in, and confrontation can all be done without saying, "You are bad," even if people are saying you *did* something bad, harmful, or hurtful.

Here's an example of a call-out that facilitated unlearning in my life: At that same conference in Eugene in 2002, I attended a workshop on disability issues where I spoke repeatedly about how I had been "blind to" what disabled people experienced and was finally opening my eyes. As it turns out, many people who are blind find this turn of phrase hurtful, and the facilitator, Eli Clare, called me out in front of the group—saying he was sure I didn't know this, but that the phrase could be very offensive, as it implies that being blind is the same as not being able to perceive something. I recall him even speaking about me personally: "Lewis is a sweet person and has really good intentions and probably does not know . . . " I was thoroughly embarrassed, and I also never thought about blindness the same way. In retrospect, I recall that the caller-outer was careful not to dehumanize me. Eli made an example of my mistake while making clear that the intent was to help me grow, to help me not harm others. He was careful to express to the whole group that he knew I meant well. I felt guilty, but not worthless. I was ashamed, but not destroyed—and, looking back, I feel nothing but wonder.

That one small moment helped me begin to think about all the many ways in which people with disabilities had been outside of my mind, the ways I had contributed to inaccessible spaces, and the ways I had participated in the dominant culture's denial that blind and deaf and physically disabled people exist and should be a part of public life. "Blind" was just a word to me, but it became a portal to thinking about *actual people and conditions,* and changing my use of the word was a portal to changing how I behaved. Others witnessed the interaction, and hopefully unlearned alongside me. That moment also gave me an example of how confronting something hurtful or problematic in a moment doesn't have to be shaming, or cruel.

At its most extreme end, shaming works directly against unlearning. Large-scale canceling, banishing, and punishing people can't create conditions for those people's unlearning because radical unlearning requires connection and relationship. People can't unlearn when they are isolated and shut down. These strategies might be helpful when the target is a corporation or a powerful individual, and the goal is to activate *other* people who are witnessing the interaction. Shaming powerful people to make a point about their behavior is a tried-and-true political tactic, and I'm all for that. My concern here is practical, not moral: if you want a particular person or group to unlearn, then shame is not a sustainable condition.

Public punishment for expressing unpopular views creates another problem for unlearning: when people are afraid to say what they really think, they can't enter into honest confrontation and debate with one another. In recent years, some wonderful writers including Ngọc Loan Trần and adrienne maree brown have gone deep on the matter of how people in a shared community can hold each other accountable and push each other to change without treating people as disposable.[6] As Trần asked in an influential 2013 blog post about "calling in," "What does it mean for our work to rely on how we have been programmed to punish people for their mistakes?"[7] Trần and brown both argue that scapegoating and humiliating—while sometimes necessary tools to address a power imbalance—are not ideal pathways to liberatory change, because they destroy rather than restore connection. brown worries in her 2020 booklet *We Will Not Cancel Us* that the use of call-outs as a tool for groupthink and public shame is actively limiting the collective investment in unlearning and building transformative communities on the left.

"I have felt us losing our capacity to distinguish between comrade and opponent, losing our capacity to generate belonging," brown writes.[8] She argues that for social justice work to be an appealing model of the world we are trying to create, we must work hard at generative conflict and confrontation, and learn to give and receive feedback without severing connection and trust. brown's framework embodies abolition and the idea (grounded in Black feminism) that no one is disposable, and that part of challenging systems of incarceration and punishment is to create a culture of non-disposability in our own communities. In the afterword, Malkia Devich Cyril writes, "While all harms are not equal, even the most heinous require a way home."[9]

But to whom falls the responsibility for providing that way home? Not everyone can take responsibility for every other person's unlearning, and the pressure often falls on oppressed people to act as teachers, or to be loving in the face of a hostile and unsupportive environment (this love-on-demand is expected particularly of women and feminine people). These lines become fuzzy in practice, in real relationships, and in real moments when we face our own unlearning. In practice, there's no "good call-out" or "bad call-out," and I'm certainly not the arbiter of either. While I feel sure that radical unlearning is our collective responsibility, I also know it's important that the burden not fall too heavily on the people who are the most harmed by dominant systems in the first place. Constantly being a "teacher" because your lived experience, culture, or reality has been oppressed and sidelined can be exhausting and embittering.

And yet, as Tarek pointed out, it may be inevitable. Oppressed people know more about oppression than the people who benefit from it, because they need to understand all sides in order to challenge it. And oppressed people have a clear self-interest in confronting oppression: "People who are oppressed are the ones with the bigger stake in changing the system," he said. But those of us who benefit or are privileged by other people's pain also have a stake, one that confrontation can help us truly feel.

For those of us experiencing harm in any form, it's important that we trust our gut: there are mistakes, harmful structures, and hurtful behaviors and comments that can be addressed through good-faith confrontations in community, and these can be opportunities for unlearning. But there are also provocateurs, bad-faith actors, and people who don't give a crap about us. These are most often the people to complain about "political correctness" and "free speech" and whine about being shamed, the bloviators who claim their freedom is limited by others' desire to be respected and who deliberately confuse meaningful critique and confrontation or calls for accountability with "cancel culture." These folks are mired in their own certainties, their own resistances to unlearning, and, more often than not, their own relative power of position, platform, or inherited privilege. While these certainty profiteers may not be disposable—because no human is—they're also not where we need to focus our most gracious unlearning energy, our most thoughtful attempts at provoking thought without encouraging shame. Everyone's unlearning is not on you, only your own—or, if you choose to become an organizer, the unlearning that happens in your community.

When folks are authentic in their willingness to address harms or question assumptions, that is the window of unlearning—which is why my questions here center around how to open that window in myself and how to recognize and support it in others, not how to "make people see" or shut people up. The people who are incapable of listening will find someplace else to keep talking. The people who want to change alongside us may take time, and may require support we can't always offer them. All of that is okay if we trust our gut. Easier said than done, I know.

I will always be unlearning whiteness and colonialism, the structures that have a way of transforming and reappearing in new shapes in the country where I live. I have internalized so many racist ideas that I'm sure I can't always see: the fear of Black women's anger; the tendency to minimize or not see racialized people's pain; insidious assumptions about meritocracy and intelligence; a deeply conflicted relationship to land and home. I have internalized the tokenistic and congratulatory tone white liberals take toward "successful" Black and Brown people, and the pitying tone those same liberals take toward Black and Brown people who suffer. I struggle to be compassionate rather than falsely pious, but all of this lives inside me.

The world is full of liminal spaces and gray areas, and the call-out and the guilt and shame that arise within it are some of the ambiguous, imperfect examples of how we might unlearn.

Without confrontation—without people taking the time and having the love and trust to point out the dissonance between my values and my words, to create tension and show me ways I might explore that tension—I doubt I would even have a commitment to unlearning racism or colonialism. Where is the self-interest if there is never a confrontation, if I never feel what's missing and remain mired in the satisfactions of privilege? Without confronting people and asking them to unlearn gender with me, and finding people who were willing and able to shift and move to understand and see me in my trans body and trans experience, I don't think I would have survived. These days, because I'm tired, I don't spend a lot of personal time educating people about trans issues—my version of confrontation is to refer folks to the many widely available resources on the internet, the guides to history and etiquette, and ask them to please educate themselves.

Unlearning is a process of peeling back layer upon layer, circling back to what we think we know and questioning why we believe it, trying to recover and respect "gut feelings" while also challenging ingrained biases. We cannot trust our gut. We must trust our gut. We cannot change. We need to change. I continually make mistakes and stumble through ideas, and I'm continually surprised by the nature of the lessons in their wake. I feel small, like a new person to the world, childlike in ways that can be wondrous or alarming. It's as if I thought I was learning to climb, but what's required is swimming. I thought I was breathing air, but I'm diving underwater.

S tories are an area of unlearning I have struggled to define or contain. Clearly they are important: Gabriel Wer used them in their unlearning work in Guatemala, Jim Henson used them to make meaning through Muppets, and many of the organizers and changemakers I've talked to see stories as an integral part of unlearning, a way to loosen synapses and invite people into conversations.

Daniel Heath Justice is a queer Cherokee science fiction and fantasy writer, and a professor of critical Indigenous studies and English at the University of British Columbia. In his book, *Our Fire Survives the Storm,* Justice articulates his beliefs about the relationship between story and resistance, story and social change.

"Indigenous wisdom traditions throughout the world hold great reverence for the sacred power of words and stories; these stories can create the world or destroy it, and each person is called upon to treat words carefully. Stories make meaning of our world, and the quality of life we find in that world depends in large part on the ethical content and purpose of those stories. Some scholars, politicians, and spiritual leaders inspire us with stories that speak to relationship and the values of generosity, kindness and understanding, while many others prefer to share the self-serving stories of fear, paranoia, and myopia that make the world a smaller, crueler place. What is 'America,' after all, but a construction of stories that have led people to acts of courage and great brutality? 'Civilization,' savagery,' 'socialism,' 'democracy,' freedom': each of these words bears its own storied burdens and possibilities."[1]

Can stories create conditions of unlearning, or are they actually the new learning itself, vessels of information and ethics? What are the meaningful differences (and I know they exist) between stories that act as propaganda and narrow our way of looking at the world, and stories that might open us up and free us?

Stories have a place in unlearning. As Daniel Heath Justice writes about Indigenous literatures, "When we question the stories that erase us and replace them with stories of both our past and current presence, we speak ourselves into an existence that reaches to the future."[2] I feel the truth of this in my bones.

When we talked, Daniel glowed through the Zoom screen. I found him funny and gentle, but with a devious edge. After speaking with him, I felt persuaded that stories can create conditions for unlearning particularly in contexts where we have trust, intimacy, or connection to the story or storyteller—and they are especially effective in this when they raise more questions than answers. I also felt persuaded of the sacred nature of story: the need to be careful, even reverent, with our words.

What follows is an edited transcript of our rich conversation.

LEWIS: How did you come to your interest in stories?

DANIEL: I was a storyteller as far back as I can remember. [. . .] I think one of the earliest memories was when I was in kindergarten. We lived in a mining town, and in the mining area, they used cyanide heap leaching, so they would pour a cyanide solution over ore and it would leach the precious metals out into collecting ponds, which are just like cyanide and rainwater. And there was one point when some horses had gotten loose and drank the water and died. And so, I'm in kindergarten, and it's show-and-tell. I didn't have anything to show, but I could tell. So I told this elaborate story about how my dad drank poisoned water and died. I constructed this entire narrative about how sad I was that my dad had died and everything. Kids were crying, and I was like, "Wow, this is really amazing."

And, the teacher called my mom and said, "Your son, he has single-handedly destroyed show-and-tell. I will never have it again with him in the classroom because he caused so much disruption." The teacher actually made me stand up in front of

the class and tell them I had lied to them. And that was really
mortifying and upsetting because I didn't lie. I told a story. It
was show-and-tell. I told a story. I didn't think of it as a true
or false thing. I thought of it as you'll tell the best story you
could, and that's what came to mind.

LEWIS: Wow.

DANIEL: Miss Chambers. I still remember her name.

LEWIS: Go away, Miss Chambers. How do you think stories relate
to unlearning?

DANIEL: Because of my work in Indigenous studies, so much of
what we do is unlearning. Because so much of what people
think they know about Indigenous peoples is just wrong. It's
based in stereotype. It's based in investment in particular kinds
of social hierarchies and privileges and claims around belonging and land. So I think the stories we tell about one another
very much inform the relations we have with one another, just
as the stories we tell about ourselves inform how we interact
with other people as well. I'm fortunate to be in a discipline
where unlearning is fundamental to the work that we do. And
it also requires us to be reflective about what we bring to the
table too—as we're expecting other people to unlearn, we have
to do the unlearning, too.

When I first started, I thought I was smarter than I do now.
Which I think, you know, that's a good thing, too, to grow
along the way. But I was more certain about a lot of things that
I am now. I approach ideas and experiences and stories with a
bit more humility than I did before. Certainty always concerns
me and I think stories treated with respect challenge any sort
of fossilized certainty. Fossilized certainty always leads to harm.

LEWIS: That's really interesting that you say that, because that's kind
of been a core grappling for me with this project is, you know,
I'm talking about unlearning in a context of justice, and of challenging oppression and visions for liberation. But there is always
this risk of replacing one framework of certainty or of propaganda with another. And now this is the story that we must all

tell, or this is the only liberatory story. So I'm curious, especially in the context of this work that you're doing, uplifting Indigenous stories and ways of looking that's inherently pushing up against colonial mindsets, how do you avoid that trap of getting into "We replace this with that," the traps of certainty?

DANIEL: I think part of it is not just presuming that there's a singular story. So bringing multiple voices into that conversation. And, you know, the great thing about Indigenous people is that we're very diverse and we have diverse experiences, and we have diverse cultural expressions even within one particular nation. We will have a lot of different approaches to issues. So there might be shared continuities. And we also talk about that. But strategies of response are so varied.

If you bring multiple voices in, you're more likely to disrupt in the attempt at certainty. And still grounded in people's experiences and realities. That doesn't mean that everything is just kind of thrown open and that there's no consensus reality. It means the consensus reality is bigger and more complicated than we imagined.

Propaganda is cynical. It's manipulative. And that's why it works. Because people want to have control over an ultimately uncontrollable universe. So it answers all the questions. Anything that answers all the questions is a lie. We're complicated creatures. We live in a complicated world. We need to be careful about being too, too aggressively certain about what is going on around us.

For me, the singular story of certainty is always about wielding power and authority over others. You disrupt that by bringing multiple voices to the table, some of whom you may not agree with, but at least they are part of that conversation.

LEWIS: Yeah, that makes a lot of sense. I also was thinking as you were just talking about fictional stories and how that can be another venue for talking about something without overdetermining it. I'm curious what your experience of that is, as a person who also writes fiction. Where does that fit?

DANIEL: In writing fiction, I often do it from multiple voices. [. . .] The singular narrator is complicated. And I think the more voices you have in there, the more capacity for empathy you have, especially with characters you don't necessarily like. It's really easy to write a cardboard villain, but the villains who stick with you are the ones who worry you that you could do the same, in different circumstances.

LEWIS: I worked in public radio for several years, and I think there's a lot of interest in that format in evoking empathy. That can be a good thing, but it sometimes falls into those same traps: here's what you're supposed to empathize with, and here's what you're not supposed to empathize with. But I guess where I'm going with that in terms of a question is, what is the usefulness of empathy in unlearning? Like, I think stories can be vessels of empathy, but then what do you think is the usefulness of that?

DANIEL: Empathy has limited efficacy. Not that it's a bad thing. I think empathy can be a really good thing. But what it often means to people is it's kind of the goal rather than empathy motivating action. Like, "I feel bad for you. I've done my work." [. . .] If empathy is unidirectional, there's something wrong with it as well, right? There's this idea that you have to be empathetic to me and my experience. But I can project all of my stereotypes and dislikes onto you. So it's just I need you to feel *me* rather than us, to see each other and think about the relationship that we are building from this point on. [. . .] It's easy to see people as cardboard villains and not to see what motivates decisions beneath them. And that's not to say that there aren't people who are horrendous in the actions that they perpetrate in the world. But most people aren't that way. And most people who have politics that I disagree with are not, they're not just irredeemable assholes, right? And they see me with fear and my politics with fear as well. And if I can't recognize that, then there's a short circuit in that narrative. It doesn't

mean that my politics are wrong, but it doesn't necessarily
mean that theirs are all the time, either.

LEWIS: What makes the difference of the story that motivates action
and engagement versus a story that provokes empathy?

DANIEL: I don't know that a writer can determine that. I don't know
that a storyteller can determine that. That actually depends a lot
on the story, and the person who hears it or reads it and what's
going on in their lives at the moment. There's a strange alchemy
that takes place with storytelling and you can't control that.

LEWIS: I also want to ask about fear. I feel like one of the things
that we are up against in the kinds of unlearning that I'm
talking about is these powerful stories that evoke and reevoke
fear in people. Whether that's about, you know, "Palestinians
are all terrorists and want to destroy all Jews" or "Trans people
are going to assault you in the bathroom." Or I could go on
with the stories that evoke fear, but what are your thoughts on
how stories can counter that?

DANIEL: Fear thrives in spaces of absence. It's not the only place it
thrives, but the problem is when we have ample stories and are
seen as an absence. So we have counterstories. We have stories
that affirm our humanity in all kinds of ways. We actually need
people to listen. We speak and they hear silence. [. . .] It's not
that we don't have the stories, we have them. It's people's willingness to hear them. Because once those fear stories find their
way into their consciousness, they're very difficult to uproot.

And, again, you can't control how a story shapes you, but
a story will change you. That's the power of it, and that's why
people are afraid of it.

LEWIS: You talked in one of your books about stories as medicine.
My impulse is to think that that maybe also could relate in
some way to unlearning. Talk a little bit more about what you
mean when you say that stories can be medicine.

DANIEL: I think stories can be very healing, but I always want to
pair that with they can be hurtful as well. [. . .] One of those

things for me is being gay. The story I grew up with was that it was a death sentence. That it was predatory. That it was disgusting. That it was subhuman. And that's a story that kind of weaves its way into your bones, and then you start to realize that, not only are your feelings not aligning with straightness, but your understanding of what it is to be gay doesn't have to be that. So in that way it can be very healing.

LEWIS: Yeah, totally. Do you remember an early encounter with a story that wasn't, you know, being gay as death and destruction and sad?

DANIEL: When I was about seventeen, a friend of mine who was a woman, her aunt bought her a gay porn magazine. I don't understand why, other than they were really cute guys on it. And she . . . shared it with me for some reason, and I was quite taken by this. I remember it was *Blue Boy* magazine.

LEWIS: Oh my God.

DANIEL: Yeah, yeah, back in the day. And I made up some excuse to borrow it. I have no idea how I did that. And she let me borrow it, and so it wasn't a story so much as I was just so entranced by these beautiful men. I'd seen a lot of straight porn. I had never seen men who were unashamedly sexual, who were beautiful, and who were looking at an implied male gaze with reciprocal desire. And I was like, "Oh, no. Oh, no." [laughter] I was like, "Oh, my gosh, that's gay? That's what gay is?" And that cracked something open in my psyche. It wasn't a story in words, but it definitely broke open the narrative.

RETELLING OUR OWN STORIES: A FEW QUESTIONS FOR REFLECTION

1. What is a story you learned that you no longer believe is true? What story do you tell yourself now in its place? What changed?
2. Respond to the following prompts:
   - *I used to believe . . .*
   - *Now I believe . . .*
3. Free write: What questions are you grappling with? Try to come up with questions that cannot be answered. Write for as long as you can, only in the form of questions.

CHAPTER 6

QUESTIONS

When I lived briefly in New York City and then decided to move to North Carolina in 2017, a number of New Yorkers I spoke to were aghast: Why would I, a conspicuously trans person, want to go there, a place that was notorious at the time for being one of the first states in the country to pass a so-called bathroom bill?

A fair question at first glance: these bills, which have since become law in some form or another in fourteen states, target transgender people by requiring everyone to use public bathrooms that align with their sex assigned at birth. In theory, anyone who appears to be in the "wrong bathroom" in someone else's eyes could have the cops called on them and be required to show ID or even a birth certificate. As a person who frequently uses men's rooms with an "F" on my ID, I would be a literal gender outlaw.

But the question still rankled me, in a few ways. First, of course, there was an assumption about New York—I guess the questioners figured I would never have a problem in a bathroom in a nice progressive place like that. Wrong there: the only places where I've personally had serious bathroom confrontations have been Berkeley, California, and a north-side gayborhood in Chicago, and I can assure you that there are transphobes everywhere, no matter the state law. The question also implicitly absolves the state of New York of its responsibility for the anti-trans attitudes of people like Donald Trump and the more recently ascendant representative Elise Stefanik, a virulent and unhinged advocate against human rights who was born in New York's capital city and educated at Harvard University.

A deeper, more troubling assumption I encountered in New York was that the people of North Carolina are somehow fundamentally different from and more backward than northerners—and that people are unchanging. Many New Yorkers seem to actually believe the stereotype that the South is full of racist, transphobic, biased people, that such people can't be found in Manhattan or Long Island, and that all this is a static state of being. The story is that some people and some places are just *that way*.

I know too much to believe that story. In some trans circles, there's a kind of macabre line of jokes about what it means to be a trans elder—basically, if you make it past thirty-five, you're an elder, in part because so many people who are trans get murdered or die by suicide, and in part because our communities grow and change so quickly, the "generations" are short. Speaking as an elder trans person (I'm forty as I write this, and I do have a single white eyebrow hair): I know better than to believe that societal views on gender are unchangeable. I have been having these conversations and inviting these interventions for over two decades, almost entirely in places that have been written off by liberals as "red states" and at least some of the time with people who are genuinely threatened by my existence or disgusted by my body. I have seen dozens, if not hundreds, of people change. I have also seen a successful phase of right-wing organizing that has deployed new forces against us—focusing on southern states and rural places because they presume these are the places they can win. In North Carolina, in fact, that wasn't even true: the original bathroom bill was repealed thanks to an enormous and unprecedented organizing effort led by a multiracial coalition that included a successful call for the NCAA and the NBA to move tournament games out of the state in 2016 and 2017.[1]

If all trans people are supposed to just live in New York and San Francisco, what about the rest of us? What about my mom and brother and niblings in South Carolina (even further into the depths of the Deep South) who are making change every day through their conversations and interventions? What about the country queers in West Virginia and the trans people in southern Ohio or northern Michigan who are my friends and comrades? Are we just supposed to give up on the places and people we love and come from? What about my grandmother?

I moved to North Carolina in 2017 in part because I knew just how important it was for me to live close to my roots in a politically right-leaning region, and to be part of the interventions and solutions in a place that didn't self-identify as liberal or progressive, like New York City. But then I had to humble myself to what those interventions actually look like. When I came out as trans to my family, it was hard but they loved me—they stuck by me through the tension and confusion of it all because of a strong, perhaps innate desire to do so, and I stuck by them through years of misunderstanding and misgendering because of the same. This combination of love and confrontation worked, and is working: we are changing together, and my family has learned to call me by my name, to view and treat trans people as the gender we identify with, and to defend us in politics and public space.

But here comes the grain of truth in the question people asked me about moving to North Carolina, the seed of compassion in others' fear (on my behalf) of bathroom bills and anti-trans rhetoric: What about the people who don't want to unlearn? What about the people we don't know, and don't love, who seem unmovable? Where do we start with unlearning when there is a wall of resistance, and sometimes a lifetime of misinformation, to pierce through first?

People in North Carolina—and across the South—were already asking these questions at a mass scale. And the questioners were finding that the answer was to ask more questions.

One of these people, Bonnie Dobson, moved to Mebane, North Carolina, from Long Island in 2010 to be closer to family. Living in rural North Carolina was hard for her; she faced racism from her neighbors, and her kids were harassed in school. In 2020, she was working as an accounting assistant and felt lost about how to respond to the police murders of George Floyd and other unarmed Black people. As a Black mother of three, "I just found it hard to keep moving during that time," she said. That was when she became an organizer with Down Home North Carolina. "I came in and I found my people."

She is now the manager of deep canvassing at Down Home, a state-wide organization that describes itself as "building power with rural working people in North Carolina's small towns and rural communities. Together, we are taking action to increase democracy, grow the good in our communities, and pass a healthy and just home down to our grand-babies."[2] The group organizes across twelve of the state's rural counties for health justice, racial justice, and access to education, as well as a variety of local issues and local and statewide candidates.

Rather than simply presenting voters with persuasive arguments, Down Home uses the technique of deep canvassing to reach people. In Down Home's language, "Deep canvassing moves beyond traditional campaign techniques by focusing on empathetic listening and personal storytelling to engage our neighbors and find shared values."[3]

Bonnie expanded: "Deep canvassing is having intentional transfor-mational conversations with folks that may not agree with you where you share your lived experience and then you ask them to share theirs, and you kind of just process that together."

I drove out to Burlington, a small, conservative town between Durham and Greensboro, to sit with Bonnie for hours and talk about what these "transformational conversations" look like in practice. We met in Down Home's humble strip mall storefront just off I-40, and sat across from each other at a fold-out table while she patiently explained.

Dobson said the process always starts with questions. For example, in a canvass she was a part of opposing the construction of a new jail in another county, canvassers asked: "Have you had any experience with law enforcement? Do you know anybody that's been to jail? And what was that like for them? When they came out, what was it like for them?"

A conversation would ensue: if they hadn't been to jail themselves, a lot of people had a cousin, an uncle, or a friend who had. Many were people who struggled with substance abuse, or mental health issues. And most people didn't recall that the jail time helped anything—in a lot of cases, it made things worse.

Then the conversation would go even deeper: "What do you think would have been different had they had the services that they needed? How would that have changed your family if they had gotten mental health services or drug services? . . . Were they better off when they got out?" In response to that last question, she said most people responded that no, people were not better off after going to jail.

Finally, Bonnie would share her own experiences—she'd tell a story about her brother, who had a schizophrenia diagnosis, being sent to jail several times. She'd talk about how hard it was for her and her family. She recounted this part of her script to me in a deliberate, warm tone. "What I really believe is that we need services in place that help folks that have a substance use disorder, help folks that have mental health issues," she'd say, "because they don't belong in jail."

Then she would turn back to the person being canvassed: "What do you think? If the services were there, wouldn't it have been better?" And then she'd ask them to consider opposing the new jail.

A lot of times, people's views stayed put—but some of the time, they'd change.

"When you have a really good deep canvas conversation, it's amazing," Dobson said. "Oftentimes you'll hear, 'You know, I never thought about it before.' 'You know, nobody ever asked me before,' or 'You've given me a lot to think about.'"

These conversations are surprisingly formulaic: the canvassers ask questions that have been tested out and refined for how well they work to get people to engage. The canvassers spend most of the time asking questions and listening. They are self-aware and nonjudgmental, careful not to react or argue. Then, near the end of the fifteen-to-thirty-minute interaction, the canvassers disclose something personal, sharing about their own experiences with the issue and how they came to the views they hold. They learn to judge how much of their own story to tell based on how the conversation is going.

Down Home's deep canvassers are systematic about measuring impact. At the beginning of each conversation, they ask for the person's views on the issue or candidate on a scale of one through ten. They repeat the question at the end and very often find, at least in the context of that conversation, that the number has moved. A Down Home study of the organization's canvassing efforts in 2020 found that deep canvassing was 120 times more effective than regular canvassing at changing people's minds, while other studies have found deep canvassing to be anywhere from 17 to 102 times more effective than traditional canvassing.[4]

I asked whether these conversations ever felt manipulative to her: "Are you pretending to empathize with someone in order to persuade them?"

She said sure—there is something that can feel tricky about withholding your own views in order to get other people to talk openly. I confessed to her that most journalists do this as a matter of course. But, like good journalistic interviewing, deep canvassing only really works if you tap into genuine curiosity and empathy. You can't just pretend to care or connect—you actually set your own opinions to the side to practice sincerely listening.

"We go into it firmly believing that we all want the same things, right? We all want to be able to feed our families, have a roof over our heads, and be safe and secure in our homes," she said, not an "us and them" attitude where you're asking "them" questions.

"If there's any 'them,' it's the government, it's pharma, it's big corporations, it's the CEOs." She invites people to focus their fear and anger towards those who have structural power, not other working-class people.

Progressive activists have been using deep canvassing since 2008, when Californian voters passed a ballot initiative that banned gay marriage, to the surprise of lesbian and gay activists—California had become the second state to legalize gay marriage following a court ruling just a few months earlier. Leaders at the Los Angeles LGBT Center became some of the first to develop a targeted methodology of in-depth conversations in place of traditional canvassing.[5]

Now this methodology is in use across the country, in campaigns about climate, immigration, trans and gay rights, and education, as well as political campaigns for progressive candidates.

While deep canvassing conversations take longer than just going around asking people for votes, they are also measurably more effective, at least when it comes to conversations about prejudice and bias—and those effects can be longer lasting. In a 2016 study of deep canvassing about anti-transgender prejudice in Florida, conversations as brief as ten minutes long were shown to create durable change in voters' views toward trans people.[6] After a few months, the people who were moved by deep canvass conversations were still thinking differently about the issue. The same researchers in 2018 published a review of studies of "traditional" political persuasion tactics (TV ads, phone calls, and canvassing) and found that, on a balance, they don't actually work at all.[7] They may remind people to vote or participate, or deepen the commitment to already existing beliefs, but these tactics do not facilitate transformation over time.

Most strikingly, these researchers found that during the deep canvassing process, three-quarters of the people canvassed were willing to have the conversation. The vast majority of people engaged in a conversation with the canvasser, a complete stranger.

"Those basic numbers tell you something about just how willing most Americans are to have an open conversation with a stranger about these ostensibly divisive issues," study coauthor David E. Broockman told Vox News.[8]

The implications are simple, but vast: even short conversations with total strangers can lead a significant number of people into questioning their views. Imagine the power of deep canvassing at a mass level—and at a community level, where we ask questions and listen to people whom we know and are in relationships with, like the people on the New College campus did with Adrianne Black and the radical Indigenous activists I met in my late teens did with me.

Deep canvassing isn't explicitly a tool of "unlearning"—it is, officially, a slow and deliberate tool of persuasion. But it has primarily been tested and used on issues that require an unlearning approach: bias against racialized people and trans people, apathy or confusion about climate or public health. And this technique works to dislodge prejudice and shift people toward compassion for groups they are not a part of, at least a little bit of the time.

But what about the people whose whole foundation for their views is based on misinformation or disinformation?

Deep canvassers have an answer for that, too: just keep asking questions.

"We never, ever talk facts," said Dobson when I asked her what they do to counter disinformation and misinformation. She described a call with a woman who believed that all of her vaccinated relatives were going to die from the COVID-19 vaccine. "I would never say to her, 'Well, they've tested the vaccine and they've done these studies,' because that's going to just entrench her further and probably alienate her."

Instead of trying to talk her out of her fear, Bonnie expressed empathy: "I am so sorry that you are living with that fear," she said.

In the interest of staying in the conversation, deep canvassers avoid debate, and avoid using facts to try to persuade people. Instead, they engage and listen—even when they believe the other person is misinformed.

This can be hard on the canvassers themselves, who sometimes have to let hurtful stereotypes or ideas go unchallenged in the moment.

"I did have a guy tell me that all Blacks were lazy and didn't want to work and just want to lay around," Dobson said. "You know, talking points from wherever he was getting them from. And I'm on the phone so he doesn't know I'm Black and I just let him finish."

She pressed on through the formula of the deep canvass. She asked questions about where he grew up—a racially diverse housing project. The man revealed that he identified as Hispanic. She asked what he remembered from being a kid, if people in his community went to work. He talked about his memories of the people he grew up around.

"And then I said, "Well, yeah, I mean, I hear you. But it's not my experience. It just isn't. And I'm Black.'"

She described an "audible pause . . . like the record player stops. And then I just explain. "You know, I've been working since I was fifteen. There were six of us. And, frankly, if I needed assistance, that's when the government should help me. It's just the way I feel,' I said. 'But, you know, I think that the powers that are controlling everything. . . . They want your group and my group, Hispanics and Blacks, pitted against one another, fighting for scraps. Because if we came together, we'd be far too powerful and they wouldn't be able to ignore us, and we could make real change in this country.' And he got quiet and he said, 'You know, I never really thought about it like that, honestly.'"

It was uncomfortable—but he agreed to think on it more. That was her ask: just think about it. "If we're curious enough to try to figure out where that's coming from, we can usually help them see something different. That's why I love it . . . it's never too late."

Talking to Bonnie Dobson reminded me of a moment I'd nearly forgotten with Mr. Yaeger, my fifth-grade teacher.

The year was 1995, and there was still mostly silence and shame about gay people in schools, even in my college town of Ann Arbor, Michigan. I knew about homosexuals as people who got AIDS or committed suicide, something that would be sad to become. You could also still be fired for being gay in most states, and many adults who worked in public schools were fearful of being accused of pedophilia if they so much as talked about gay issues. I was not aware of knowing any "out" gay people at that time.

One day in our bright little classroom on the second floor of Angell Elementary, a kid named Gary started calling someone he didn't like "gay," making a face of disgust. "That's so gay" was a common slur in the '90s, but I didn't know it yet—as I remember it, our relatively diverse small public school had very little tolerance for bullying behavior, and hurling insults and slurs was rare. Even though I barely knew what being gay was, I knew just enough to believe that I might be (when I was nine, I wrote in my journal, "I might be a lesbian but I'm not sure yet"). So, being me, I jumped in and started debating Gary, telling him he was wrong to insult gay people like that, and asking him (rhetorically) if he actually knew anyone gay? Or what? (Also being me, I believe I had a small crush on Gary—it would be years before I reconciled how it was that I could have a gay crush on a boy, a whole other unlearning.)

The argument quickly escalated (I didn't know about deep canvassing yet . . .), and Mr. Yaeger jumped in.

Tom Yaeger, whom we called "Mr. Y," was a scruffy guy, a former factory worker from southeast Michigan who became a public school teacher and stayed in that same corner classroom near downtown Ann Arbor for decades. He constantly brewed himself coffee and buzzed around the room with a mug in his hand, he laughed easily, and he took us all very seriously. He was the only person we knew who did yoga, through classes at the YMCA. And this is important: he loved us. We all knew he loved us, because he paid each student careful attention—we kept letter journals with him where we composed letters every week and he wrote us each back.

Mr. Y jumped in on the conversation with Gary about "That's so gay," and instead of shutting it down or punishing me or Gary, he paused the entire class from whatever group activity we'd been doing, and started to ask questions. What did we know about gay people? Did we know any gay people? Had we heard of homophobia? What did we think that was? Why might it be hurtful to use "gay" as an insult? Could we think of a better way to get across what we were saying? Mr. Yaeger shared about gay people in his life, people he knew and loved. And he empathized with me, little weirdly gay-friendly Lewis, for feeling hurt by the use of gay as an insult. But he also empathized with Gary—as a result of Mr. Yaeger's questions, it emerged that his parents, who were very religious Christians, believed it was morally wrong to be gay and Gary was grappling with it. The entire class of twenty or so fifth graders talked together about all of this for a long time, sharing openly. Gary wasn't punished for using the slur, and I wasn't punished for arguing with him about it.

I wish I could know the impact it had on Gary—of course part of me imagines, or hopes, that Gary is gay and that this confrontation saved him years of anguish down the road. But I do know the impact it had on me. Rather than shrinking in the face of people like Gary (and there would be many by the time I made it through middle and high school as an out gay teen), I began to develop an interest in them, compassion for them. I saw that conversation could reveal what they were afraid of and where they got their ideas. Even when I was being bullied, I could see everyone's inherent power and inherent vulnerability—Gary, in another context, could have been seen as a bully, but questions and conversations cast him in an entirely different light. While bullying can threaten and harm, there's always something behind or beneath people's defenses and power plays, a reason why people act aggressively or repeat bigotry. I was never a shrinking violet in the face of a homophobe, but Mr. Yaeger's teachings about the power of asking and listening made my challenges and confrontations over the years more curious, more compassionate. I learned to wonder what was underneath, and saw the power of disarming people rather than fighting, when it's possible.

This kind of conversation, the kind that allows for conflict and discomfort over controversial social issues, is so threatening to the status quo, and particularly to right-wing conservatism, that many states and the federal government are now actively attempting to ban it in schools. They are passing laws against conversations about race and gender, even the most open-minded and even-handed conversations, claiming that even *talking* about oppression causes an intractable division among people. I believe the attacks on "critical race theory" and "gender ideology" prove what a threat our movements for justice pose to right-wing power: prejudice and exclusion cannot stand up to the simple tools of curiosity and openness, the power of transformative conversation in public classrooms. These tools, some of the same tools that deep canvassers use, destabilize the pillars of our seemingly strong systems of oppression. Thus they must discourage simple curiosity and accuse the Left of being "thought police" for desiring curious conversation. (This is not to say the Left is immune to incurious conversation, or to acting like the thought police—an affliction deep canvassing tries to overcome, much as Mr. Y did for my fifth-grade class. The fact that Gary was not punished for antigay slurs is an important part of the story.)

Nearly thirty years after my transformative classroom experience with Mr. Yaeger, Bonnie Dobson shared an almost inverse story about her daughter, who, in the twelfth grade in North Carolina, heard someone using a racial slur on a field trip with a school club. She was the only Black person present; when she told her mom about it, Bonnie approached the principal of the school.

"I thought, *Oh, this is such a great opportunity for kids to learn.* We can give them some words because sometimes kids just don't have words just to say something as simple as 'That's not nice. Don't say that anymore. Don't call people that.'" She assumed everyone would agree that racial insults are problematic. A conversation would teach the person who used the slur about the impact, and teach others how to name when and why something is hurtful.

After weeks of silence from the principal, she followed up. He said: "I talked to the parents, and they're just not willing to have that conversation."

Bonnie was floored, not least because she knew the white children and parents involved, and had known them for years. "I'm not trying to get these kids in trouble," she said. "I'm trying to teach them something. And, as an educator, wouldn't you want that opportunity as well?"

Not necessarily: the education system has become a battleground in this country for precisely the ideological debates Down Home is stepping into through their campaigns—race, gender, class, and power. The right wing is targeting "critical race theory" and "gender ideology" in public schools; in many parts of the country, they are succeeding at shutting down these conversations through fear and disinformation. They use rhetoric that warns of dangerous and greedy transgenders who ruin sports and spoil bathrooms. They claim that teachers are cruelly inflicting white guilt upon innocent children when they are forced to learn the true history of slavery. They stir up fear about migrants and vilify non-English languages. As of 2024, more than eight hundred policies had been introduced in US states and local districts banning conversations about race, racism, and oppression since 2020, and hundreds had passed.[9] In 2023 alone, over five hundred anti-LGBTQ bills were introduced into state and federal legislatures, many targeting education and schools.[10] In early 2025, Donald Trump began issuing executive orders that threatened to punish any school system where support for trans students and teaching lessons about racism and diversity continue to be the norm.

In South Carolina, where my niece and nephew go to school, it is no longer permitted for publicly funded programs to teach that "an individual, by virtue of his race or sex, is inherently racist, sexist, or oppressive, whether consciously or unconscious," and schools are also banned from suggesting that "an individual should feel discomfort, guilt, anguish, or

any other form of psychological distress on account of his race or sex."
In other words: no anti-oppression education, no white guilt. The same
bill disallows schools from requiring children to wear masks in order to
prevent the transmission of the deadly COVID-19 virus and other rapidly
contagious viruses. The former governor of South Carolina, Nikki Haley,
was on record saying that children should not be allowed to talk about
sexuality or gender in school, period—not without parental consent.
In that scenario, a transformative conversation like the one Mr. Yaeger
facilitated in our classroom in 1995 would never be allowed to happen
at all, effectively privatizing a debate that very clearly has public implications. The conservative movement is creating another generation of
people who will have to face unlearning if they are to live in a multiracial society, accept the existence of transgender people, and stop being
afraid of one another.

The fear that is constantly deployed in these campaigns, the fear
expressed by Bonnie's daughter's school principal about even holding
a conversation about racism—that fear keeps power structures ticking,
and encourages unthinking deference to dominant systems as well as
insensitivity to actual members of diverse communities. But it's refreshing to imagine that the tools for pushing back on this can be as simple
as a set of careful, empathetic conversations with young people. These
are tools we can all access, although the specific line of work might
not be for everyone. I know, for example, that if I tried to deep canvass
people around transphobia I would be a big flop. I have too much hurt
and pain and rage, too much impatience, and too much of a need to
compartmentalize in order to make it through my days in a world with
so much animus toward me and people like me. But I'm beyond re-
lieved that someone is out there doing that work, especially right here
in North Carolina.

"If you pull people into their own experiences, in a loving and compassionate and curious way, you can dispel fear, dispel anger, hatred,"
Bonnie said to me, with the quiet confidence of someone who has actually done this. "I don't know any other way."

Decades after the successes of the civil rights and feminist movements for equal rights and an end to legal segregation, the US is still a segregated, scared, sexist place. People still get shot by police daily, and people increasingly come out of their houses and shoot each other, en masse, in public. Transgender people face rising rates of violence even as we become more visible and make limited legal gains.

The feminist, Black liberation, anti-racist, abolitionist, and trans liberation movements have stoked mass unlearning—and they have forced key structures to change. But these movements call for nothing short of liberation. As structures crumble, power pushes back, and we are in a moment of powerful, existentially threatening backlash.

The right wing and its capitalist cronies have found a loophole, one that's supported and upheld by our increasing reliance on remote work, remote school, and privatized technologies to communicate. No one can unlearn if we don't talk to each other at all.

As I drove out to meet Bonnie Dobson, I was struck by the individualism of the landscape: we are each in our cars on the highways. We stay in our cars through the drive-through. People here place their orders online for home delivery from Amazon and stick to their homes after work, behind wide lawns. People watch the news and it's all about shootings and public menaces; people are afraid of each other, afraid of race war and immigrant invasions. For whole swaths of this country, the landscape and the media are constantly teaching "every person for himself," reinforcing isolation. These learnings are the wall we're up against in the collective unlearning required by movements for liberation. What does it look like to unlearn an entire matrix of fear and alienation? How can we cope with the disappointment and despair?

Bonnie still struggles with how isolated she feels—not just as a Black woman in a mostly white, rural place, but as someone who feels a responsibility to make change happen. She bears the weight of the cumulative cynicism of our society.

"People think, 'If it doesn't affect me directly, what do I care?'" Questions and deep conversations are not a fast or easy way to overcome that apathy. And I struggle with them, myself: it's hard to be patient and inquisitive when you feel isolated, threatened, and tired. But, over time, leaving our apathy behind and getting into the muck with people works.

"I'm not saying that everybody has to do that," Bonnie said. "But can you imagine if more people did? Makes me cry."

Bonnie did cry, looking me right in the eyes, as I teared up from across the table. "It would be a different world, wouldn't it?" she said. "I would want to live here."

UNLEARNING INTERVIEWS: A TEMPLATE

This is a template of most of the questions I asked the people I interviewed for this book. Each interview focused on seeking a personal story about my core questions, and most also explored each person's work in the world to some extent.

For a while, if anyone lit up around me when I mentioned "unlearning," I would ask them for an interview. I highly recommend interviewing people as a personal unlearning practice, particularly elders or people in your life who grew up in different places, generations, or ideological backgrounds than you. Deep and active listening turns on our most receptive mind and can prompt unlearning in ourselves. Remember to seek affirmative consent before any recording or documentation takes place!

1. Unlearning is about letting go of deeply held beliefs or ideologies or worldviews—not just changing our minds, but changing our way of thinking and reacting. How do you relate to that concept? What does it bring up for you?
2. What is a story of something you used to believe deeply, but don't believe in anymore?
3. How did you unlearn it? What prompted you to want to unlearn?
4. Is there a moment you remember when you knew you needed to unlearn? [Note: most people said no to this, in my experience! It was often an ongoing process. Still, I like to ask this question in case it prompts a memory or story, as it did in the case of my grandmother seeing Bull Connor on the TV.]
5. Who or what made your unlearning possible?
6. What do you believe created the conditions for unlearning?

7. What is the relationship between unlearning and [your practice of art, teaching, activism, etc.]?

8. How have relationships and love shaped your beliefs? Are there relationships that have contributed to your unlearning, and how?

9. How has community shaped your beliefs?

10. When you know you need to unlearn something, what do you do about defensiveness?

11. What helps when you have a fearful or defensive reaction?

12. What kinds of practices have supported your unlearning?

13. What practices do you believe support unlearning, in general?

14. What does unlearning look like at a collective level? How do you believe it is best facilitated?

CHAPTER 7

SOMATICS

*The body is the shore
on the ocean of being.*

—SUFI saying

We were meant to have a somatic session after the protest in DC, because the protest in DC had gone completely wrong. Nine of us from Durham drove up for the day, attended an afternoon-long workshop on direct action, and went to the street outside the Democratic National Committee (DNC) headquarters at the appointed time. The plan was clear enough: groups would post up outside of side doors and exits, and our Durham affinity group's job at this direct action, just five weeks into the Gaza genocide, was to stop congresspeople as they emerged from a gala and ask them, "Do you support a ceasefire?" with iPhone cameras rolling. No matter what the answer (at that time very few had called for a ceasefire), we would have visual material with which to hold the congresspeople accountable.

But before any representatives could emerge from the dinner taking place inside, before the media cameras were fully set up to take in the spectacle we had planned with two hundred protesters and thousands of candles representing all those dead so far in the assault on Gaza, just as we set up around the DNC building, the DC Capitol Police turned up by the hundreds. Rather than the standard response to planned disruptive protests (which was generally orderly arrests following several verbal warnings), the cops seemed to have been instructed to attack and cause mayhem. Our group of nine went from quietly planning how to approach emerging congresspeople and get them on tape rejecting Jewish constituents asking for a ceasefire to locking arms in defiance of a police attack on the front steps of the building. Police tear-gassed, shoved their bicycles through the crowd, and came up the steps in rows to break the human barricade. One by one, they pulled us apart and dragged or threw us down the stairs of the DNC headquarters.[1]

I remember just a few things from that night, which started out cold and cheerful and ended up terrifying: I remember screaming, "No," and holding tight as my friend was pulled out of armlock with me by two armed officers and dragged away. I remember a young Black police officer standing in front of us, slowly putting on latex gloves as all the cops did before assaulting us, and saying, out loud, "I don't want to do this." I remember my friends around me yelling out, "You don't have to do this!" I remember seeing the cement steps in front of me as I was thrown to the bottom by two sets of gloved hands, face-first, a flash of bracing for pain. Landing maybe painlessly, maybe too much adrenaline to know (later I was bruised, but not badly injured). Being picked up by two officers who escorted me toward the edge of the protest as I hollered, "Am I under arrest? Am I being charged with something? Let me go or charge me!" They let me go.

Of the two-hundred-some protesters present that night, only one person was arrested. But around ninety of us, including nearly every member of my group, were assaulted in some way—grabbed and thrown to the ground, tear-gassed in the face, dragged across the grass, or slammed into trees or cars.[2] There was screaming and separation and fear in the eyes of the people I was with. Some of us turned noisy and verbally aggressive, while others stood back, unsure. Our group was separated; one person fainted, and some of us watched as the cops carried her out by her four limbs and deposited her on the other side of a barricade. She came to, crying and screaming.

The Capitol Police told the media it had been a violent protest, even claiming that demonstrators had tear-gassed *them*. But every ounce of chaos that occurred that night came from the cops.

Afterward, our group reunited on an almost unpleasant adrenaline high and continued to try to find congresspeople and tape them coming out of the building. But the building had gone on lockdown, an absurd rumor having been started that anti-war protesters were "January 6th-ing" the DNC. Hundreds of officers in riot gear cleared the block and escorted the Democrats out later that night, barricaded off from having to face our questions directly. The only congresswoman we managed to catch up to on the way in, Jan Schakowsky of Illinois, had dashed through a side door and slammed it in our faces as we videotaped. We shared the tape to social media. The following week, she joined the call for a ceasefire.[3]

A couple of weeks later, our group came back together in Durham for a somatic healing session facilitated by two Generative Somatics practitioners in our community, Yashna Padamsee and Eliana Rubin. At least one of our group members was skeptical—"What *is* somatics? I'm not into, like, meditation and stuff . . ."—and I felt some of that skepticism myself. I didn't want to cry about our assault by officers. I wanted to get mad, to defend and react. I wanted to keep fighting, but I was also waking up at night with cold sweats and bad dreams, screaming as I processed the noise and violence in my sleep.

The session, which took place in a friend's living room, started with our two facilitators clarifying that the goal of their work with Generative Somatics was not individual healing or making everyone feel better. The goal was strengthening all of us collectively to continue to be active—to process the incident through our bodies in ways that allowed us more options for how to act and react in the future. The goal of "healing," so unlike much of the contemporary social media and advertising rhetoric about healing and therapy, was not individual self-improvement, but collective power. I felt my shoulders relax in relief. *I can do this*, I thought.

The workshop began with a simple series of actions. We practiced moving around the space and noticing our bodies. We practiced facing one another, walking toward each other, and saying "No" with varying levels of firmness, pushing one another away. We practiced standing at each other's backs, feeling and noticing the support of another body behind us. I was good at saying "No" and pushing people back—the same skill I'd showed in defiance of the cops a few weeks before.

Eventually, Yashna and Eliana had us move our bodies into formations that resembled how we had been when the Capitol Police attacked us: arms locked, facing outward. As a full group, we practiced reacting with the fullness of rage and pain we felt in that moment. Our bodies were allowed to move as they wished, to comfort and protect each other. Things became blurry as we flashed back to that night, following the facilitators' straightforward prompts. At one point I found myself outside of the circle of my comrades, crying in a ball on the couch. Someone came and got me, pulled me back in, held me. We acted out physically supporting and shielding each other, actions that had been impossible when our group was pulled apart that night. We got to feel what it was to react fully, to allow completion of the feelings that were only halfway expressed in that quickened period of assault. For those who had gone quiet, there was a chance to practice assertiveness and rage; for me, who had been noisy and rageful at the protest, there was a chance to get small and notice that I had also been hurt and afraid.

If I'd been told that a somatic healing session meant partially reenacting the traumatic events themselves, I would probably have avoided it altogether—my mind gives a hard no to the idea of reliving trauma as a path to healing. But because Yashna and Eliana were people I knew and trusted, I was open to what they offered. That night, I felt something almost miraculous happen. Through this collective, embodied interaction, I felt my body letting go of fear and tightness and hurt I had been unable to process. I felt myself return to a sense of safety, let go some of the vigilance that had stuck with me in the days since the protest. After this embodied session, I felt the incident settle out and dissipate in me. My body had moved through a cycle it was meant to, not just raging but grieving, not just defending but also being held and feeling safe.

While the session itself was remarkable because of how effectively Yashna and Eliana physically moved us toward collective grief and healing, what was even more noticeable was the way the group coalesced afterward. Rather than being divided or embittered by the trauma we'd experienced together, the nine Durham protesters were bonded, aware of what the incident had brought up for each other, and able to continue on in our activism (which often puts us in confrontational and high-risk situations). Later that week, we attended an online debrief with others who had been present and saw people bringing their unresolved reactions into that space, harshly critiquing the organizers of the protest for the actions of the cops, going off in the Zoom chat, complaining, and turning on one another. Our group, released from the feelings we'd been holding onto, participated in no such dramas and instead came out fortified to continue and more deeply trusting of one another.

At this time, I had been reading about somatics as a potential way to create conditions for unlearning, but this experience showed me exactly why a full-body approach to unlearning is so important: lessons and healing processes that are felt and embodied actually last, changing something in us often much more efficiently than the transformation that comes from simply talking through an experience or feeling. And, while somatics is often spoken about as an approach to individual healing and therapy, there are many people today approaching somatic practices as a part of collective political work, designed to change not just how people think but how we act together—to strengthen organizing, movement building, and cooperative efforts. The two people who turned me on to this process from the inside are, not coincidentally, leaders in this movement for politicized somatics.

"I've had a big journey around using my voice," said Yashna Padamsee gently. We were sitting on my couch in Durham, her legs folded under a blanket, watching my pitbull pace the floor and periodically interrupt with frantic face licks.

Like I do with most of my interviewees, I'd started by asking her about something she unlearned and how she did it. She talked first about shame, an unlearning process she said she was still in the midst of. But, she said, even before her work on shame, she had to unlearn silence.

In her early twenties, she joined a collective called Ubuntu that was formed in Durham in response to the nationally publicized incident of rape committed by the Duke University men's lacrosse team: Ubuntu was a groundbreaking group of women of color, mostly queer women, practicing transformative justice to address sexual violence. "Part of why organizing with Ubuntu was so powerful was because we were speaking as a collective voice and I didn't have to find my own voice," she said. "I could speak as part of a collective. So that was one part of my healing journey."

But while she became an organizer around sexual violence and racial justice, and found her place in a collective, Yashna struggled with finding her *own* voice. The root of this was her experience of sexual assault as a young person.

"One aspect around surviving this sexual assault was I was silenced around it," she said. Family members of the assailant told her not to speak up or something bad would happen. Now, if she was fearful or triggered or unsure, silence was still her default.

"When I was under pressure, small or large, I would get quiet," Yashna told me. "That would be an automatic response in my body to not speak—that could have been as small as choosing not to talk, or as intense as, like, literally, my body would shut down and I couldn't get words out."

Through her work with Ubuntu, she encountered Generative Somatics, an organization whose programs "engage the body (emotions, sensations, physiology), in order to align our actions with values and vision and heal from the impacts of trauma and oppression."[4] Yashna has since become a leader in this collective methodology of transformation, training in somatic healing, somatic coaching, and Embodied Leadership for the last sixteen years with Generative Somatics (GS).

At GS, the first step in the training was to look honestly at your own responses.

"First comes the somatic awareness," she explained. "Somatics," here, simply means the whole body—an integrated body that encompasses the mind, the self, and our physical being. She started by becoming aware that silence and feeling voiceless is her body's default under pressure. "That's a huge realization, and I see it play out in all of these areas of my life. And, in this opening, I have an opportunity to do something about it or not."

For the first several years of her training, she said, this awareness was the focus. "And then came slowly the somatic practice of speaking up when under pressure in low impact ways, low stakes ways," she said.

She began practicing using her voice with friends, then at work, and then with her spouse. "Now I can speak in front of hundreds of people."

Just the night before our interview, Yashna and I were both at a protest where I was playing the drums and she was leading chants and rallying hundreds of people outside of a contentious city council meeting. Her voice was wide and powerful. She said it was still a struggle; she woke up the next day with feelings of shame after using her voice in such a forceful and public way. But, through the years of diligent somatic practice, she had unlearned her automated shutdown of her own voice. That work was integrated into her organizational work: Yashna led embodied leadership training with survivors of labor trafficking at the National Domestic Workers Alliance and brought somatic practices into her organizational development work and her work supporting other social justice leaders.

Yashna had introduced me to somatics when we worked together at the movement journalism collective Press On—she would guide us through a common somatics exercise called "centering" at the beginning of meetings from time to time. Coming into it, I understood the general idea, but not the specifics; somatics was body stuff that you do to get more grounded, I guess? Like meditation and taking deep breaths? I was fascinated with the neuroscience of how people can heal internal wounds through engaging with the whole body, but I still didn't really get what somatics *was*. Yashna guided us to find our gravitational, physical center, and then to pay attention to our bodily sensations from there—as Yashna phrases it, "reconnecting to the dimensions of your body: length, width, depth, and center." Each centering practice is slightly different, but, in general, it is a guided process of noticing our bodies and reflecting on their (our) dignity, history, visions, and community. In learning how to stay centered, we also learn to notice when we are not centered—when we are directing energy forward or outward at the expense of noticing what is behind or within us, for example, or when we are shrinking back in response, or ignoring what is at our sides. Centering was not so much focused on quieting the mind as on paying close attention to the body and its sensations, learning to notice our current state and automatic tendencies.

———————

Richard Strozzi-Heckler, one of the driving forces in the practice of somatics in the US today, defines the "soma" in the Greek sense of "the living body in its wholeness." Strozzi-Heckler explains: "This is not the sleek, airbrushed body on magazine covers or the Cartesian notion of body as beast of burden that ferries a disembodied mind to its intellectual appointments. Nor is it the mechanical, physiological body of modern medicine or the religious formula of flesh as sin. The body, in the somatic sense, expresses our history, commitments, dignity, authenticity, identity, roles, moral strength, moods, and aspirations as a unique quality of aliveness we call the 'self.' We cannot act or live in the world without the body, or the self in this sense."[5]

Somatics describes a set of practices informed by both ancient and modern traditions, from Chinese medicine to Ayurveda and yoga, from Buddhist meditation to Western psychology, and it draws on knowledge produced by the quickly blooming field of neuroscience that has informed much of our discussion of unlearning in this book.[6] While the term as it is used now was coined by Thomas Hannah in 1972 and often appears in therapeutic and New Age spaces, somatic practices in the broad sense exist in every culture; if somatics simply means engaging the full body, the soma, in healing and transformation, one could argue that everything from religious dance to drumming to healing massage encompasses somatics. There is no single organizational or cultural claim to somatics, although there are multiple traditions.

Yashna practices what Generative Somatics calls "politicized somatics."[7]

"Asking the general population about somatics, you hear it more in a therapeutic context," Yashna said. Somatics is depoliticized and presented as a one-on-one approach to personal healing. "It's really thinking about the individual body, which I think only takes you so far. I feel really lucky to have been trained in politicized somatics, which understands that the world we live in, under systems of oppression, shapes our experiences and our responses and reactions."

Politicized somatics places this personal work in context of the systems and structures of power that surround us—meaning that unlearning shame or silence can be understood in the context of unlearning rape culture or racism, and healing from trauma can be understood in the context of recognizing the systems that caused the trauma. Our individual practice is always linked to the collective. Politicized somatics sees the goal of the work not as self-love or self-improvement, but as transforming both individuals and groups so that we can show up better in movements for justice and prefigure the world we want to create. As Prentis Hemphill of the Embodiment Institute says, "The kind of change we are after is cellular as well as institutional, is personal and intimate, is collective as well as cultural. We are making love synonymous with justice."[8]

Internalizing change through the body, rather than the mind alone, allows us to integrate those changes so that they are long lasting. Generative Somatics cofounder Staci Haines defines somatics as "an intentional change process by which we can embody transformation, individually and collectively. Embodied transformation is foundational change that shows in our actions, ways of being, relating, and perceiving. It is transformation that sustains over time."[9] GS cofounder Spenta Kandawalla brought a long history of community organizing to the work, making GS a key meeting point for somatics and politics: "I want us to contend with the centrality of organizing to our transformation," Kandawalla said on the Generative Somatics podcast. "Both [healing and organizing] are necessary for our well-being and to build power together, to shift conditions, and to live with more freedom."[10]

Politicized somatics is based on the belief that transformation can be not just a mental process, but a deeply embodied change. Ideas, concepts, history, reeducation—all of these are not enough if unlearning isn't integrated by the body, because the body and the mind are not separate and the body often determines our reactions in spite of what our minds may want. I imagine my grandmother, shriveling in disgust at seeing gay people holding hands or backing fearfully away from a drinking fountain after racial integration—her mind told her not to fear, but her body was trained otherwise.

"Our automatic ways of reacting, relating, and thinking are driven from much deeper in our brains, hearts, and muscles than our ideas about them," writes Haines. "These embodied patterns will persist (that's what they are built to do) until we take action to get support, heal them, and engage new practices."[11]

Our automatic responses also have a way of creating problems in social justice movements, as collective efforts devolve into harsh inter-personal conflicts or fall apart over instances of harm within groups. In the last couple of decades in the US, many activists—particularly people working on transformative justice and interrupting cycles of sexual assault and domestic violence—have gravitated toward somatics, and, even though I resisted at first, I have now joined them. I felt it that day when we healed collectively from the police attacks: embodied transformation takes root more deeply than just prompting people to rethink. Embodiment can thus be both a condition and a tool for unlearning, a way to make unlearning accessible and lasting.

Eliana Rubin's somatics story started in a very different place: with her journey of beginning to unlearn Zionism. She was raised in a liberal Jewish family in San Francisco and went to Jewish day school. She said positive messaging about the state of Israel was a nearly daily part of the curriculum, and it was often spoken about in concert with lessons in fear—the message she received, over and over, was that Jewish people were under attack, and the state of Israel was the only way to keep Jews safe. Because there is a state of Israel, she and the other students were told, Jewish people should feel safe—and any threat to or even critique of Israel should be read as a threat to that safety. She remembers feeling that something was not quite right during those lessons.

"As kids, I feel like we have more access to a holistic way of thinking," Eliana said. "And so, it was like something in me didn't add up. They're telling me I should feel safe and comfortable, and I feel very unsafe and uncomfortable."

In her early twenties, as she became more exposed to people and ideas that questioned Zionism and the ideology behind the state of Israel, she began questioning these lessons from childhood. But this questioning didn't become embodied until she decided to see Israel and Palestine for herself. Even though she was already questioning Zionism, she got a "birthright" ticket to the region—meaning her trip was paid for by the propaganda arm of the Israeli government that encourages Jews around the world to move to Israel, engages in soft diplomacy and cultural outreach, and sponsors visits and tours of the country for young Jewish people. These tours expose people to the best parts of how Jewish Israelis are living, without acknowledging the illegal occupation, apartheid laws, and violent border expansion that makes that life possible. Eliana made plans to abandon the birthright tour halfway through and join up with other solidarity activists.

"I went, I participated in a few days of the trip, and, again, that feeling arose in me that I had in school, where I was like, 'Something's so deeply wrong here, and I feel unsafe,'" she said. She remembered driving on a bus past the relatively newly constructed wall at the border of the occupied West Bank, "and these people are telling us to literally look the other way when we're passing the apartheid wall, to party and enjoy the life in Israel. I felt a lot of shame and disgust in that experience." Seeing the Israeli military occupation and the border regulations with her own eyes alienated her from her own background. The version of Judaism she had been taught no longer seemed honest to her, because it was so intertwined with Israeli propaganda.

"When I had my bat mitzvah, it's very common that you get a tree planted in your name in Israel through the Jewish National Fund," she explained. She recalled these stories she'd been told, that Palestine was a land without a people for a people without a land, and that Israel was "making the desert bloom" by planting these trees. But, during the birthright tour, she went to a park with a plaque that said these trees were planted by the Jewish National Fund.

"You can see the rubble of old villages, and there are just trees planted over it," she said. "And I was like . . . 'I did that.'" Eliana saw that people had actually lived there, right up until a very recent displacement. It wasn't a desert, it was a town; it wasn't a land without a people, but a land whose people had been violently removed. "I felt very opened by that. It kind of crumbled the infrastructure of Zionism and Judaism, the Judaism that I had learned. And in a way it validated those younger parts of me."

She ditched her birthright tour and ended up working on a Palestinian farm for a few months and then participating in a protest that led to her and several others being arrested by Israeli police and jailed. At the end of her incarceration, she was told she could either make Aaliyah—which means agreeing to Zionist ideology and accepting her place in the state of Israel—or she could leave the country and face a ten-year ban on returning. She is now banned from returning to current-day Israel or occupied Palestine.

Coming home from that experience in her early twenties, she was contending with emotions that were overwhelming. "I felt a lot of rage," she said. "I felt betrayed and deceived and angry."

And that anger showed up in her conversations, what she called "gnarly debates" with family and community members as she tried to unravel the myths of Zionism and the Israeli state with them. She had been there and seen it with her own eyes, and she strained and struggled to express what she had seen, to help people override the stories they'd been told over years of religious education and cultural training.

"There was no amount of facts or conversation or debate that would move them," she said. Confronting that obstacle was how Eliana, who is now the author of *Taking the State out of the Body: A Guide to Embodied Resistance to Zionism*, came to politicized somatics.[12]

As she saw how stress or even trauma reactions were dominating her conversations with other Jewish people about Zionism, Eliana said, "I started to notice, I'm not having a conversation with this person's intellect or reasoning. I'm having a conversation with their trauma response and with a very deeply ingrained wiring towards survival." People were afraid, and in their fear, they could not hear either rational arguments or new information. Her passion and intensity following her time in Palestine was going in one ear, out the other.

"We have to address that core need for safety," she said. A collaborator at the Arab Resource and Organizing Center in the Bay Area suggested Generative Somatics to help address this. "So that's when I got really into somatics as a tool for change and unlearning."

First, Eliana had to get clear on her own commitments and reasons for having the conversations. "I want safety for Jewish people and I want safety for all people, and I can be Jewish and I can be anti-Zionist."

And she had to find a way to stop pressuring people to change, which meant developing an awareness of her *own* activation first. When she started feeling her heart rate rise, her palms get sweaty, her voice get frantic, she would pause, and center.

"I think since learning somatics, it's much easier for me to see those moments, because I know when something just got activated," she said. "It could be that someone's fucking with me or hurting me, and I need to defend myself. Or it could be that there's an invitation into something that's actually more values aligned. And so I want to recenter and actually be more receptive to that."

She now teaches this skill through a somatics exercise they call "the grab." Working in pairs (and with full consent), two people attempt to "grab" and activate each other—both physically and emotionally. Then, when you are grabbed, you figure out what you need in order to stay out of activation and choose how you are going to respond. I witnessed this exercise in a workshop Eliana gave with two other people about somatics and unlearning Zionism. If I were the one being grabbed, I would instruct my practice partner to say something to me that I found upsetting or difficult to respond to nondefensively. As my partner said the offending phrase, they would literally grab my arm. My job, instead of fighting or immediately formulating a response, was just to notice my reaction, the physical and mental feeling of being grabbed. "Let yourself have that reaction. Get to know it, what is the reaction? If we don't address the core, whatever core thing is getting kicked up by that, we're not actually going to embody the change. We might be able to perform something different, but we haven't deeply shifted in a lasting way."

After being grabbed, we were guided to pause and simply notice the feelings coming up. Then we did the centering exercise that is taught to everyone in Generative Somatics: that first exercise I had learned, in which you take deliberate time to notice your body, where it is, what it is doing and feeling, the space it takes up and the space around you, and find your physical center of gravity. You also recenter in your reasons for doing the work you are doing, your commitments and communities. After centering, which can take seconds or minutes, you choose how you want to respond to being grabbed—this time, with a fuller awareness of what is coming up for you. In that process, the initial reaction to "the grab" becomes tempered; in this workshop, people found themselves taking deep breaths, pausing before reacting, and gaining clarity on how they wanted to act.

"The pressure is still going to be there, but you're able to turn and feel into that with more resource in your body and therefore more choice," Eliana said. "From there, you can choose a different pathway and be like, 'Well, if what I really care about is the liberation of Palestine, chewing this person out who just told me I'm a self-hating Jew is not going to get me any closer to that.'" She emphasizes that the goal is not to be gentle necessarily—it's to be centered enough to consciously choose your response. "Sometimes you might recenter and then choose, 'I want to yell at you right now,' and that's great. The point is to just do it choicefully and not out of reaction."

There's a slightly counterintuitive but beautiful logic to these teachings in Eliana's work around Zionism. She is facilitating unlearning, but the person she focuses on changing is *not the other person*. The unlearning takes place inside of her—her role is to expand her and others' ability to respond with intention to people who might be activated, angry, or accusatory when she challenges them on Zionism. This is based on the understanding that even the best argument, the clearest information, the most compelling human story cannot land if the other person is in a dysregulated state, and that we can support people to move out of that dysregulation by remaining centered and compassionate ourselves, regulating our own nervous systems and entering into a kind of limbic resonance or connection that makes for transformative conversation. Rather than trying to talk them out of fear, our job is to learn how to hold that fear and respond to it with empathy without losing sight of the larger goal.

These somatic modalities are pointedly *not* about adopting one specific form of communication, or learning or unlearning one discrete thing. Many people assume that somatic practices are about becoming gentler, or softer, embodying a particular New Age style—as Eliana said, "I think there's a real misconception, as somatics gets more popularized and other, body based healing traditions have been whitewashed and colonized. There's this idea that embodiment means you always *talk like this*"—Eliana shifts from her usual firm and direct style of speaking to a soft hippie voice—"and you're very at peace with everything and kind. . . . There's these ideas of what that looks like. And I think they're wrong. The lineage of somatics that I was taught is, we can be embodied in anything. So when we center, we're not centering to feel calm. We're not centering to feel complacent under the conditions that we're facing, we can center in our rage. We can center in our grief. We can center in any of it."

The goal is not to avoid anger, but to challenge our own reactivity so that whatever we express and do is more fully aligned with our commitments, she said. "I find that there's a different quality, when centered rage moves out—that has a really different impact than a reactionary kind of anger."

While the actions employed by somatic coaches and facilitators can seem simple, the science that explains these practices is complex and continually being updated and debated. In Dr. Bruce Perry and Oprah Winfrey's book *What Happened to You,* the authors explore the neurological implications of childhood trauma—itself a relatively new area of study for neuroscience.[13] As Perry, a child psychiatrist, explains, the human brain is organized hierarchically. At the top of the nervous system hierarchy is the cortex, responsible for creativity, thought, language, and abstract conceptual experiences like time and hope. This part of the brain organizes experience into linear memories and narrative stories; without it, we wouldn't have human culture or education as we know it. The next layer down in the hierarchy is the limbic brain, responsible for the experiences of reward, memory, bonding, and feeling—this is the area where we experience love and attunement, resonance with others, and the senses of connection that can be so important to unlearning and rethinking.[14] Below that, the diencephalon is the boss of arousal, sleep, appetite, and movement. At the base of the hierarchy, the brainstem controls temperature, breath, and the heart. These lower two layers are at times referred to as the "lizard brain," because they are the oldest parts of the brain in terms of evolution; the higher parts of the hierarchy are notable in that they mainly exist in mammals like us. These lower parts are also the layers of our brain's system that are the most closely connected with the rest of the body: the senses, the heart, and the gut. The lowest levels keep our basic functions (heartbeat, breath, sleep, appetite, movement) ticking along, and they collect information and respond to it, generally without any "conscious" thought.

These unconscious neural systems are also the first stop for most of our interactions in the world.

"Input from all of our senses—vision, hearing, touch, smell—first comes into our brain in the lower areas," says Perry. "None of our sensory input goes directly to the cortex; everything first connects to lower parts of the brain."[15]

Our automated responses are key to our survival, allowing us to have good reflexes under instances of immediate pressure such as a car pulling out into the intersection in front of us, or a threatening look from another animal. Because we need reflexes for survival, Perry says, "our brain is organized to act before we think."[16]

Importantly, when we go into a fear or shutdown response based on the reactions of our so-called lizard brain, we temporarily lose our ability to reason.[17] "Fight-or-flight" arousal, an overwhelming anxiety in our gut, or the complete shutdown mode of "freeze" that is cued by neural pathways out of our conscious control—all of these make it difficult for humans to respond to immediate stimuli using our full range of mental capacities. When we are activated in this evolutionary way, we lose access to creativity and problem-solving, and it can become hard to connect and bond with other humans. The love, community, and connection we need in order to be open to personal transformation become inaccessible.

Once the acute trauma or stimulation is over, we can generally restore or shift our sense of connection through touch, eye contact, light, motion, and attention to what we are feeling—much like we did in the somatic healing and processing session after our assault by police in DC. But during a full takeover by part of our brains designed to keep us alive at all costs, we cannot rationally consider ideas or possibilities. Our hearts pound, our palms sweat, and we react without conscious thought or intent. Psychologists call these states "dysregulation" or "activation"—and they can become a trap.[18]

These insights about the potential for healing trauma through somatics have led to breakthroughs in psychology and psychiatry, but it is not only trauma patients who experience activation—we are all susceptible to the reactions that put us under the control of our bodies and out of control of our conscious minds, which is why understanding the process is so important to creating conditions for unlearning. The neural networks trained to help us survive under threat send the same signals, and our bodies have the same reactions, regardless of whether the threat is imminent—for example, if we have been told our whole lives that transgender people are dangerous, we might become activated the first time we encounter a transgender person, no matter how sweet and unthreatening that person is. Or, as Eliana Rubin noticed as she began to unlearn Zionism, many people acculturated to the intergenerational fear of anti-Jewish attacks are susceptible to full-body fear responses even when they are not facing an immediate threat.

Eliana explains this ongoing pattern of reactivity succinctly: "To the nervous system, there's no distinction between a perceived threat and a real threat. So you're activated whether someone is attacking you or not."

While not every instance of unlearning requires confronting patterns caused by trauma, the reactions we may encounter in a situation of intense defensiveness, ingrained bias, or cognitive dissonance—increased heart rate, sweaty palms, reduced rational thought, intense fear, the desire to fight or run away—are physiologically similar to activated trauma responses (albeit with wide variation in how intense the reactions are and how long they last). Whether being stuck in one's ways is a result of years of indoctrination, acute experiences of trauma, or simply habituation by the dominant culture, the path of confronting that stuckness can be rutted with reactivity. The fact that PTSD and childhood trauma patients are healing ingrained patterns through somatics presents a hopeful opening for all unlearners. Even reactions that are out of our conscious control can potentially be grasped and changed.[19] But we cannot transform ourselves or each other while we are actively in fight, flight, or freeze mode, abandoning choice for reactions that may feel like the only thing keeping us safe.

While Eliana and Yashna immediately saw the connection between somatics and unlearning, they were both somewhat resistant to the negative frame of "unlearning"—their concern was not eliminating some old way of being, but opening up new approaches. Both spoke about the importance of choice.

"Somatics is literally about creating new pathways," said Eliana. "And so when I think of unlearning, it's like those parts of you probably never go away. But the less that I run the neural pathway of 'I feel unsafe, Zionism is the answer' that was ingrained in me, it's going to slowly die off. And the more that I build pathways in my body toward 'I feel unsafe. How can I get wide and feel for the collective that's holding me?' that's going to help me invest more in the visions of culture and community that we're trying to build."

Trauma response and activation also never fully go away, said Yashna. "They are there waiting in the wings. Because often we've had lifetimes of that particular way getting set in our bodies, in our organizations, in our families, generations, you know," she said. Somatics practitioners talk a lot about "blending": taking your first knee-jerk reaction, accepting and seeing it for what it is, and slowly allowing it to blend with a reaction in which you have more self-determination. "The blending and the curiosity is the first step among many to find new patterns, new learning. These practices help give you more choice."

As she explored her voice through somatics, Yashna began to find moments of choice. That didn't mean always speaking up or being loud in every context. "When can I choose not to speak? And have that be a powerful choice versus, like, 'Oh, my body just is shut down and it won't let me speak.' Or 'The conditions around me are shutting my body down.'"

These moments of choice, to me, resemble the desire lines of the mind that are core to unlearning. If the well-trodden, prescribed path is the sidewalk, somatics can help to first notice the sidewalk, then question the sidewalk, then physically bring ourselves into a state of active choice. Eventually, we can learn to walk along a new desire line. Somatics helps us access neuroplasticity, not by calming or emptying the mind but by bringing attention and eventually self-determination and collective choice to how we act, move, and think. Allowing our bodies to fully process their reactions makes space for our minds to see options. Doing this collectively, with an explicit goal of releasing past patterns that harm our ability to work collectively for justice, is a complex unlearning practice supported by decades of study and experimentation.

Somatic practices can interrupt ingrained patterns of action, heal trauma, and give us tools to change our inner landscapes and to get better at facilitating unlearning in others. And, in a sense, almost every practice is somatic: the soma, the whole body, is connected to our nervous system in a constant conversation, with the body and its senses and reflexes telling the mind what to do perhaps even more often than the conscious mind directs the body. The beauty is, somatic practice isn't just a thought exercise. Through somatics, radical unlearning can become something that we do not just by reflecting and then acting, but a process that emerges *because of* action. But this kind of somatic transformation only works with repetition—with dedicated, intentional practice.

INTERLUDE: "COMING OUT OF THE FOG" AND EMBODIMENT THROUGH DRAG

Tori Grace Nichols embodies the joy and hopefulness of unlearning: drag performer extraordinaire, student of comedy and screenwriting, singer and actor and community organizer, Grace—who performs as the genderqueer drag king G-Clef—embodies the hope and belief that people can change in everything they do, including making people laugh.

Grace has also been through the wringer of unlearning, themself: as a baby, they were adopted from a Filipino family by a white woman who was a teacher on US military bases overseas, and they grew up moving around the world within that intersection of nationalism and colonialism. In 2008, they moved to the US and slowly became politicized around their adoption experience—an unlearning process so common among adoptees that it has a name, "coming out of the fog." They have also come out through their life as queer, trans, and genderqueer, and they use their performances to evoke silliness and possibility. They are also my friend, and a member of the Durham SeaRealists collective as well as the legendary drag troupe House of Coxx.

We talked about unlearning over many months and on two occasions we recorded our conversations—once, sitting in a adorable wooded cafe, the second, sitting together on my couch. I was particularly taken by their explorations of mental health support, embodiment, and theater and performance as portals to unlearning. Here's some of what we talked about.

LEWIS: Tell me about "coming out of the fog."

GRACE: In the adoption world, "coming out of the fog" is a kind of unlearning, or undoing, of any type of narrative that an adoptee might have received about their experience. And it's not necessarily like this for everyone, but the majority of folks who are adopted experience this because, culturally, the adoption

narratives are "Adoption is an amazing lifesaving thing in
which a baby got saved and put into a good home out of an
impossible situation." In short, adoption saves lives.

LEWIS: Isn't that even like a TV ad, explicit propaganda saying that?

GRACE: Absolutely. So coming out of the fog is recognizing it's not
a fairy-tale situation that a lot of people have placed on us. And
placing this "You were saved" narrative [on adoptees] creates a
lot of guilt and pressure. Lots of adoptees also do a lot of writing and creative works around gratitude. Because another thing
is like, you should be grateful you weren't aborted. You should
be grateful that you didn't grow up in poverty. You should be
grateful you didn't grow up in a "third world country."

I was adopted from the Philippines when I was seven
months old by a white woman who was a teacher overseas on
American military bases. . . . I'm interested in this concept of
unlearning and learning because, on the one hand, I know all
of the white women meant well, and I know they all loved us in
their own ways, and I want to give them grace and understanding for that. On the other hand, I really wish that they also were
open to hearing how harmful their actions were and are.

LEWIS: What was going on in your life when you started to come
out of the fog?

GRACE: It was probably not until I was about twenty-seven. And
this is really closely connected to identity development because
I had never really considered individually what it meant to be
Asian, what it meant to be from the Philippines. I felt so distant
[from it]. I didn't actually see that as a part of my life.

It happened when I attended a conference. I was working
as a staff person at a small liberal arts college in Georgia and
had taken some LGBT students to a conference. The keynote speaker there was [healing practitioner and leader] Yolo
Akili, and he was giving a speech. He was supposed to be the
keynote speaker and he just spoke so honestly that he was
having a really hard time. He's like, "I'm supposed to give this
big motivational speech today," but instead he was like, "I'm

tired, I'm sad. I have a lot of grief." In being authentic, he really encouraged us to think, "What are the untapped places of grief in our life?" I'd never even thought about that. I honestly had a little bit of a crisis, a lot bit of a crisis after that, because I've never thought about what kind of trauma or grief I had experienced . . . and I had never thought about my adoption as trauma, or my separation as something to grieve.

If I have never thought about what it means to be Asian, how is that possible as an Asian person at twenty-seven? A big part of coming out of the fog was not only learning about broader aspects of the adoption industry but the specific lies in [my] own experience.

The bluntest thing that we can say about the adoption industry is it's human trafficking. By another name, painted up as if it's not, as if there's not an exchange of money for a human, and that trickles down into everybody's consciousness. People feel perfectly justified paying money for a human because they think it's a good thing.

Now my understanding around race dynamics, around power dynamics [is that] more often than not, a birth parent, a birth family, a family or culture of color, or generally labeled "Third World," are coerced into giving their babies up because they're already prelabeled as unqualified to take care of a baby, because they are impoverished. The deeper unlearning I think we all have to do involves asking what caused the impoverished circumstances. Where is this notion of worthiness coming from? Why is it assumed that a white family, a Christian family from the US, is going to be able to care for this Black or Brown baby better?

We should be asking these questions in a much bigger way because, you know, an unfortunate reality is the abuses that happen in adoption and foster care. Because the assumption, again, is that [a] white Christian family could never do any wrong. But lots of wrong happens. The biggest example we have are the Indigenous boarding schools.

LEWIS: And then how did you come out of that period of crisis? What changed and moved for you?

GRACE: To begin with, it was finding the type of mental health support that would just stabilize me at first. And then it was kind of a confrontation with my own codependency. Confronting the codependency feels pretty crucial for trauma healing, because it just feels like figuring out how you can take ownership back of your own life, regardless of what has happened, you know? And it's my understanding that [for] folks who have been through a lot of trauma, it's hard to be in our bodies. It's hard to take responsibility for ourselves. So the easiest next thing is just to focus outwards. And just that makes relationships really fraught.

And a key part for me was also not really being able to access all of the hurt and rage that I felt. So part of it was definitely taking responsibility for my own actions, but also giving space to the harm that I experienced [by] allowing myself to acknowledge the impact of difficult things that had happened. Putting a name to them. You know, if everyone's saying, "Adoption is amazing" and "You should be so grateful that you're not sleeping on the floor in the Philippines."

LEWIS: And at that point, when all that was happening, where were you with your queerness and gender identity, how did that interplay?

GRACE: My queerness absolutely helped me along that journey. Because I had already more or less had this process of figuring out I'm different and figuring out how to navigate the world with being a bit different.

It felt like a much longer process around gender and similar examples around messaging that I received that didn't align with my actual experience. So I had always been tomboyish. I always felt pretty comfortable not conforming to gender expectations as a young girl. And so when I learned the language— genderqueer, nonbinary—that made a lot of sense. And I was really excited about that. But I didn't identify as trans until some years later, because the messaging around transness is like, "You're in a wrong body, and you want to move from one gender to another gender." And not only that, it's like a torturous experience. You hate yourself. And I'm just like . . .

LEWIS: You're like, "I don't hate myself, so I must not be trans?" That's so upsetting. But so true.

GRACE: I remember luckily being able to meet other trans people, and I kind of remember, unfortunately, having an experience of pity, just being, like, "Oh my God, I couldn't even imagine having so much internal conflict." I didn't realize there's so many different expansive options of transness, of gender identity in general.

LEWIS: So my big question and exploration with all of this has been what creates the conditions for unlearning. If you were to look at your experience of unlearning these really deep things that require all this change in you, what do you think created the conditions for that in your life?

GRACE: I think with change in general, there are ways that it can happen kind of abruptly, sometimes, violently, and in difficult ways, and then there are ways sometimes that it's just super incremental. And you just kind of feel like you've arrived somewhere different. The adoption bit definitely felt like the former. I was hit with all this information.

I mean, definitely the first thing that comes to mind is lots of mental health support. It's just really unsettling.

LEWIS: And it sounds like for you, there was a lot of grieving or a deep emotional process to go through that. I think humans are smart and we don't do those kind of things, if we're not in a situation to do them—we're good at repressing if we're not in a safe situation to go there.

GRACE: Yeah. I know so many people now who do grief rituals, which is so nice because then it just makes it more of a human experience. And then it doesn't have to be so violent.

I just keep coming back to, like, therapy. Connecting with other adoptees was pretty crucial, of people who were able to tell me like that my feelings were real and valid. [. . .]

Probably similar for transness, it was just meeting and connecting with a lot of other trans people. I learned a lot from
younger trans people—who were just like, "Yeah, this is who I
am. This is how I express."

And then, learning about precolonial Philippines, as I
tried to search for ways to reconnect with my birth culture,
I got to learn about queer and trans presence since the beginning of time and specifically in Philippine culture. . . .
Gender-expansive people are really revered and honored and
had very important roles in our communities. People don't
realize our existence since the beginning of time.

LEWIS: I'm curious to hear more about the work that you're doing
now, both around screenwriting, but also drag and performance and how you feel like that relates to unlearning.

GRACE: I started drag in 2010 . . . I just loved it. I mean, it certainly
helped with my gender identity stuff, being able to express
in different ways and just sort of drop into a different experience, the way that you're able to just develop a whole different
persona. And to get to embody that is a really transformative art form. And then my politicization has taught me [that]
drag performers have always been on the front lines of LGBT
movement and community as like the loudest, sparkly people
who are like, "Yeah, we're fucking queer." Like, "What are you
going to do about it?" . . . It has been really interesting to see
the very specific attacks on drag performers, and I'm excited
for the future when we look back on this moment and are like,
that was the opposition's biggest misstep, to try to come after
drag performers . . .

LEWIS: Who are beloved, who, like, everybody loves . . .

GRACE: Beloved in the community. And I say this often, what I love
about drag is, like, yeah, it's not joy for just the LGBT community. It's for everyone. It brings delight and joy to an entire
community.

LEWIS: And it seems like you get to embody things that feel maybe
harder to access in day-to-day life?

GRACE: Yeah, the embodiment aspect I feel like is also one of the
key elements to a condition of unlearning. And, actually, the
really great cultural workers of AgitArte, based out of Puerto
Rico, do a lot of guerrilla theater, and big creative, direct
actions, they would always emphasize that you kind of have
to feel liberation on a cellular level. . . . A common practice
is, you know, doing political theater and making a thing like
a tableau or a machine and doing the oppressive version of
that . . . so you might have a jail. And then on the flip side,
there's, like, community gardens and education and health care
and even getting to experience that with a small group of people creates so much possibility because then people can feel
what it's like. Maybe that's not emphasized enough. Particularly
in movement.

All of us are always bringing all of our traumas to movement. And so I think we're often just looking outward: We
want to change the world, want to change this, want to change
that, but what would it be like to start more internally and
have these very small liberatory experiences? And try to create
more wholeness within ourselves? Our movements are broken
because we are broken. But if we were to create wholeness for
ourselves, we could create more whole movements because
we would be different in movement. All of our petty fights and
conflict and scarcity mindset, we don't have to do that. It feels
instinctual, but there's many other possibilities.

LEWIS: I love that.

CHAPTER 8

PRACTICE

Denise Perry had a simple practice that she did every morning, an experiment in unlearning and release: she brushed her teeth with her left hand.

Denise is right-handed. At night, so she didn't get bad teeth during the days, weeks, and months of practice, she would brush her teeth using her right hand, and then in the morning, she would switch to the left.

"I've been doing this for almost two years now because I want to test it for myself," she told me with an almost-ironic smile. "I said, 'How long will it take for me to be able to brush my teeth with my left hand and feel equally satisfied, natural, and easeful with the outcome?'"

We were sitting on her couch in a rural part of Durham County, where she lives on a couple acres of land. Behind her, there was a framed poster with a screen-printed cocoon that said "Transformation"; behind me, there was a wall-to-wall shelf full of books about Black feminism, organizing, somatics, and transformation.

I didn't come here for stories about tooth brushing, but it turned out to be the perfect anecdote: I came because Denise has worked for over a decade teaching Black social justice leaders how to transform their own leadership through practice. She talks a lot about practice, she facilitates "practices," she invites people to practice. She and the teaching team she works with often repeat the mantra that it takes three hundred repetitions for the body to know how to do something, and three thousand for it to become embodied—an assertion of many somatics practitioners.

But she wanted to see for herself: could she show her mind and body how to change a practice, or even embodied muscle memory, by simply changing her daily routine?

It worked, she said—after nearly two years of daily left-handed practice.

"Now I find myself sometimes brushing with my left hand when I don't have to." The repetitions formed a new way of physically doing something, and that new way formed a series of synapses, and with repetition, the discomfort of left-handed brushing was unlearned, replaced with a relative fluency in this narrow, specific task.

"Practice is transformative because you begin to embody new ways of being," said Staci Haines and Ng'ethe Maina of Generative Somatics. "Through repetition what was a new practice becomes natural, easy, a new habit. You are in fact beginning to become somebody new. You will begin to see more clearly and quickly the choice that opens up in the moment about how you want to be. We are what we practice. Are we practicing what is most aligned with our vision for the world, for justice? This is where we want to continue to hone ourselves, organizations and work."[1]

Radical unlearning is about what we do, not just how we think about things—which means radical unlearning requires us to identify how we want to act, and then engage in a practice to build that new embodiment at every turn. Denise said it's important that we choose these practices, and that the practices expand our choices in general. "We want to be discerning, thoughtful and purposeful to help us have choice which is a form of freedom. Therefore we engage in receiving assessments, identifying what we most care about, and build our practices to serve what we most care about."

Practice, on the surface, certainly seems like an expression of unlearning (and learning) and a way to deepen and continue it. But can practice itself create conditions for unlearning? Can the actions themselves take us through to the other side?

————

Denise began our discussion of unlearning with a revelation about what she is struggling to unlearn in her own life, something I resonate with deeply: she said she was unlearning perfectionism and opening up to vulnerability.

"I'm battling it all the time, the idea that I have to take care of and fix things . . . that I am trying to get everything right." Like most of us with our ingrained ways, she comes by it honestly—her parents, of Cape Verdean descent, relocated from Boston, to LA, to Maryland, to follow her father's work as a pharmacist and then union organizer. They were devout Catholics and sent her and her brothers to Catholic school, where they learned discipline, rigidity, and the constant performance of not making mistakes. She was a middle child and the only girl, and, even though she left the church as a teen, she learned at a young age how to navigate between people and worlds, how to slide into respectability politics and perform as expected.

By her mid-twenties, Denise was also a union organizer, and she described how crushed she was by her first campaign. "I was driving from central Florida back to Maryland without stopping, in great tears and sadness, because the first organizing campaign that I ran with my coworker, with some nursing home workers, we lost. I was devastated."

She got to Maryland and her coworker, who was training her, asked what she was so upset about.

"We've probably ruined their lives," she replied without hesitation. "I mean, they lost. They may get fired and who knows what happened. And it's, you know, it's our fault."

Her mentor gently and firmly reminded her that the people they were organizing were grown folks, with their own choices, who opted into the campaign and made their own decisions.

"Unless you lied to them," he said, "you have nothing to worry about." This kind of failure generated powerful, lifelong lessons, and there would be many more mistakes that paved the road to being an effective, confident organizer. But for Denise, this part of the job was deeper—in order to be a good organizer, she had to unlearn her need to simply win. She had to trust the people she was organizing.

Denise told me her stories with a wry, low voice and a humorous sparkle in her eye, her curly salt-and-pepper hair hugging her head. She wore black-rimmed glasses, jeans, and a plaid button-down, and apologized for her dog named Bandit traipsing around the house and making shy eyes at me. She talked as if we were already friends, the way many organizers are trained to do, and I was grateful, relaxing into the conversation as she did.

"I'm almost forty years older than I was at that point," she said of her revelation about losing her first campaign, "and still practicing. . . . I want to get to where I'm not afraid to try something for fear of the mistake, but the mistake is the information that I need. What I see as a mistake may not actually be a mistake but an opportunity for growth and information."

The idea of practice as a portal to unlearning is simple. As stated by Ruth Wilson Gilmore: "Practice makes different."[2] Or, as adrienne maree brown puts it in *Pleasure Activism*, "We are what we practice. We become what we do over and over again."[3]

Practice is an age-old way to learn and become competent or expert in modes of thought or physical skills—and it is beginning to be recognized as a key to unlearning, too. Somatics practitioners and students of trauma healing modalities are at the cutting edge of this line of thought, as the last chapter explored. The assertion of the new neuroscience is that by intentional and precise repetitions of action, we can not only create new synapses, but encourage our minds to abandon the old. As Thomas Lewis, Fari Amini, and Richard Lannon write in *A General Theory of Love*, "Experience methodically rewires the brain," creating the well-worn pathways that make actions and ways of thinking easier to repeat. "The more often you do or think or imagine a thing, the more probable it is that your mind will revisit its prior stopping point."[4] Practice is the somatic experience of taking control over that wiring—identifying and choosing which pathways we want our neuroplastic minds to cultivate.

A well-known exercise of neuroplasticity is practicing a sport or an instrument. This highly physical form of practice leads to change in our brain's abilities and our physical capabilities. The more specific and targeted the repetition, the more effective the learning.

"A key principle of neuroplasticity is specificity," explains Bruce Perry in *What Happened to You?* "In order to change any part of the brain, that specific part of the brain must be activated. If you want to learn to play the piano, you can't simply read about piano playing . . . you must put your hands on the keys and play."[5] The same principle applies to unlearning, but with an additional moment of awareness and disruption—as you feel your hands move towards an old way of playing, you adjust your position to the new way. As you feel your mind fall into a rut, you adjust your thought patterns. Simply having new information (I am playing this wrong; I have understood this wrong) is typically not enough—you must repeat the unlearning/new learning pattern, over and over, until the old reaction ceases to be habitual and the new one emerges. Practices that interrupt thoughts and facilitate new behaviors can be anything from poetry and creative writing to breathwork, physical touch, music, meditation, and rituals of centering like the ones described in the previous chapter on politicized somatics.

Both somatic practice and unlearning are at the core of Denise's work as an organizer. For many years now, she has been co-leading Black Organizing for Leadership and Dignity (BOLD), a national organization that serves as "a catalyst for transformative, embodied leadership. Through training, project incubation, and network cultivation, BOLD supports the infrastructure of powerful and coordinated movements."[6] The people who participate in BOLD's trainings are leaders in social and racial justice efforts around the country, and BOLD's vision is a strong, multiracial justice movement in which Black-led organizations play a key role.

BOLD describes its work as having three pillars: Transformative Organizing, Political Education, and Embodied Leadership, and they train up to a hundred people per year in intensive sessions. They aim to transform individuals and organizations who then work to transform

society. They believe leaders within these organizations need to address their own internalized forms of oppression, their own (inevitable)
messiness, and their access to choice. BOLD doesn't believe people are
bad and aim to change who they are; rather, their trainings help people
identify and build their capacity to choose how they want to be. They
can unlearn and build skills that help transform their organizations and
the world—the part of the work that BOLD calls embodied leadership.

Rather than taking the stance that there is a particular methodology
or approach that will work for all these leaders, the trainings at BOLD
focus on the needs and limitations of each person. Each individual
identifies their own commitments and personal areas for growth, and
during the training they develop their own *practices*—actions that will
bring them through the embodied experience of showing up differently.
Denise explains that they start with questions: "How are we showing up
and how is that impacting ourselves? And is that how we want to show
up? What is our commitment to who we want to be, how we want to be?
And it doesn't mean we erase who we are by any stretch."

It's like her left-handed toothbrushing, but for the movement: one
person's practice might be to take a breath and get grounded every time
they enter a new room, while another person's practice might be tai chi
in the mornings, and someone else's might be changing the way they
listen when other people talk. The approach isn't to shame or blame
people for how they've done things in the past or try to prove that there's
a better way, but to systematically carve out new ways of behaving that
align with each person's political goals and commitments.

Following on the teachings of Generative Somatics, one of BOLD's
training partners, these trainings embrace the idea that the brain isn't
separate from the heart or the hands. We are an integrated whole—the
soma—and we know we have unlearned when we react, respond, and
behave differently. In the process of this embodied, practiced change, the
goal shifts from perfection, analysis, and language to practice—practice
not just in the sense of repetitions and preparations, but also in the sense
of how we show up every day and attempt to make change.

Denise said in BOLD trainings, as in Generative Somatics, the practices start with simply noticing. "There's a practice where we walk toward

another person," she explained. As you get closer to the other person, you notice how their physical presence affects you: "How are you feeling? What's happening? Do your fists clench up? Do you close your eyes? Do you back away?"

As they begin to notice their own embodied responses to other people, she said, "then they have choice."

BOLD's approach is sensitive and humanizing, but it's also systemic: once they see what their own reactions or actions are that they want to change, participants choose practices to embody on a daily basis. After they complete a course, they become a BOLD alumni and can continue to participate through a thirty-day practice check-in that's offered soon after the training, through joining regional alumni groups known as Cumbe's, or through advanced training with BOLD. And the organization follows up to evaluate the effectiveness of the training in the years after, systematically observing and asking whether and how these leaders have changed their practices, how they have run successful campaigns or projects, whether their organizations are still thriving, and how they and others see their leadership. Overwhelmingly, participants in BOLD persist in their work, bring the practices with them, and stay in their organizations as leaders.

It's successful, she believes, because it's chosen, it's embodied, and it's part of a community of people practicing together.

"I don't think we can make someone unlearn," Denise said. People have to choose unlearning, and repeat themselves until it sets in. This is done, she says, "for the sake of what they most care about, for the sake of having choice, for the sake of sharing the best of who they are in this work. This is not a short process or something done alone—it requires an accountability buddy, a community of practice, and a North Star."

Sometimes practice feels like it takes forever, like a trudging series of repetitions. But sometimes practice makes change quickly. When we show up for the practice, it's not just that we can unlearn through repetition, but that we can unlearn in a moment, by having an experience that rewrites our bodily expectations of what is possible.

Take this story that Roxy Manning, the author of *How to Have Anti-racist Conversations* and an organizer and antiracism trainer, told me—it starts when she and her friends left a restaurant late at night in downtown Oakland, and saw a couple of unhoused people fighting on the street.[7]

"We decided we wanted to intervene," she said. "This is a huge moment of unlearning. You see people arguing, you walk away, you stay safe. You know, you don't engage. You don't do that, especially if they're unhoused. They might be dangerous, you know? And we were just like, 'Wait a second, no, this doesn't feel good.' We were worried about gender violence, a whole bunch of things."

She and her friends—a man and two women—split up, and the man approached the guy in the fight while the women approached the woman. They gently separated them, and started to talk, "really bringing in everything that we'd learned about empathy and connection and, like, not judging or shaming," she said. "It would have been easy to be like, 'What are you doing?' But it was more like, 'Oh, what's going on? It sounds like y'all are really distressed.' And it turned out the tension was one of them had forgotten the shopping cart, and now they'd lost the shelter spot and there was no place to stay. They were both so frustrated and angry and taking it out on each other, and so we helped them come up with other strategies."

At the end of the conversation, the man and woman walked away, having refocused their attention on their shared problem. For Roxy Manning, this was a pivotal moment in her own unlearning—she had been studying and writing about nonviolent communication, but it was rare to have a chance to apply these skills so directly in an escalated situation.

"Taking this learning that was in our head about how to empathize with people and how to have these conversations and actually stepping into something that might be scary and dangerous, was really important," she said.

It worked—they were able to help. "But then also the feedback that it had an impact, we were actually able to change the situation, was so reinforcing. Now I know that I can walk toward conflict in the future, right? It was a huge support for being able to move from thought to practice."

This interaction reminds me of the feeling that something has "clicked," that you get when you're learning to ride a bike. When it clicks, it becomes a practice that you can choose again and again—the muscle memory of doing it safely and successfully getting stronger at every go.

As I wandered the halls of other people's unlearning in the fall and winter of 2023 and into 2024, the genocide in Gaza committed by the US-funded Israeli military was unfurling a living nightmare on a place and people with whom I felt a deep connection. For anyone with a connection to occupied Palestine or Israel—and for many without—it was a scary and activating time. In those months, as I protested the ongoing genocide between bouts of attempting to finish this manuscript, I found myself unlearning hopelessness and cynicism—by practice.

I had been through a fair amount of learning and unlearning about Palestine before, mostly through friends who were anti-Zionist Jewish activists and through the leadership of Palestinian American writers and organizers. I was a fan of Edward Said; I had followed the Boycott, Divest, Sanctions (BDS) movement; I had spoken out in anger following the Israeli military murder of journalist Shireen Abu Akleh in 2022. My close friend Micah Bazant went to Palestine in 2006, and I myself visited with a group called Eyewitness Palestine in 2018.

My ten days in Palestine changed me: we traveled the occupied West Bank, watching men stand in line to make awful border crossings through high-security Israeli terminals at 4 a.m., watching kids build gardens in refugee camps where they had to protect the plants from the IDF's frequent use of teargas. I bought old Palestinian coins near the stagnant and symbolic apartheid wall, coins that showed that Palestine preexisted the 1948 Nakba, that people had been there. We met youth activists in al-Khalil who cooked us beautiful meals and begged us to go home and tell what we saw. We met the founder of the BDS movement, Omar Barkouti, a brilliant, principled, patient man. Finally, through the Ford Global Fellowship, I made some new friends in 2021 and 2022 who were Palestinian and Lebanese, or living in Jordan, and who had family and friends in Gaza and the West Bank—second- or third-generation refugees.

All of which is to say I did not need convincing that another Israeli siege on Gaza funded by the US was wrong. The unlearning in 2023 for me was about something else. Many people know that Palestine is occupied, that Palestinians are not "terrorists" or "animals," and a lot of people don't believe the racist propaganda about Palestinians even if they have been exposed to pro-Israeli propaganda (I, too, am constantly unlearning the racism embedded in the messages that Israel is a democracy, that it's less homophobic than the rest of the Middle East, that it's a source of safety in the Middle East, and so on). But even if you unlearned those biases, and saw through the propaganda, there was another ideological frame that urgently needed to be unlearned in the context of the US: the framework of apathy and passivity, the sense that we have nothing to do with this and there is nothing for us to do about it.

The people I knew in 2023 who believed that our actions don't matter did nothing. The people I knew who believed that it matters to show up in protest, even when you might not "win" or the situation seems hopeless, showed up in unprecedented strength and numbers. In DC that fall, I joined hundreds of young Jewish protesters taking over the Capitol to demand a ceasefire, and later joined tens of thousands of people, mostly Palestinian or Arab, taking to the streets in the largest pro-Palestine demonstration in US history. Among them, I imagine many who, like Denise Perry, were practicing the vulnerability of knowing that we might not win, but also seeing that there is a larger purpose to demonstrating anyway.

So much of the time, participating in protest, participating in movement spaces, I have felt like, "What is the point?" I hate the way so many marches feel dull and aimless, the people whose minds we are trying to change never seeming to be shaken by our noise. I have struggled to believe in it, even though of course I believe in it, and my whole life in many ways is a result of other people's risk-taking in the streets, other people's faith that things could change. And yet, and yet, the US military, the US empire, the capitalist forces and barely hidden oligarchy that benefits from militarism—all these wear you down with their sheer size. The more you know about dominant systems, the more helpless you can come to feel. "What would be the point of doing anything?" I had wondered—many times. In 2023, simply showing up at a protest and putting my body on the line was a way of coming out of that fog.

The practice became the unlearning. Driven by feelings of love for Palestine and my friends who are from there, I didn't wait for the cynical side of me to change before I went to a protest, or bargain with the voices in me that didn't see the point. I dragged myself out of the house, unmoored and furious. In the early days of the genocide, we refused to leave Congresswoman Valerie Foushee's office in Durham, joining a mostly Jewish group piling up small stones in the hallway and reading the names of the hundreds of Palestinian children already killed by Israeli airstrikes, less than a week into the siege. We organized to go to DC; huge groups of us got arrested on the Capitol, my first arrest in my life. We came home, called our congresspeople, marched through downtown, flew kites in honor of the thousands of children who had been killed. We went back to DC and got beat up and dragged out by the cops; it was all caught on camera, but nothing happened. We painted posters in our basement in Durham. Protest became a practice. Somehow, after twenty-five years in social justice movements, this was still a new experience for me.

During this same period, I came across longtime climate justice activist Joanna Macy's work with Chris Johnstone on "active hope." A clear-eyed take on what is required of us in a time of global climate collapse, extinction, and the horrors of war and genocide, all coming to us live on Instagram, Macy and Johnstone echo Mariame Kaba's idea that hope, rather than a feeling, is a discipline—something you can learn.

"Active Hope is a practice," they write. "Like tai chi or gardening, it is something we *do* rather than *have*. It is a process we can apply to any situation, and it involves three key steps. First, we take a clear view of reality; second, we identify what we hope for in terms of the direction we'd like things to move in or the values we'd like to see expressed; and third, we take steps to move ourselves or our situation in that direction."

Active hope, for me, has become an area of unlearning—a study in how I can change my insides by simply showing up. "Since Active Hope doesn't require optimism," they write, "we can apply it even in areas where we feel hopeless."[8]

And it worked: every time I showed up in a place where we were doing something to try to stop the genocide, I felt my heart get a little bit bigger. Sometimes the feeling was physical—the reality of injustice or the words of a particular speaker or the simple presence of a huge crowd would flow through my body, expanding inside me. Through this practice, I had a much-needed breakthrough: it's not all drudgery and self-righteousness and sitting through meetings where nothing happens. It's not all calling your congressperson and then feeling put out when nothing changes. There's a selfishness to practice, because these practices of collectivity and solidarity can give life meaning. I believe I felt more connected than the people I know who did nothing, more clear on my purpose in a moment of global insecurity and doubt, less helpless, more connected. I called my congresswoman's office over and over, and I often cried on the phone with the random interns who answered, not in a way that was put on, but out of felt grief. I could feel my vulnerability moving them to cognitive dissonance, to discomfort, or even empathy. "We'll talk to her," they'd say.

We still don't know the end of this story, but I believe our actions helped—they helped get aid to Gaza sooner, they helped Palestinians know that the world had not abandoned them even if powerful governments had, they helped keep a fire alive in the belly of the beast. Telling our stories from Palestine, reading the stories from Palestinians, practicing and connecting with people, participating as part of a global anti-war and anti-imperialist movement changed me, resensitized me to something that, despite my strong opinions, I had come to accept. I felt hopeful again.

It feels vulnerable to even talk about this change from within, because I have learned over and over again from the dominant culture that it's naive to think that our small acts of protest matter. On the other hand, I've learned from activist and movement-building culture that these acts are supposed to be done selflessly, with absolute faith. I have never showed up selflessly for a protest, as I used to think I should. But now I think the fact that we get something out of it even when we don't win is part of the magic that makes persistence possible. Protest sometimes leads to structural change and always leads to change in the people who participate. There is a reason for showing up that is deeper than whether our demands are immediately won.

Our demands did not go over immediately. But, in Durham, we campaigned to get our congressperson to call for a ceasefire and eventually, she did. By then, thousands of Palestinians had died, but only a few dozen congresspeople and one senator had even said the word "ceasefire" publicly. I got the news in the airport that we'd won our local campaign—"Valerie Foushee said ceasefire!"—and I cried and called my parents and cried even harder, proud and devastated. In that moment, I had this gutting realization that we had done all we could, and it still wasn't going to matter—it would need to be *every* congressperson, it would need to be *more*, to have the impact that we wanted it to have.

The weeks and months ticked on. We wrote letters and made calls and signed petitions. The South African government brought a charge of genocide against Israel, and the international court at the Hague affirmed that a genocide was likely underway. The death toll surpassed thirty thousand, half of them children. Almost everyone in Gaza was displaced.

There's truth to both feelings—that participating in protest doesn't matter, and that it does. Protest doesn't always produce the results we need, and the structures that we are up against can feel (and be) intractable and scary. But the history is unfolding right now, and our bodies are shaping that history. There's also the truth of what it means in the broader arc of history to be voices of witness, to slow the grind of the war machine, to create a world in which not everyone accepts genocide even if many people do, often by way of apathy and cynicism. Around the world, in 2023, people did not just watch a genocide happen, did not just watch innocent people, including children, having their lives uprooted and destroyed and being brutally murdered and displaced on our social media feeds, and do nothing. Everyone who did something in that moment in my country, the United States, hopefully unlearned some of the training that we are all receiving to just go along with things. Our acts of protest made a difference to how we related to each other, to Palestinians, to our own spiritual lives in the face of massacre. And by showing up, we allowed ourselves to be changed. We opened up new possibilities for how to relate in the future. We became less cut off in general, more in touch with this world in all its messiness.

That's the kind of unlearning that you can't think your way into. There's no right way to go about it. You can't say to someone, "Go to this protest," or "Do that action"—we have lives, we have needs, we have limits. There's no rule book—what I'm talking about is deep, ancestral, spiritual work, asking: What does it mean to me to show up in my life, in this world, in the fullest way that I know how, and what do I have to unlearn to make that possible? And, for me, that terrible year was about unlearning cynicism, intellectualism, and the complete falsehood that our personal actions are futile.

In a globalized era, it can be overwhelming to learn new facts about the world—we are inundated with information from the internet, and we can start to feel small. So much is happening and everything is bad. But it's also the first time in human history that we've been able to know, in such intimate detail, this atrocity is happening over there, *and* there's something I can do about it. I want to believe there's something transcendent about that, to know that you are part of a global undercurrent, to be able to see the videos of mass protests for Gaza all over the world, to be able to speak to people directly and say, "We are with you." Me locking arms with my friends in front of the Democratic National Committee office in DC is actually me locking arms with people across the world, in defense of Palestine and in defense of a world we know is possible. Locking arms is a practice; repeating it will undoubtedly change me, help me continue unlearning the constant narrative of cynical giving-up that dances before our eyes in this country. The genocide continued, but not without a hopeful and persistent global attempt to end Israeli atrocities.

Mariame Kaba had said it, adrienne maree brown had said it, Joanna Macy said it, a zillion beautiful leaders said it. Denise said that February day: It's the practices, it's the practices. I was finally listening. In the background the bombs were still falling, the Israelis were preparing to move in on Rafah, the very place where they had told refugees they might go to be safe. But I was practicing, preparing for a life of facing these realities without flinching, learning through action how to not look away—unlearning the apathy that draws a well-paved pathway across our hearts in these times.

Denise talked a lot about choice, and conscious decisions to unlearn and change. A question that follows me around is the problem of whether unlearning can happen by practicing *without belief*. Could you repeat a pattern so many times that you unlearn your old pattern without consciously challenging the underlying ideology? For example, if someone who hadn't consciously "unlearned gender" called me by my correct gender pronouns over and over again on repeat, even though it goes against their instinct and beliefs, might the underlying ideology of the gender binary crumble inside of them, in turn? Or, to take my own example around apathy: Can I unlearn it by simply showing up? It feels like there's a kernel of possibility, that maybe practice has the power to override the entrapped mind.

I put the question to Denise on a whim, assuming she would have some kind of wisdom. After all, as a trainer she asks people to learn and unlearn truly deep habits and beliefs—lack of self-love, distrust in others, internalized oppressions. Can someone undermine an idea simply by adopting a new practice? Can a transphobe use the right pronouns and unbecome a transphobe?

Denise, who was often circumspect and vulnerably unsure in our conversation, surprised me with a definitive answer: no. The underlying desire and intention matters, she said. Someone might use the right pronouns because they don't want to offend or be deemed insensitive. But if they're doing it just to appease, she said, it's not really unlearning—it's a performance, a game of social etiquette. At the neurological level, she's speaking to something that is not well understood, but that humans are good at grasping intuitively. We might say something different, act a different way, because of social pressures or a desire to not offend. But something in the hidden layer, in the synapses we can't see or understand, belies the difference in the *way* we do our practices. If

I had shown up for all those protests out of obligation, or to perform for my audience on Instagram, the act of showing up might not have humbled me quite the way it did. Saying the "right words" or even doing the "right actions" is not the practice of unlearning—the practice must include realigning ourselves toward the shifting meaning of these words and actions.

By way of example, Denise brought up equine therapy—the horses can tell when we are anxious, performative, or distant, and the conversation with the horse is about establishing intuitive and somatic trust. The horses can tell if we are really embodying the change, if it's practice for practice's sake or something deeper.

"How we show up with that horse is so sensitive—that horse is not going to giddy up and go if it doesn't trust you," she said. "And there's a deep feeling there. . . . 'I'm not going to giddy up and go, because that shit you're giving me right now is not embodied. And I don't want you to just get my pronoun right. I want you to actually look me in the eye and connect with me about it. That you're saying it not for yourself, but you're actually saying it because you respect me.' So, the pony ain't going to get up and go."

Practice makes different—but there's a somatic difference between the practice of trying to *seem* different or inoffensive, and the practice of engaging ourselves to holistically unlearn an ideology. We might "slip up" in terms of language, but when the change sets in, it is a deep change. I can actually see this in myself around other trans people—in the early days, I would fret about calling people the "wrong" pronoun, habituated to certain assumptions about their assigned sex and genitalia, whether I wanted to be or not. These days, when someone tells me how they identify, they completely become that in my eyes. There is no system of synapses in place to support my assumptions about what they "really" are anymore. Unlearning binary gender wasn't overnight—it was a practice of learning to see myself and other trans people as we are. But the practice went to the core of my beliefs about the world, changing not just my language but what I see when I look at others' beloved bodies.

It seems unlearning can't be accidental or forced: it requires noticing a well-worn pathway inside ourselves, and choosing to change not just our view of one thing or another, but our *way* of thinking and acting. Still, I suspect there is a place for diving into the practices while we remain unsure about the ideas—start using different language, for example, and there's a good chance a deeper unlearning will open up. Start showing up at the protests, and active hope might unfurl from that act of possibility. Take a deep breath as you enter a room or a conversation, and see what comes out differently.

Certainly, practice is a way of unlearning, and it can facilitate transformative change. But what makes us *want* to change? What helps us with the devotional drive it takes to unlearn?

The question is becoming its own circle, cyclically returning—why do some people choose to engage what other people ignore? Why do we see wrong in ourselves but then refuse to devote ourselves to changing? Practice might make different, and practice can be taught, which means anyone can devote themselves to a new way of interacting with the world. But what creates the conditions of devotion? Denise pushed me to think about joy and freedom as a part of unlearning. Can there be pleasure and play in unlearning?

CHAPTER 9

POETRY AND SURREALISM

*Always we need the audacity to speak for more freedom, more
imagination, more poetry with all its meanings. As we go
deeper into conflict, we shall find ourselves more constrained,
the repressive codes will turn to iron. More and more we shall
need to be free in our beliefs, as we come to our forms.*

—MURIEL RUKEYSER, *The Life of Poetry*

I n my late teens, I wandered the blocks of the Heidelberg Project in
Detroit, where artist Tyree Guyton had taken over abandoned building
after abandoned building, painting broad bright polka dots on the edi-
fices, hanging shoes from the trees by their laces, piling shopping carts
full of the detritus of capitalism's violent assault on the city.

It was an eerie reimagining of what had been, could be, and was.
After hundreds of years as a marshy Anishinaabe trading site on a wide
riverfront, in the twentieth century automobiles and industry had transformed the landscape. Detroit boomed. The whole thing was built up
so that masses of Black people and Italians and Poles could be paid just
enough to build cars for the country and the world. Wealth accumulation
exploded, people moved there in droves, the wide streets were full of
Cadillacs and Fords. Then Detroit infamously busted: by the time I was
born, in the 1980s, it was known as a place where the river ran orange
and caught on fire, and where homeless people were left wandering
through gutted mansions. By the end of the century, the water didn't

run and the lights didn't come on for blocks and blocks of houses. People lived off the land even though the soil was leaded. There was still a middle class, but it was shrinking, and white flight and globalization meant Detroit, the Blackest city in the country, was often pictured as a land of potholed streets, toxic brownfields, and violence.

Detroit had become racial capitalism's poster child, and I'd grown up forty-five minutes away in what was effectively a different reality. Detroit was either a pariah, the "dark ghetto" where, as one of my parents explained, "you might get mugged just for being white." Alternately, and more popularly, by the late 1990s, Detroit was talked about in nearby white enclaves as a charity case, a sad place where I was taught that people were barely surviving, resources were scarce, life was dangerous. Notice the passive voice: people weren't doing anything, nor was there anything being done *to them*. It's just how it was. People from my white liberal town would go to Detroit for the purpose of helping: running afterschool programs for poor Black kids, giving out food, "bringing" artistic culture.

Tyree Guyton, a Black Detroiter, didn't see some idealized beauty or redemptive sunflower field of dreams in his city, but he also didn't see the pure miserabilism of the white liberal gaze. As he and his wife and grandfather and kids from the neighborhood cleaned up the abandoned lots around his childhood home, he saw the raw material at hand.[1] They made art out of all the "leftovers," a statement in itself about the people who'd been left in a city with shrinking infrastructure and growing debts. The sudden transformation as you walk down the cold, sprawling blocks—from rundown houses to funhouse mirrors—takes visitors to another place, playful and grieving. Still, that place is Detroit—a surreal vision, which is to say a vision of what is already there, just beyond or above the "real."

Though I would never have identified it at the time, it was there at the Heidelberg Project that I began to unlearn "Detroit." The idea of a Black city as a site of desperation transformed into the idea of a Black city as exactly itself, a multifaceted place, a place of homes and art and artists, protest and truth-telling, a place that did not need saving but deserved self-determination. Walking through Heidelberg, the juxtaposition of the soles of shoes with Detroit's open skies, of fresh paint with rotted homes, of the shiny hopeful metal of shopping carts with dust-encrusted piles of plastic toys and home decor, jolted something open in me. It opened up room to feel more than one feeling at once: angry and spooked, and then mournful and amused. It made Detroit real and the story of disinvestment less one-sided; it said, in Guyton's Black surrealistic voice, this unreal, too-real place is ours.

Walking through Heidelberg challenges not just the idea of a Black city, but the idea of space within cities—what is an "empty" lot, one begins to wonder? What is an "abandoned" building? What power do people have to change the geography, to make new desire lines and expressions and new kinds of public space? The possibilities were part of the ambiguity, because, as you walk down these blocks of the Heidelberg Project, there is no plaque, no reason or explanation for all this art. The charge is just to pay attention, to witness it and enter into the questions.

By contrast, when the liberal environment around me taught me about Detroit, I learned the people were impoverished, but I never learned why. I didn't learn about people in Detroit organizing; the long history of class struggle against the titans, Ford and General Motors; the federal government with its strict redlining and sharp highway slicing. I didn't learn about the powers that together made Black life, on average, shorter, harder, and more dangerous than white life. I didn't learn about the righteous anger that can emerge from the other side of oppression, or about the art that invariably does. I didn't learn about Black Surrealism. In offering an opening to a new way of seeing, Guyton's work at the Heidelberg Project offered one of the most important anti-racist interventions possible. Unlearning the flatness, the devastation I associated with the city, made Black life complex and creative in my eyes in ways that white people, the most segregated racial group in the world, often manage not to perceive.

It seemed clear when I embarked on this project that there should be some link between art, poetry, and unlearning. And there are many: anyone who has practiced and worked at imaginative endeavors like painting or poem writing has probably felt the floor fall out from beneath them at least a few times, felt the perspective-shifting power of witnessing and making art. But, as with any of the conditions explored in this book, art is not *necessarily* an unlearning portal—it's just one of the ways we can come to unlearning, if we are open to it. I have chosen to focus my study of art and unlearning on surrealism precisely because the Surrealists, as a movement, have always aligned with the idea that art *should* change us. They are experts in art as transformation and they share my interest in creating the conditions for radical change by undermining hegemonic ways of seeing. Surrealism demands participation and consciously attempts to change practitioners and audiences alike—it's not art for art's sake, but art that seeks to uproot dominant ways of thinking and looking.

Tyree Guyton's work, as I would later learn, was a continuation of an expansive and international Surrealist tradition that was concerned with radical unlearning from its very beginnings. In the early part of the last century, the Surrealists were among those to notice that capitalism had far surpassed its role as an economic system: it was a system of dominance, an ideological framework, a machinery in control not just of our daily lives but of our thoughts and feelings. This totalitarian tendency was most obvious from the standpoint of the parts of the world that had been colonized by Europe. Colonization and capitalism had become total projects, encompassing visions and value systems that Europeans and the US imposed on the colonized around the world. At this point, any resistance, it was becoming clear, would have to address both material conditions and inner lives—the colonization of the imagination and the soul, and the grip of imperialism on the mind.

Surrealism as a literary, cultural, and arts movement embraced this problem from its very beginnings. French intellectuals like André Breton and Paul Éluard explored the resistance of the mind in intense manifestos. Thinkers like the Martinican poets and political leaders Suzanne and Aimé Césaire saw the relationship between imagination and resistance, and they inspired the Surrealists in the belly of the beast to see it, too: revolution required imagination, and imagination required submitting to the poetic and the unexpected.[2]

Contrary to what is often taught, Surrealists were not just interested in dreams and the subconscious, or art that goes beyond "the real," and they were not just white painters of strange landscapes and melting clocks (not unrelated: many of his contemporaries in the Surrealist movement saw Dalí, he of the drippy clocks, as a sellout and a fake).[3] They are indeed students of dreams—but they have also been students of changing how we think, scholars and strategists of unlearning through artistic praxis.

It's not a coincidence that surrealism is often depicted as a nonpolitical European artistic phase rather than as the international and multiracial political art movement that it was. Robin D. G. Kelley, author of *Freedom Dreams: The Black Radical Imagination*, has played a role in bringing that full history back to life.

"The surrealists not only taught me that any serious motion toward freedom must begin in the mind, but they have also given us some of the most imaginative, expansive, and playful dreams of a new world I have ever known," he wrote in the introduction to *Freedom Dreams*. "Contrary to popular belief, surrealism is not an aesthetic doctrine but an international revolutionary movement concerned with the emancipation of thought."[4] In a later interview, Kelley elaborated: "Surrealism is committed to the real, to the now, and to action. . . . It's not exclusively about transformation. It's about revolution."[5]

Surrealism in its original manifestation centered around the practice of changing how we think and see. In an issue of *Tropiques* published in 1941, Suzanne Césaire argued that surrealism was a "permanent readiness for the Marvelous." Césaire wrote about surrealism as an invitation, a practice that opened up "the domain of the strange, the marvelous and the fantastic, a domain scorned by people of certain inclinations. Here is the freed image, dazzling and beautiful, with a beauty that could not be more unexpected and overwhelming. Here are the poet, the painter and the artist, presiding over the metamorphoses and the inversions of the world under the sign of hallucination and madness."[6]

The Surrealist movements, first labeled as such in France and Martinique in the 1930s, embraced the "Marvelous" and undermined the

"Miserable" through studies of dream, through automatic writing and painting that tapped into the subconscious, through games and collaborations, through listening to impulse and desire and following ideas without attachments to where they might lead. Surrealism was never just a vision or style, but a method that also recognized its predecessors in African and Indigenous art traditions. As Kelley documented, the Surrealists in Paris protested against colonialism in the 1930s, calling for "Revolution Now and Forever" and referring to French liberalism as "Murderous Humanitarianism."[7] The surrealists were critical of Marxism for its racism, and critical of socialism for its acceptance of the powers of the colonial state. They questioned everything.

Even that early, white and Black surrealists intermingled and created alongside one another, the Europeans taking inspiration and lessons from the knowledge and arts of Afro-diasporic cultures. The anti-colonialism and anti-racism of surrealism is a continuous thread, reflected again in a remarkable 1998 journal issue called "Surrealism: Revolution Against Whiteness" spearheaded by the Chicago Surrealist Group. "Surrealism is first of all the liberation of language and imagination: the direct application of poetry to the solution of humankind's fundamental problems," wrote Chicago surrealist Franklin Rosemont. "Now as always, we strive to tear down the walls separating dream and action, conscious and unconscious, the real and the imaginary, thereby creating situations in which real freedom can develop."[8]

Surrealism has produced poetry, art, stories, and manifestos of mental resistance for nearly one hundred years. "Surrealism gives voice to desire's telepathy: It is oxygen, the weightless weight of thought, perpendicular flight, a wheel of black fire, the true alchemy of our time," wrote Penelope Rosemont of the Chicago Surrealist Group in 2019, adding that Surrealism was less interested in aesthetics than solidarity and mutual aid—an expression of activism through art.[9] The Heidelberg Project, I would later learn, was a part of this ongoing tradition—a fine example of Surrealist thought in action, as it explored the Miserable and the Marvelous through visual juxtaposition to pose a political challenge. In 1992, self-proclaimed Surrealist artists and groups from all over the world signed a letter defending the Heidelberg Project and the work of Tyree Guyton, calling his revamped homes "marvelous assemblages." The city had a program of demolishing these houses, and much of what he'd initially created was named blight and destroyed—twelve homes to date have been taken down by demolition or arson. The Surrealists' statement quoted Guyton as saying, "I see art as a way of saying, seeing, and feeling all the things I never had a chance to do when I was coming up. . . . It's the kind of magic I dreamed about as a boy, but am only now able to express creatively."[10]

Surrealists—still a roving and self-defined movement of artists, writers, and thinkers with an antiestablishment bent—were aghast at the city's attack on his haunting manifestation: "At a time when the 'official art' of the US is mired in ludicrous irrelevance, Tyree Guyton has hurled a bright red sackful of monkeywrenches into the repressive machinery of white racist America's politico-cultural vapidity. His first houses have been reduced to rubble. But every day more houses are abandoned! And what are all the bulldozers in the world against the unfettered imagination?"[11]

Surrealists talk a lot about poetry, and they don't just mean written words in poems—they often discuss the poetry of daily life, the poetry that can be found in juxtaposition or in music, the poetry of random chance and play. The Surrealist definition of poetry as a practice and a way of life connects it closely to unlearning. After all, poetry, like visual art, has the option to lie flat on the page; it can be rote and meaningless, depending on how it is written and how we read it. It can be droning, rhyming, even silencing (say, in the context of a classroom teaching classic poetry as if it is the only poetry worth reading). But the *life* of poetry, the practice of poetry as a constant reverence for the unconscious and a mode of connection to the Marvelous, as a way of interacting with art and one another, has the potential to change the fabric and shape of how we think. The Surrealists believed radical imagination and fearless interaction with materials and the built environment can facilitate unlearning and reorient our minds. And key to this belief was the idea that we can't just spectate, look at art or read poetry or watch games being played. Surrealism is insistently participatory. As Surrealist predecessor Lautréamont put it, "Poetry must be made by all."[12]

Kai Lumumba Barrow's work exemplifies this participatory prerogative. In adrienne maree brown's *Pleasure Activism*, poet Alexis Pauline Gumbs describes Kai as follows: "Kai Lumumba Barrow is movement. . . . Even when she sleeps, Kai is listening. Maybe Kai is our movement, our whole fragmented Black abolitionist nomadic futurist Black feminist movement. Like if earth and flesh made an installation of what it looked like, using one person's body, life on earth. Our movement aware and urgent, creative and critical and never the same and always the same and beyond understanding."[13]

I share this because I can't think of a better way to describe the iconic presence of Kai.

When I proposed to Kai the idea of surrealism as a condition for radical unlearning, she said that unlearning might better be thought of as a kind of agency, as "practicing self-determination."

Kai's personal practice of self-determination is evident in everything she does. In the early 2000s, she was a founding member of the leading national abolitionist organization Critical Resistance, and before that she worked with NYC-based organizations such as Student Liberation Action Movement (SLAM), FIERCE!, the Free Mumia Abu-Jamal Coalition, and the Direct Action Network. She was a staff member of Southerners on New Ground (SONG), a liberation hub for Southern queers, and is now a Forever SONG member. She has supported political prisoners and fought for Black feminist causes for decades. More recently her works have focused largely on art: her installations, collages, and public creations are collisions of saturated color, found objects and trash, natural and environmental materials, and political and Black mythologies.

When I asked her what she was personally unlearning, she surprised me: she said she was striving to unlearn, at age sixty-five, her own tendency to tolerate pain. She had chronic migraines, and it took her years to realize that if she just pushed through the pain, they got worse and worse, but if she paused and slowed down, noticed the pain, and stopped what she was doing, she could actually interrupt the cycle. "I don't have to feel pain all the time, I don't want it. I can change it," she realized. But it required her to stop accepting searing pain as something that she should just suck up and tolerate. "I think that's the case with a lot of habits or social behaviors," she said. "We're just kind of going through it. . . . We normalize it."

Unlearning the way she dealt with her headaches and learning a new set of habits became a symbol for Kai's unlearning in a more expansive way. In herself, she discovered not fear, or cowardice, but profound avoidance—a tolerance for her own pain and suffering that she had deeply internalized. "That's very microcosmic, but it expands into such a large kind of body," she said. "It becomes part of the body politic in the scheme of things. I'll take it. I can handle it. This will be over in a few. I'll just keep moving. I don't have time. It's not that important."

In a related unlearning, Kai said, she has been working to get better at listening to her own intuitive wisdom. "It's actually a legitimate way of understanding phenomena around you and what is likely to occur given the amount of experiences that you have over a lifetime," she said. "[I'm] unlearning the dominant social ideas that my knowledge, that what is perceived as women's knowledge or primitive knowledge or whatever, is not valid knowledge and comes from nowhere."

It was Kai who taught me that Black Surrealism—also a practice of self-determination—is different from European surrealism in how it embraces the surrealism of everyday life. Black Surrealists recognize jazz music, Black intuition, and the many absurd juxtapositions of Black life in deeply anti-Black societies as a part of surrealist insight. Black Surrealism is both a lived experience and a skill. "It's a muscle," she said, one that requires learning "to be constantly in a juxtaposition, like living in a juxtaposition, and you're actively surfing the juxtaposition, right? You're going back and forth within it."

Her work insists that its spectators and participants surf the juxtapositions, too.

"Surrealism is something you have to be involved in," Kai said, filling the room with energy after I asked her on a video call how surrealism might relate to unlearning. Her intentionally nomadic art project, Gallery of Streets, is a deliberate provocation. The project rethinks and unlearns the concept of the art gallery as a private, rarified space. Gallery of the Streets, led by Kai and her partner Jazz Franklin, describes itself as "an evolving network of artists, activists, organizers, scholars, cultural workers, and community supporters committed to exploring radical possibilities within Black geographies."[14]

The project juxtaposes visual, political, and interactive elements in all of its work. For example, as we spoke, they were getting ready to launch a roving pirate radio project with a community-based cooperative called Cooperation Gumbo. Gallery of the Streets would use a reconstructed adult tricycle and microbroadcasting technologies to communicate "hidden histories" of BIPOC cooperative markets in the Third Ward community of New Orleans. The next phase of their Radio Outlaw project would travel by reconstructed minibus throughout the Black Bible Belt in rural Alabama, working with Black women farmers to tell stories of sustainability despite their experiences with overlapping environmental, racial, and gendered capitalism.

"What we try to do is be true to the name Gallery of the Streets and be engaged with people in the creation of the work," Kai told me. "We can all make art together. We're trying to unlearn art and art making as selective and for the few and not to be touched, but only to be consumed and commodified."

The current opus of Gallery of the Streets, called b[REACH]: Adventures in Heterotopia, is conceived as a visual opera in three acts: the first, the Book of Dirt, manifested as a public "abolitionist playground" made of found materials in New Orleans. The second, the Book of Air, is manifesting as pirate radio partnerships with Black community organizations across the South. The third, the Book of Water, is a site-specific installation both above and underwater in St. Croix and Durham, North Carolina, in partnership with a BIPOC and queer group of artist-intellectual scuba divers called the Durham SeaRealists—a group of which I am a member. These multifaceted collaborations, Kai said, are "an ongoing process of unlearning. Unlearning dominant ideas of what is art? What is culture? What is organizing? . . . b[REACH] is really rooted in humor, play, and provocation."

The visual opera in three acts has something of a plot: in the b[REACH] mythology, a group of twenty-five incarcerated women have staged a rebellion, based on the true story of the Bedford Prison Uprising in 1972 led by Black lesbian activist Carol Crooks.[15] This group of women is in the process of being transferred to an all-male "institution for the criminally insane" (this part really happened in history), and, in the process of the transfer, their bus crashes. Only twenty-four of the prisoners make it. One of them, dubbed "Prisoner #25" for the purposes of the opera, disappears. She then joins a group of fugitives who guide her on a journey away from Miserabilism and toward the Marvelous.

The characters start out seeking justice for Prisoner #25, but, as they move through the Book of Dirt, the Book of Air, and the Book of Water, they begin to wonder, "Can you really have justice in miserabilism? What is justice in an unjust society?" As the fugitives seek justice, they encounter more and more absurd examples of it, and their journey undermines the norms of justice, fairness, meritocracy, right and wrong. These assumed understandings of society are what Kai hopes b[REACH] will undermine by requiring people to participate—to actually get involved with the art and to play, as people did in a literal physical way in the abolitionist playground in New Orleans.

"Play is an interesting idea because it doesn't demand permanence," she said. "There's a temporariness to play. It doesn't demand answers. How often do we just gather to be playful, to be silly with each other?"

In an earlier iteration of the [b]REACH project in 2020, Kai launched a presidential campaign—her persona DJ Trickster ran for president against Donald Trump and Joe Biden under the slogan "Let's Get Stupid." On the day of the 2020 election, members of Gallery of the Streets including the Durham SeaRealists met baffled voters at the polls. In North Carolina, we wore sea creature costumes and bore an enormous psychedelic kaleidoscope fabricated by Catherine Edgerton and Jodi Hart, with a stained-glass wheel constructed of images of the sea, slides of the Bedford Prison Uprising, and found objects like snake skins, pill bottles, and cicada wings. We invited people to look through the kaleidoscope, and asked questions seemingly unrelated to the "outcome" of the election: *What new things do you see through a kaleidoscope that you couldn't see before? How does the kaleidoscope change your view? What have your dreams this week been telling you about our world? What do you want to see in your community?*

The kaleidoscope helped people to look differently; the conversations were meant to document the connections and ideas that came out of that seeing. Other members of the network took over abandoned lots in New York, made a light-projecting bicycle and rode it around New Orleans showing abstract films on walls, and shot films in the Great Dismal Swamp, a southeastern nature preserve that was once the most notorious site for maroons, people who escaped slavery and created their own secret communities in the forest.

The elusive DJ Trickster didn't win the election, but every encounter with her pointed out the strangeness of the 2020 election through Surrealist juxtaposition. Who really "wins" elections in a society without justice?

I threw myself into these same surrealist waters when I traveled to St. Croix in early 2024 with the Durham SeaRealists to create, we thought, an underwater tableau about abolition and the sea for the Book of Water. Kai had been leading us for years through what felt to me like a maze of the artistic unknown. We would twist this way and that, down hallways and up stairwells of confusing artistic visions. On a retreat in Oak Island in 2022, she explained everything empathically: "[b]Reach is a visual opera, but not opera like Italian ladies singing, not your mother's opera, a Black surrealist visual opera with arias and a libretto."

We're working on the libretto, she'd explain, weaving us into the nonlinear plot. Our scene, the SeaRealists, was just after Prisoner #25—named Peaches for this episode—escaped from the bus, and Peaches would appear underwater and be taken in by a Chorus of Outlaws, played by us. Catherine Edgerton had certified most of the group as scuba divers to make this vision possible. We would show Peaches liberation through some kind of performed welcome, offer underwater spaces of joy and grief, and we would each be in a character representing a tarot spread that Kai had created, or was going to create—unclear. A living tarot spread cum visual opera cum liberation libretto. I didn't fully "get it," but I was energized by the concepts. Kai talked about heterotopias, worlds within worlds. Our job was to create one.

We started creating costumes and sets and characters for each of ourselves. Mine was Octocordion (an octopus whose body is an accordion), and my partner, Catherine, was Glass Eye (a kaleidoscope-making fish). The rest of our crew—all queer activists in Durham—played with shimmering scales and performances in the form of jellyfish or seahorses or sting rays. Nearly two years after our first meeting, we had created a lot of costumes but had no form or rhythm to our performance. There was no libretto, and the scene still didn't make sense in my head. But having all trained in scuba and talked about the Book of Water and the libretto for years, we made plans to go to St. Croix that January and film a tableau.

"What's a tableau?" someone asked at one of our meetings. The process was like that—circular and evasive. This story required unlearning in me because of what was happening in my organized, linear, logistics-oriented mind throughout this watery artist process: I was freaking out. Sure, I wanted to push my creative edges and make something revolutionary and also unlearn whiteness and linear time and what have you. But this? We were flying eight people to the Caribbean to make an underwater film with no plan. I understood the words Kai said, but I didn't understand the meanings behind her twists and turns, the constant unveilings of new ways of approaching the opera, the libretto, the whole thing. First it was a feature film of an opera, then it was a surrealist documentary, then it was a feature film and a documentary about the making of the opera, then it was a series of live installations, then it was a series of tableaus, one of which, the Book of Water, was to be our performance in St. Croix. But we got all the way to St. Croix and I still felt in the dark.

On the way to St. Croix, Kai assigned us all to read parts of Saidiya Hartman's *Lose Your Mother*, a book about the transatlantic slave trade that doesn't offer solutions or easy ways out of the devastating legacies of slavery. Hartman, a Black American, goes to Ghana in search of some sense of familial or ancestral connection, intending to tell the history of slavery by tracing a path of what might have been her own ancestry. But she's unflinching in the telling of what she sees and does not see; in Ghana, rather than finding her way home, she finds a series of contradictions, an unresolvable question. She finds that to be enslaved to another people's country and way of life is to "lose your mother," to forget your own name and place of origin, and that loss may be unredeemable, that severance may not ever be healed—certainly not by transatlantic travel across lines of structural inequity and gulfs of cultural difference over generations.[16] It was, for me, an uncomfortable and captivating read about the problems of power and agency and "home" in the wake of colonization and slavery.

Reading *Lose Your Mother* (a book I could not put down) something opened for me about what Kai was trying to do with her artistic leadership. In the fine and sometimes confounding tradition of Surrealism, she wasn't leading us *toward* something. She was leading us to get lost, to enter collectively into unknowing and play as a form of self-determination, in direct opposition to the unknowing that was imposed by enslavement. In St. Croix, our crew, mostly Black women, went through a portal at a legendary baobab tree, met the relatives of a political prisoner they'd been looking for on the island, and created a tableau at the golden hour of our friend Grace becoming the light in an abandoned lighthouse tower, dressed in a gold crown of their Filipino ancestors. Everything became magic and possible. I was quiet a lot—even though I'd been invited through my relationship to Catherine and the other SeaRealists, I couldn't believe I was a part of this.

The tableau, the Book of Water, took form as abstraction—we went scuba diving and shot videos underwater of pea pods in motion, blue beads sinking, burlap sacks and black lace dancing, looking alternately like bodies and cages, white veils perfectly neutrally buoyant next to dying coral reefs and swimming sea turtles. What we began to make as a collective was strange and unruly, unmoored from before and after, embracing grief but not entirely about it.

But this path for me was filled with discomfort. I kept looking for a role, something I could research, or do, or grab on to. *I can make spreadsheets! And send emails!* I had thought. I was stuck in that same objectifying, white colonial perspective, clinging to linear reality—I needed something that was mine, that I could feel clear about. More than once, I annoyed and alienated my collaborators with my pummeling emails. And throughout the project, I felt lost. What was my role? Where was Kai taking us, with her roving brainstorm sessions and big words and irreverent tangents? I disliked not knowing what was going to happen.

When we finally came together in St. Croix, though, the results were alchemical. I realized that letting go of control was a giant unlearning, a giant step off of a precipice I didn't think was even available to me anymore. I used to feel that unmoored magic as a teenager. But as an adult, I'd become so darn linear. I figured I would always play more or less the role I'd fallen into—the wrangler, the facilitator, the leader. Being led by a sixty-five-year-old Black woman whose entire breath and life were given to liberatory ideas, who didn't care what time it was or whether we had a food plan, brought me to my edges of nonlinear discomfort. But allowing myself to lose time and a sense of direction opened me up to be part of a collective artistic process unlike anything I've experienced. And maybe what felt to *me* like getting lost or entering unknowing was, for others, a way of being found or known.

I also felt as it unfolded that this letting go was yet another way of unlearning whiteness—I was no longer trying to think differently about Black people or attack the lessons of my childhood, but being invited to think differently about *myself* and the ways whiteness manifested in my own body, my own ideas about belonging, my own sense of comfort or unease in a situation. In a Black-led, mostly Black, intuitive artistic process, my whiteness stood out to me not as a superficial presentation but as a deep cultural and power differential; my desire for control was revealed and felt suddenly small and even egotistical. Kai and her whole crew were also not interested in whiteness as a subject—my role was as a scuba diver (Catherine's assistant), as a journalist and researcher, and as an abolitionist artist and dreamer. It's not that it didn't matter that I was white—but my whiteness and Catherine's were not the center of the room, or the creative process. We were there to make a thing about abolition that centered Blackness and the sea.

The unlearning took place through the process, through humility and sinking in, through the wordlessness of artistic exploration and immersion. With so many decades of experience behind her, Kai was skilled in leading by wildness and creative confusion. But I wouldn't have been able to come along if I hadn't let go of my own need for answers, plans, and linear visions. Just weeks before the trip to St. Croix, I privately told myself that I was done with the disorganization of it all, that I would finish this trip and then quit. But pushing that voice to the side, and letting another one come in—one that can accept unknowing even if it's uncomfortable—made me briefly into Octocordion, made me a part of an ensemble and a student of Black Surrealism, made me unlearn yet again—as Kai had said, "surfing the juxtapositions."

People are surfing the juxtapositions all around me: Catherine Edgerton, who brought me into Gallery of the Streets, is a surrealist painter, kaleidoscope maker, and scuba diving instructor whose goal in her work is "to invite other people into the vulnerability and surrender of an embodied art practice that challenges what we think we know about the world, specifically about white supremacy, insanity, and punishment." She's also a long-time student, friend, and collaborator of Kai's.

Kai's 2018–20 Black Surrealist study group changed how Catherine thinks about learning. "My process toward learning had been about nailing something down, and through my initial grasps to understand Black surrealism, it got so exhausting that I realized that that grasp in itself was a type of colonization of the mind," she said. "I was trying to understand it in a way that I understood understanding, that I could articulate or pass on, or that I could show my authority on. I think the unlearning in that was a moment of surrender: I really don't understand this, and I'm not meant to understand this in the way that I think I'm supposed to. It's meant to be elusive and magical and unbridle-able. And it's meant to be contradictory and nomadic and playful. It's meant to be not capturable. And so, to unlearn, I had to learn how to deeply and intimately build familiarity and curiosity without pinning it down."

That unlearning of authority, sureness, and clarity in favor of magic and the contradictory is what Catherine believes is needed in social justice movements. As Catherine put it, social justice work too often asks us to change the world around us without changing how we think, our internalized ideas of correctness, superiority, understanding, and truth. Groups advocating for change often replicate capitalism and the logics of incarceration and punishment even as they are trying to curb their consequences. "In movement spaces that are trying to undermine or change society through a lens of social justice, I haven't ever felt free from those internalized patterns of thought or ways of being, or ways of organizing," Catherine said. "Whereas surrealism, even just thinking about it is a relief. It's like walking into silence after being in a crowded train station . . . it offers more possibility for actual change. For freedom. For moving toward, surrendering to something bigger."

The way around narrow thought, in a surrealist cosmology, is not to "rethink" or reprogram, but to loosen the reins on thought itself. Automatic writing, which is the practice of writing (or making any art form) by opening up a direct channel to the subconscious and unself-consciously following its cues, is one technique. Games like the Exquisite Corpse (a surrealist parlor game where multiple people collaborate to make drawings but cannot see what the others are drawing until the end) also accomplish this by juxtaposing seemingly unrelated visions in a visual relationship. A favorite of mine, the "question and answer game," is one I've been playing since I was a teenager: a group of people writes a set of "answers" (to any hypothetical question, of any kind) on scraps of paper and then scribes an unrelated set of "questions," also about anything. Then, a Q+A is held in which a question is drawn from a hat, and an answer is randomly read in response. The surrealist method of "objective chance" is given center stage—seeming coincidences become hilarious, or magical, or unpredictably insightful. I have seen Black feminist poet Alexis Pauline Gumbs perform a related practice in her public talks in the form of a "poetry oracle": audience members pose questions of importance to them, and Alexis answers them with randomly selected statements or passages from Black feminist poets and thinkers, honoring and remixing their history and wisdom. We practice surrealist games, including the poetry oracle, frequently at home—letting chance and randomness, which are always present, take center stage and inspire new ways of thinking.

"If you take the meaning, or the desire for meaning out of something, you can no longer be egoic about it," said Catherine. "Like if you're juxtaposing things, and you're doing exquisite corpses or found poetry, all these things where you can't control the outcome . . . you can't be a perfectionist because perfectionism requires that you have a forethought about what it's gonna be."

It is through these surrealist techniques of juxtaposition and tapping into the unconscious that Catherine does almost all of her art: a combination of collage, work with glass and light, and oil painting. Catherine's most recent solo art show applied these principles of surrealism, play, and juxtaposition to the problem of whiteness. As she frames it, on the one hand, whiteness is a hoax and a myth—but, on the other hand, it's a source of real material power, an enforceable reality with consequences for people and the planet. As a white-bodied person, there's a challenge in attempting to unlearn the mores of whiteness without denying its enduring power in the world. In other words, we can't simply "decide" we are not white, or disidentify from cultural dominance—because as long as the system continues to protect white bodies at the expense of Black and Brown ones, whiteness will matter regardless of what we have unlearned in ourselves. Surrealism, shaped by the wisdom and legacies of Black and Brown artists, has room to hold this contradiction.

Catherine's work addresses the contradiction as an embodied paradox, by placing bleached coral—a white object which is also a consequence of climate change—next to white people who wear the masks of animals, icons of power and vulnerability such as the dog, the lamb, the rabbit, the snake, the pig, and the rat. Her "white-skinned" people (modeled from photos of her own body) are ironically elaborate in terms of color—purples and pinks, browns and blues—reminding the viewer that "white" is a construction, not a skin color. Her bleached coral, on which her "white" bodies lean carelessly, is a gutting show of the consequences of global racial capitalism. Her animal masks remind us of the consequences of whiteness for white people—in a society structured on exploitive power relations, what is it to be or become one's "true self"? How can white people expect to relate to ourselves, to humans and animals at large, without first being honest about the global harm our human-centric racial myths have caused?

But the approach, the how and the why of making art, is more important to Catherine (and many Surrealists) than the images themselves. She is an evangelist of found poetry, automatic writing and painting, and remixing imagery through cutting up, collage, and play, releasing the hold on the "real" in favor of the surreal through sculptural book projects, grotesque self-portraits, and playfully glorious kaleidoscopes. She also teaches people how to make glass arts and found poetry, and how to scuba dive—another surrealist practice in that it exposes us to the real-unreal of the underwater world, reminding us of our intrinsic relationship to the below and beyond.

At the core of all of these practices is the simple idea that we cannot make change without a powerful practice of reimagining—and imagining is powerful because it is something anyone can do, even under (sometimes especially under) the harshest of circumstances. Surrealism as a practice can create conditions of unlearning in repressed societies and conditions for battling totalitarian and imperialist thought, but it doesn't comfort or assuage or instruct. Ideally, it explores, questions, and undermines through imagination and curiosity. As Indigenous queer surrealist Ronnie Burk wrote in 1998, "Surrealism is an excellent guide to seizing the means of production because that is where the experience of surrealism begins—seizing the means of production of *language itself.*"[17]

Is the idea that everyone should become a poet, that everyone should practice art as a means to unlearn? Yes. As the prolific twentieth-century poet and activist Muriel Rukeyser argues in *The Life of Poetry*, "art prepares us" as participants in society and transformers of our surroundings.[18] The practice of art, automatic writing, poetry, any unfettered creation, can tap into the ineffable and visually rich worlds behind our own conscious minds. This practice uses the same muscles we need to prepare for all kinds of unlearning. The Surrealists assert that art is something you do and that everyone should do, because it prepares us for freedom, to behave and think more freely. Surrealism is a way to practice opening up, unlearning not by forcing a new set of ideologies through the narrow passageways of the mind, but by preparing ourselves to live with and beyond false dualities, to "surf the juxtapositions." Art can be a practice for making the world anew.

"Surrealism, itself, is an attempt to get beyond false contradictions, such as waking and sleep, reason and madness, objective and subjective," writes Penelope Rosemont in her book *Surrealism: Inside the Magnetic Fields.*[19] In embracing its practices, we cannot be "wrong," because, as Muriel Rukeyser asserts, "you cannot imagine falsely."[20] Rescued from the pressures of ego, control, and accuracy, we are free to melt the synapses, to juxtapose, to dream. Surrealism asserts that "good" and "bad" art are not about expertise or skill, but about honesty. It is a way to tap into truth within the self and, therefore, to undermine inherited knowledge or reclaim lost inheritances, to find the roots of ideologies and loosen and unearth them. This approach to art reveals previously unseen and uncharted desire lines and gives us a way to practice following them where they lead.

WHAT IS IT LIKE TO BE A BOAT? A REVERSE PRESENTATION

"What do you do in your daily routine?"

*"It's a huge responsibility, carrying all these souls.
So much pressure to be hole-less and full."*

—ANONYMOUS Q&A

In a workshop I created to explore radical unlearning while writing this book, I had participants play with surrealist games and imagination in order to prompt explorations of their own unlearning. Here are the prompts for you to use or adapt as a party game, a solo or paired practice, or a workshop of your own. Remember, as Muriel Rukeyser said, that you cannot imagine falsely!

MATERIALS NEEDED

- A bunch of paper cut into small scraps (I recommend dividing an 8.5" x 11" piece into eight pieces, or you can work with scraps you have)
- Pens and markers
- Paper or notebooks for each person to write in
- Two hats or baskets
- Thirty-second timer

SET-UP

Gather participants (two or more) in a circle. Give participants ten scraps of paper each, with pens and markers.

PART I: Q&A (TAKES ABOUT THIRTY–FORTY MINUTES)

1 Read the following prompts, and give everyone thirty seconds per prompt to write down their answers. Encourage them to put down

179

the first thing that comes to mind in response to the question and not to think about it too hard.

What is it like to be a boat?

What's something that makes you uncomfortable?

If you asked your mother something, what would she say?

What are you unlearning right now?

What's one thing that makes you happy?

2 Fold and put all the answers in a hat!

3 Now give participants thirty seconds per prompt to write down their questions. Again, they should just put the first thing that comes to mind in response to the prompts—but this time, write them in the form of a question.

What is a question you are grappling with or wondering about right now?

What question would you ask your favorite author if they suddenly appeared in the room?

What question would you like to be asked, but never have?

What question would you ask an octopus?

What's a question you have asked in the past that embarrasses you now? Out loud or otherwise.

4 Put all the questions in a hat!

5 Q+A Readout: now for the fun part. Give one hat to someone on one side of the circle and one hat to someone else. Going in a circle, one participant draws a question and reads it aloud; the person opposite them draws an answer and reads it aloud. Pass the hats around until you've exhausted your questions and answers, or are satisfied with the outcome or run out of time, whichever happens first.

Note: The traditional surrealist variation on this parlor game is to simply write "questions" and "answers" with no other prompts. They can be about anything, though generally we recommend steering clear of yes/no questions. Then read aloud the results in a circle, and silliness usually ensues.

PART II: WRITING AND REFLECTION

1 Read aloud this prompt: *Think of something you would like to unlearn—a belief, habit, or ideology you want to let go of to make space for new ways of thinking and being. Think for a minute, and write down the thing you are unlearning or want to unlearn.*

Now we're going to imagine that it's a thousand years in the future. And this very thing you are trying to unlearn no longer exists; it's just not a concept or belief in your culture anymore. The whole conception or practice has disappeared. Immerse yourself in that future in your imagination. Now your task is to explain this thing to a child who has never heard of the concept. Then, tell the story of why it's no longer around.

You have fifteen minutes to free write on this prompt. If writing is not your thing, feel free to draw or meditate/conjure visions. You won't be asked to share this unless you want to, but we'll take a few minutes to pair off and discuss so you'll have the option of sharing.

2 Split into groups of two to four people to discuss the following questions:

> *What were you unlearning? (Read your writing aloud if you choose to)*
> *What was the experience of the writing exercise like?*
> *What insights did you glean?*

3 Come back to the full group and ask for a few reflections. Ask participants: *What are you unlearning? How was it to try to imagine a world without that thing?*

CHAPTER 10

IMMERSION

U nderwater, the mundane can become full of wonder—bodies that would fall down on land are floating, swaying. I once watched a dry seed pod dance and rise. Air moves in visible spheres that glitter, dividing into stars and galaxies. Fish make eye contact and act inquisitive. Breath is loud and rhythmic and reassuring.

When I learned to scuba dive with the Durham SeaRealists, my body, which for me had felt so often like a burden, became weightless, a vessel for equilibrium rather than judgment. Sunken artifacts like an old airplane became homes for the absurd, as we swam through the pilot room or collided with its wings. I watched my friend Grace, who is just under five feet tall, slam dunk a weighted basketball in slow motion. The water that day was cold and dark, and from inside of it, I could hear myself laughing into my regulator in delight.

But learning to scuba, for me, wasn't an immediate unleashing of wonder. It was largely an experience of disorientation. I lost my map and I had to unlearn navigation.

I was used to having an aerial view. I could picture north, south, east, and west, place myself at the little dot that says, "You are here," copy the outlines of a route or map to memory, and know where to go. I learned to read a map before GPS and Google Maps, and I prided myself on this skill of orientation—if I can get a mental map of a new place, I feel like I know where I am, especially if we stay on a city grid. The aerial view is shaped by the colonial view: in my house growing up, my parents had maps from when colonizers first came to what is now called Michigan, the area where I grew up that belongs to the Anishinaabeg peoples. These maps erased their names and their understandings of things, putting in their place the names of the French and English people who settled near Detroit, who fought and killed the Indigenous people who inhabited the land, a two-hundred-year campaign of extermination. The word Huron—the name of the most beloved river and lake in my young life—referred to a tribe, though I only just learned that Huron was a French colonizer name ascribed to a people who called themselves the Wendat or Wyandotte. In falling in love with the cool clear waters of Lake Huron and the easy flow of the Huron River, I knew a land and water devoid of its people and context: land without its true name, water without its true keepers. This was the map I had memorized, and over and over again in childhood I rode north on I-75, over the Mackinac Bridge, and back south again home. This is what loving land meant to me—highway trips to a house on the lake in a place lost to its original peoples.

When I learned to scuba dive, that map dissolved: I found the dimensions of up and down distracting and complex. Catherine, who taught scuba with an abolitionist lens, encouraged all students to give up fussing with the compass and pay attention to our surroundings, navigating by sight and feel, but I struggled. Everything is slightly different when you're immersed—in addition to the two extra directions, you're thinking about breathing, your motions are slowed, your sight is magnified by water. You look up and can't tell which lights are which and where the sun is. The feeling of "I don't know which way I'm going, I'm not oriented to what's next, I'm not in control" was almost dizzying.

And yet washing away my mental map ushered in a feeling, one that I later identified as a portal to unlearning. I saw, for example, that not all minds harbored the same discomforts as mine. For some of the people I learned to dive with, it was easy—I'd see them pop down underwater for the first time and explore happily, naturally returning to where they started or fearlessly surfacing someplace else. Maybe they never oriented to the land with "maps" the way I did—it is a colonial construct, after all. I floundered toward a new way to navigate. I was not gratified or at ease; letting go of maps felt almost like releasing a part of my identity. It felt like I was sand on a rock and a wave had just hit and that wave was sloshing down, washing some of me away.

This is what immersion can do, by virtue of being both disruptive and encompassing, disorienting and sustained. It can wash away the synapses that make us feel like ours is the only way of looking at a thing. It is another condition that can open up unlearning.

Immersion is known to be a powerful mode for learning language and culture. Many people who have moved to a new or foreign place can also identify the *unlearning* that seems inevitable in that context—challenging our most fundamental assumptions about space, time, relationships, language, logic, syntax. It can also be surreal, playful, or frightening. In immersive experiences, including scuba diving, up can be down, and words can change in their meaning, or become useless altogether. Confusion is often a factor, and immersion probably requires a degree of confusion if it's going to lead to unlearning (in other words, I am not talking about immersion in things that are totally familiar, like a US resident going to Disneyland). Immersion also can't allow for complete passivity if it is going to facilitate unlearning, say, a virtual reality game, overprescribed tourism or even some of the art "experiences" being touted as fully immersive. I have nothing to say about unlearning, for example, following the touring "immersive" Van Gogh art show I saw in North Carolina, which was basically Van Gogh projected onto walls. And many, especially from positions of global privilege, travel to new places and ensure that their comfort and orientation are constantly curated, leaving the possibility of unlearning behind.

The immersion that is useful to unlearning engages the senses and requires response or interaction—it imposes a whole new palette on our brains. This sort of immersion, almost like the water in my scuba diving experience, creates enough confusion and disorientation through all the senses to disrupt existing neural connections. Resurfacing, I am caught off guard—I think, "What was that exactly?" Or "How am I going to explain this?" Or "What do I have to compare this to?" Immersion creates the conditions for unlearning when it fosters a feeling of overwhelm and discontinuity that, eventually, reveals a space for a new way of going about things.

Anyone who has ever fully immersed themselves in a foreign language may know the feeling, and the pain of how prolonged it can be to adjust to an immersive experience when it challenges our brains, pathways to thoroughly change. Immersion to create the conditions of unlearning can take the form of performance art, of surrounding oneself with a new culture, or simply of entering into an architecture, landscape, or public space that is unfamiliar and staying awhile. These experiences are not all rosy: we can also be immersed in a jail or prison, surrounded by conditions that cause fear or rage. We can be immersed in a location that strikes delight or stokes anxiety: a desert, say, or a chaotic open-air market, or a city subway system, or a bucolic college campus. Regardless, in so many of my conversations about unlearning, immersion in some form has been a factor—the moments or situations where we are in a lived, multisensory experience so encompassingly unfamiliar that our senses themselves become conduits of surprise and disorientation.

Whether they are positive or negative, I suspect that the kinds of immersive experiences that challenge our assumptions about the world have an outsized tendency to be transformative by comparison with their less immersive counterparts—watching a film about a place is just not the same as *being there*. But travel is not a particularly accessible condition for most people; I'm interested in the conditions we can cultivate wherever we are. Here, I will focus on intentionally immersive experiences I have encountered—scuba diving (which I practiced with a community group committed to accessibility), and several mixed-use art and political spaces created in part with unlearning in mind—because they provide examples that can potentially be explored and emulated. When have you been immersed in something that challenged you to change? What did you see, smell, taste, or feel?

I first got the idea that immersion might create conditions for unlearning from my friend Chantal Wong, a creative force from Canada who lived for two decades in Hong Kong. Her interest in working outside of and beyond the frame by creating immersive experiences started in her childhood and expanded when she studied art history in school. She told a story about unlearning as a young adult when she traveled to the country of Lesotho and had to unlearn her assumptions about the people and culture there—and, in general, she told me as someone who had lived around the world, immersing in different cultures has made her less inclined to universalize her point of view.

Chantal is small, and she seemed sweet when we first met, but I quickly came to perceive her as a powerfully unbridled person, full of questions and curiosities—not so much sweet as fearlessly interested. In 2014, Chantal founded an art space in Hong Kong that responded to the growing Umbrella Movement, the name for the rising pro-democracy movement in the city at the time. But her goal wasn't necessarily to build that movement; it was to question who was being left out, often foreign domestic workers, asylum seekers, and refugees. The space brought in activists as well as members of these highly marginalized communities—not necessarily with a prescribed idea of what might happen, but with an assumption that sharing a space might open up new ways for both groups to engage.

"How do we create the conditions for these sparks and tensions to exist?" Chantal said. She was interested in doing that in physical spaces, engaging the senses, and making it accessible to diverse populations. She took that same vision for sparks and tensions into her next project, Eaton.

Eaton was Chantal's heart work and heartbreak: a hotel in a diverse neighborhood of Hong Kong that in 2014 was converted from a drab three-star business hotel to an experimental art project. Eaton, which has another location in Washington, DC, would become a 24–7 site for arts and culture while still functioning as a hotel. This effort was funded by wealthy investors who saw the potential for a hotel to operate as a self-supporting cultural and arts space, inspired by the surrounding community. As the director of culture and driver of programs at Eaton,

Chantal created a space that was both a refuge for activists and change-makers, and a site of experimental and immersive art.

Again, her intention was not to manipulate a certain outcome.

"It's less to force these conversations to happen than to create the conditions for people to reside next to each other," she said. "There are these exhibitions. There are artists. They hang out till three in the morning. And then in the room next to it or upstairs or in the same space, we would bring these young asylum seekers together to have classes about how they want to transform their communities."

Eaton made use of immersion because both residents and staff found themselves surrounded by projects and ideas they didn't anticipate: while one person came to their day job in hospitality, a women's festival with drag queen performances might be going on, and open conversations about sexuality might be taking place. While someone enters a hotel as a guest, they might find themselves in the middle of an installation or immersed in a performance as both audience and participant, conflating prescribed roles. The use of the full space has the potential to engage all of the senses and upturn expectations. Rather than being a turnoff for guests, Eaton's surprising environment was popular with travelers from around the world.

"I think what is transformative is that in that moment of potential, wonder is created," Chantal said. Something can be beautiful without creating wonder; the wonder comes with the element of surprise or the unexpected, wordless encounters that shift perceptions of what is possible. For example, Eaton once held a twenty-four-hour movement festival, a dance event that echoed the changes in the city, the occupations and actions on the streets below, that roamed through the entire space of the hotel, rather than just appearing on a stage. A dancer on a stage twirling, she said, might not evoke wonder. "But if you wake up at three in the morning because you're jet lagged and you see in the hallway that somebody's twirling, that's an element of wonder and magic. . . . It's how we've decided to disrupt the quotidian, or the broken: with seeds of magic."

People were skeptical and tired of property developers and displays of banality and wealth in Hong Kong, especially of property investors.

But Eaton's function as a cultural space that welcomed both regular people and risk-taking community leaders and creatives gave the surrounding community a feeling of connection to the place. It also opened up a new form of hope that even the wealthy might share an interest in creating something for the greater good of Hong Kong. In 2017, Eaton put up a series of billboards encouraging passers-by to think about their own belief systems and values, prompting people to think about climate justice, feminism, and labor rights. "What does your revolution look like?" and "What if you could choose the person you love?" the billboards asked. Using billboards for art and messaging was rare in Hong Kong, where profitable advertising space rarely goes to waste. In 2020, as the protest movement grew, these messages took on new meaning—the word "revolution" became associated directly with the political revolution. Eaton chose to replace the billboard. But simple questions, as we know, can be a threat—they, too, can provoke unlearning. Even though Eaton Hong Kong was a private enterprise, the potential of the space was clear.

Between the political changes in the city, the tensions surrounding the uprising, and collective hopelessness and helplessness people experienced during COVID, Chantal began to feel it was impossible to continue to practice her work catalyzing new ways of seeing and questioning the world. In 2020, she said, Chantal experienced a breakdown in her beliefs—in her sense of sureness in general.

"I'm somebody who always has the answers. For the first time in my life, I have no idea. And it's super scary. All the structures and the things that they relied on and the things that built them and how they responded, just stopped making sense. I couldn't compute them anymore. I thought: *I don't have any answers.*"

She made the difficult decision to leave Eaton, and Hong Kong, to pursue her creative work elsewhere. After this painful leap from creating an immersive arts hotel to living in exile, Chantal began to rebuild her identity, piece by piece. She adopted a practice of meditation—the only way she said she could see through the problem of no longer knowing what was "right" or what was true.

———————

Hashem Adnan looks at people intently. He holds himself carefully, like a dancer or a horse, sure but somehow delicate. It's unsurprising to learn he is a performance artist: when I spoke to Hashem, I felt that forceful presence just in casual conversation. Our interview encompassed many of the conditions for unlearning we have already explored: Hashem's sites of unlearning included relationships, crises, child's play, and theater—although he proposed that there is nothing you can do specifically to make theater a site of unlearning, as people will engage with it how they choose. Another thing he said might help is total experiences—immersions of a sort that demonstrate that another way of life is possible.

He got into theater, he said, "through alcohol and my uncle." An uncle of his when he was a kid liked to sit around and drink arak, and he would pretend to give some to Hashem. Then Hashem would play along, pretending to be a drunk little boy in front of the whole family. He found his way to the character of the fool, the clown.

But he said these games had a serious edge—they were a way to survive in a time marked by war and instability. He was born in 1984, during a war in Lebanon that didn't cease until 1992.

"During this kind of childhood, it was always also about using the idea of gathering, of being together, of sharing stories of playing games," he said. "I held this with me. Later on, I was very much interested in performance also as a political statement and action. Slowly, slowly I decided that this is what I really want to do. I want to recreate the world through theater. And sometimes to recreate a world, you need to destroy an existing reality."

Now, he said, the focus of his unlearning is individualism in his efforts at organizing and art. "It's very super hard, you know, because we come from a very individualistic background," he said. "This is engraved into us through the first, the patriarchal model that gives the individual-slash-hero-slash-good person a very strict form. And at the same time, there's the old liberal and neoliberal culture, a very consumerist culture and a very individual kind of thinking."

He has been trying for years to build collectives, to experiment with producing solutions to problems in community rather than relegating them back to the field of the individual. The problem was acute in Lebanon as we spoke in 2023—with the precipitous and damaging devaluation of Lebanon's currency that started in 2019, many people's access to basic supplies like electricity had become restricted. Mutual aid efforts to collectivize that access had also largely failed, he said.

"And if you take Lebanon now after 2019, after the uprising, after the fall of the uprising, and after the pandemic, and after the explosion and everything, and then the deep state of collapse that we have, individuals were completely left alone to deal with all of this," he said. "Most of the attempts of collectiveness, of solidarity, of building alternatives, didn't really reach anywhere."

This gets at a problem I've been puzzling with, the role of crisis or catastrophe in unlearning. While some people name crises as potential catalysts for rapid personal or social change, such change is not inevitable in a crisis—and, oftentimes, it's also not lasting. People might "unlearn" their individualism for a few months of frantic mutual aid, but then go back to the old ways in the aftermath, when things are somewhat more settled. That's what Hashem had seen in crisis after crisis in Beirut.

"In moments of urgency and crises, many people can start a process of unlearning. For it to be able to continue, we need to have a network of places, spaces, collectives, people, possibilities and resources that are accessible for us," he said. "We need to be able to enter into a way of living in which we challenge ourselves in how we are the consumers of the ideology and the culture of the system. This cannot happen only theoretically."

And here is where Hashem, too, proposed immersion: a project he was part of, Mansion, attempted to give people a way to enter this way of living by spending time and participating in an alternative space.

Mansion was just that—a literal mansion in a neighborhood in Beirut that was loaned to a collective of activists and artists by a wealthy person. It had fifteen rooms for private use, and five public spaces: a main hall, a garden, a yoga room, a rooftop, and a kitchen. It was open from 9 a.m. to 7 p.m. and all of its operations were collectivized—artists, activists, and NGOs paid monthly fees that helped cover the bills and maintenance. For a few years, it became a center for performances, play, creativity, and activism in Beirut, one that defied the capitalist categories of public and private.

"We need to create living experience, living experiences of daily life that are healthy for us, that help us grow, that help us work, help us meet, help us party, help us enjoy, help us support each other, help us find collective moments that *we* propose, not only collective moments that come as a reaction of a certain attack happening on us," he said. In a space like this, unlearning might be sustained—the immersion and ongoing-ness of it would allow people to explore collectivity and challenge individualism beyond the moments of acute necessity. For him, Mansion was a refuge through several periods of crisis and became a collective and artistic home for his work—and his own unlearning. "It really proposes a space where people can live time in a different way, can relate to their work and to the work of others and to the social existence and to their professional existence, in a less capital-centric way," Hashem said. "We need such attempts."

Unfortunately, in 2023, the Mansion collective lost the mansion as the wealthy donor took it back to develop. They are now looking for a new space to carry on the work. But Hashem suggested that immersion need not only happen at places like Mansion that are wrested from the hands of property owners (or places like Chantal's Eaton, a private hotel).

"Mansion is an example of this idea of creating living models. Other places that can also work and function in this way are public spaces . . . also spaces like, like forest spaces, give this sense [that] when you are in nature, when you are in the forest, it's not about private property, it's not about consumption. When it's not about this world," he said, "something else emerges."

There is a sadness in Hashem that I also see in my friend Chantal—and that I feel sometimes in myself. The three of us met through the Ford Fellowship and spent a lot of time drinking whiskey and wandering through conversation, about our role in the world, about whether our work has a reason. There's something we have in common, something paradoxical because it feels like it's about loneliness in the context of constantly working in community—a bodily alienation, a discomfort with our own place in it all. And perhaps it's also a sense that the world we know is possible, the magic and wonder, is not the world we see before our eyes—and, in fact, our spaces and ways of wonder are being actively dismantled and repressed, because power structures know just how dangerous it is for people to feel the connection and the pleasure that they can feel in a place like Eaton, in a place like Mansion, or in the ocean. I know what it's like to breathe underwater, and when I explain it to each of them, they look at me like they completely understand. But behind the understanding, there is hunger and disappointment and even a little rage.

Immersion engages all of our senses, and creates a total experience that has the power to take us away from our default definitions and shapes. I experienced this in direct ways while living in France during the early stages of this project—I grappled with the language and culture, but I also physically entered into spaces that called my own idea of space into question.

In a round theater inside Luma in Arles, France, a film shifted across the walls, a wall rose up to cast sudden sunlight and returned to the floor, and a soundscape that seemed to be emanating from the ceiling turned out to be an elaborate system of echoes, prompting the people in the room to begin playing, making clicks and singing to see how the ceiling's echoes would reply. Together in that room we found a rhythm. I thought I didn't like "things like that," but I was consumed by this installation at Luma. And Luma itself was immersive and strange, a free space that didn't describe itself as a museum or a gallery or a workshop for artists or a center for studies of ecology, yet seemed to be all of those.

Later, I thought about the video installation and about Luma overall. "I don't know *what that was.*" I had dinner with Chantal, who was living in France at the time, and told her about it. Over mediocre seafood stew, she shared with me how much her experience of always being an outsider has shaped her unlearning—so many weeks, months, and years spent living in unfamiliar places have led her to question her assumptions about everything, to constantly have pointed out how much the shape of our thoughts is cultural and ideological.

Just a couple of weeks later, I wandered alone through a space that, like Luma, defied my own existing categories. People had said, "You have to go to La Friche Belle de Mai," and I looked up all the individual words and still couldn't make meaning of it—*la friche belle* means beautiful wasteland; *Mai* means the month of May. I knew it was in an old tobacco factory, which felt resonant because the town where I live is also an old tobacco town. One day, at the end of a long walk, there I was. It was an enormous campus; there were warehouses and steel staircases and cement block buildings covered in graffiti. There were gardens and messy playgrounds that looked like they'd never be allowed back in my litigious country. I wandered through a cement tower with pavilions where kids were break dancing with a boom box, as if it was the '90s. I saw a bar and restaurant, the doors to a theater, and then came out of a section of what seemed to be artist studios into a courtyard full of families. It was extremely diverse, reflecting the real makeup of Marseille—a city populated by Algerians, Tunisians, Lebanese, Somali, and Syrian immigrants, people from West Africa, people from Iraq, and white French people.

In this courtyard, enormous groups of children romped with seemingly no adults attached to them. A handful of adults drank beer from glasses (the French! With the day drinking! It was about 2 p.m.). The kids played soccer; music boomed from a speaker somewhere. I came down the graffiti-covered stairwell and walked through this wonderland, confused. Was it a park? Was it a community center? Who was in charge? I went through some double doors and found myself in a bookstore stocked with French art books and political posters. My French wasn't good enough to ask, to understand. So I just listened, and walked.

La Friche Belle de Mai was some Marseillais's reimagining of public space to be covered with art, gritty and wild, accessible and weird. Unlike the reimagined tobacco campuses back in North Carolina, this place didn't try to cover up the grit or prevent the graffiti. It combined professional, large-scale art and design with street art, unexpected juxtapositions everywhere. And it wasn't privatized: the space was publicly funded. I saw zero chain stores, and the bar and restaurant on the campus were run by La Friche to benefit the public spaces. There was no part of it where you had to pay for entry. I tried to picture a place like La Friche in the United States, and I couldn't—everything was too regulated, too litigated, there was too much liability in just letting children play and paint the walls. Everything was too expensive and public resources were decimated by deliberate government divestment. A place like this would inevitably come with corporate sponsors, a Starbucks at the entryway. At La Friche Belle de Mai, in the confusion of immersion came the unlearning.

My simple assumptions about what spaces are, what art is and where it can exist, what "public" might mean in action, were transformed in just a couple hours of wandering, as if underwater, through the beautiful wasteland, wishing everyone could have access to a place like this.

Radical unlearning emerged continually, like a fractal pattern that expands and echoes and changes—the conditions could be as simple as love and community, or as complex as an elaborate immersive public space in a foreign country or the skill of scuba diving. Still, none of it feels out of reach—even the magnificence of Mansion and La Friche and Luma were built with collective effort and budgets that are dwarfed by war budgets and fossil fuel economies. It shouldn't be a radical proposition that everyone *should* have access to immersive, creative spaces that hold the potential for unlearning. And yet access is perhaps the simplest, most important condition of all—so simple I almost missed it.

CHAPTER 11

ACCESSIBILITY

L earning to dive, immersing in strangeness, surrealist art, and loving connection can all loosen us up to explore unlearning. So can our practices, our bodies, the questions posed by those around us, and the experiences of confrontation and cognitive dissonance. And unlearning might be scary, but it doesn't have to be thankless: because radical unlearning frees people from paradigms that claim that we are inferior, less deserving, or naturally predisposed to being oppressed or marginalized, it can make our lives more liberatory and possible. This is especially true for people who are currently oppressed, whose bodies are written out of the dominant stories and spaces. When we can find our way back to our bodies, to cultures of belonging, to stolen traditions or robbed dignity through unlearning, it is not so much a burden as an unburdening. We can be free to connect with knowledge that has been denied in the service of dominant systems.

Sometimes, the main condition required in order to unlearn is simply that the new information, worldview, or way of thinking is accessible. This occurred to me first as I was having conversations about unlearning with friends in prison, who were invariably enthusiastic about the project of radical unlearning. Most people I have met who are incarcerated for long periods of time are extremely hungry for any and all forms of outside information, and they are deeply motivated to unlearn. After all, the teachings of their surroundings have not liberated them, but literally confined them: a constant curriculum of distrust, militarism, and violence surrounds people in the US prison system and teaches over and over that certain people are disposable, irreparable, and unworthy.

But many people in prison are not duped by this. They know their own worth, but it requires a constant rejection of the messages perpetuated by their dehumanizing surroundings. The prospect of collective unlearning for them doesn't inspire fear—it's a peek at possibility, an affirmation of reality that prisons and carceral systems try to deny. In my experience, when political education or structured unlearning makes its way inside of prison walls, people lap it up—especially those with long sentences or life sentences, who are often deprived of educational programs altogether, since those programs when they exist at all prioritize preparing people for reentry.

It's therefore no coincidence that prisons are the site of the most intellectual censorship and knowledge control anywhere in the United States. For incarcerated people to unlearn is a threat to the entire structure of class, race, and gender that allows people to be put in prison in the first place. My comrades in prison often can't get books on abolition, on public health, on women's bodies, on racism; they are subject to some of the most extensive and seemingly arbitrary systems of book and magazine banning known to humankind.

The situation is almost the inverse of the privileged white suburban person for whom unlearning might drain their sense of self and belonging, or the sequestered religious cult member for whom unlearning could mean losing a sense of identity or community. Some of the people I grew up around have all of the access, but little of the desire to unlearn—because it would mean giving up power. Unlearning in a situation of extreme structural oppression where your body is the target can be a way to *restore* a sense of self, to return to belonging. It can confirm gut feelings and inner wisdom.

Reflecting on this while I was driving in the car and listening to a podcast one day, I realized that accessibility is possibly the simplest of all the conditions for unlearning. Radical unlearning, after all, is a disruptive form of learning that looks to the roots to understand our bodies, our lives, and the situations we are in. The curriculum for unlearning is ideally accessible to the people who need it most—whether it is a curriculum of immersion in a new space or place, a curriculum of re-thinking history, a curriculum of decolonizing or deconstruction. And when that curriculum is made accessible, plenty of people will not be resistant to unlearning at all but instead eager to enter. I think of myself as a trans teenager, unlearning binary gender with a great zeal, or of folks in prison, begging for people to send them books, invite them into study groups, challenge them in political conversations. Even the hungry college students challenging racism and studying Black and Palestinian liberation like their lives depended on it are a good example of this. In many cases people's lives do depend on it.

This condition is so fundamental I almost missed it. But it's also perhaps one of the easiest ones to cultivate.

Accessible modes of unlearning have an extensive history in social movements across the world, from Augusto Boal's Theater of the Op-pressed workshops in Brazil, to Indigenous reclamation projects around land and culture in Indonesia, to the Freedom Schools of the Black liberation movement in the US—even an overview would be a whole other book. One key theme across these popular education models for unlearning is that the bar for entry is low: they do not cost money or they are sliding scale, they take place in locations people can reach, and they are inclusive and do not require higher education to understand. Ideally, they focus on the people with the least access to other sites of intervention—people who can't just sign up for a class in critical peda-gogy or gender studies, because they are poor or incarcerated or living on the streets or too young or too old. The podcast I was listening to when all this flooded in was *For the Wild*, hosted by Ayana Young, and the guest was Anjali Nath Upadhyay, the founder of Liberation Spring, an adult education program focused on radical unlearning, and host of a decolonial feminist podcast called *Feral Visions*. Inspired by her way of speaking about accessible education, I reached out for an interview.

"I've known that part of my purpose has to do with offering adult education for just about the entirety of my adult life," Anjali said into the Zoom screen. She was living in Ecuador, speaking to me from a pink room lined with books. Anjali was tattooed, with long black hair, and her way of speaking was serious and direct, but open. She told me she'd always been a self-identified nerd, and that her first path as an educator was through graduate school, where she trained in political science and philosophy.

"And yet, on the side, I was always doing popular educational projects and political education, whether it was having consciousness raising circles in my living room or documentary nights once a week at an intentional community that I lived at in undergrad." As a result of this extracurricular education, she wasn't as easily sold on the careerist messaging that surrounded her. She was not persuaded that the most valid forms of education took place in rarified spaces like universities rather than grassroots, accessible locations where anyone was welcome to participate.

These autonomous spaces were the seeds for her later unlearning projects, she said, but so was what she witnessed growing up.

"My mother passed away prematurely in her fifties in 2007, in part from an abusive relationship with my father," she said. And that left her wondering about the missed opportunities for unlearning in her mother's life. "What if my mother, as someone who didn't graduate from tenth grade, had access to feminist consciousness-raising circles that could have felt accessible to her, especially as a mostly single mother? How could that have changed her life? Could she still be here today, if she had had access to those kinds of supportive community spaces?"

Access is central to everything Anjali does now: she didn't want to pour all her educational energy into a space that never would have mattered to so many people she loved, people like her mother who were never inside the ivory tower. "I did not want to be just another academic publishing critiques of academia in academic journals while the world is on fire."

In 2015, she left academia and founded Liberation Spring, a grassroots education and unlearning space "in the service of decolonization." As the website explains, "This (un)learning can support you & your community in facing political, economic, social, & ecological challenges.

Gather with a constellation of folks who are showing up to this precious moment in history with integrity. Our courses fuse consciousness-raising, popular education, & other approaches to learning that will aid you in embodying the liberation you're seeking."[1]

Anjali wasn't interested in competing with her friends and respected peers for limited professorships and fellowships in academia, and she didn't want her own teaching to stay forever behind a paywall. "I would rather offer something that is unambiguously and unapologetically housed in community," she said. Liberation Spring classes are sliding scale, and no one is turned away for lack of funds. "That to me is non-negotiable. It's most assuredly not from some kind of charitable model at all whatsoever, but rather a class analysis and honoring the necessity to show anti-capitalist ways of doing things within this project," she said.

The courses at Liberation Spring are interdisciplinary and heavy-hitting: this season's class is called Gaslight the System; last season was Technoskepticism, and the one before that was Kitchen Counter Intelligence. The courses meet for a semester-length period, a few hours a week, with sections that are BIPOC-only and sections that are open to all.[2]

Anjali has an expansive definition of accessibility, which involves being financially accessible, geographically accessible (in her case, all classes take place online since COVID), and accessible to people with physical and mental disabilities. She also has commitment to making her decolonial courses accessible to people for whom learning and unlearning aren't comfortable—either because they had traumatic encounters with educational systems, or because they were afraid of confrontation, or because they had been taught to act like they already know it all.

"Accessibility also means having the utmost respect for the resistance that comes up in an unlearning process, people's skepticism and misgivings, suspicions, critiques, principled disagreement," she told me. The goal of her courses isn't to avoid the tension that's inevitable when our deeply held beliefs are confronted, but to encourage and explore it. She doesn't want people to pretend they know what's going on all the time, or fake agreement with what's being said in class. "In a conflict avoidant culture like the mainstream US, a lot of folks can have sort of affective edges come up for them around naming even a disagreement—like, 'Is this going to change the vibe in the room? Will there be some tension that's so thick that you could slice the air? Will you be able to sense that people are less comfortable with you, or that there's been some rupture or break in the sense of community that's been forming?' This isn't a space where people are pressured to all kind of smile and nod."

Radical unlearning gets to the roots of social and political propaganda and tugs at those roots—a process Anjali calls "pulling weeds." But that work can't be done without confronting the presence of the propaganda in the room, identifying the weeds and discussing what we want to cultivate and why. That means in a collective unlearning space, people can't be afraid to speak about their own doubts and ingrained beliefs. "We're here to do this tender labor of looking at that and getting into it, not hiding it, or being afraid of bringing something up," she said. "That consistent, rigorous encouragement of disagreements, and of principled contrast, is something that also makes sure we're not just perpetuating echo chambers."

Pulling weeds also means identifying the ways that sometimes, a weed is feeding us. "Folks are much less likely to unlearn something if their livelihood is contingent upon them adhering to it," she said. Many people have grown up with what Marx called "false consciousness," beliefs about our own position in society that are self-defeating but that feel true—for example, the idea that people in prison are "bad" or that poor people are poor because they are inferior or undeserving, ideas that encourage oppressed people to accept their position and blame their peers, rather than their oppressors, for their situation. Undermining these—whether it's about class, race, ability, religion, or career—can undermine our sense of self. "It can be terrifying. This is an invitation into the unknown, right? And we all have different relationships with the unknown. It can require a heaping dose of humility."

I keep coming back to my friends behind bars, the ones who cannot go home, who cannot live on the land, and for whom the mere practice of seeking knowledge might come with physical safety risks—this, too, is an accessibility issue. My friend Tashiena Combs-Holbrook, for example, is an avid unlearner of her own dehumanization as an incarcerated Black woman. And yet, when she talks to other people in prison, when she tries to agitate and organize around the routine strip searches—a form of gendered violence—she and the others she's locked up with risk facing even further violations of their bodily autonomy. Others of my comrades in prison have faced heavy tickets and days in solitary confinement simply for joining collective unlearning spaces by phone. Radical unlearning can provide tools for resistance, but we must face that such unlearning might not be able to provide immediate safety for the people doing it. To create conditions for unlearning, we need to challenge the policies and practices that most aggressively try to prevent unlearning from taking place at all.

Cultivating accessible spaces for unlearning, then, must mean advocating for all people to have access to public and collective knowledge resources; access to libraries and adult schooling and study groups and free internet; and advocating for all people, especially those in prison, to have the safety to explore ideas without repression or punishment. Unfortunately, right now in the United States a full million people have routinely restricted access to all these things, and many millions more are kept from public space through the acts of the carceral state in a given year—they are in jails, or foster care, or psychiatric wards, or detention centers. Tens of millions beyond that are exposed to education systems and workplaces daily that punish and discourage critical thinking or following gut feelings, and that degrade and demote those who bring subversive or threatening knowledge to the surface. Access to public libraries, free extracurricular education, and other no-cost common spaces for critical engagement should be central to our advocacy for radical unlearning.

The mind doesn't lose its ability to resist in prison or in repressive schooling, mind you—I would argue that quite the opposite can happen. At least some people become even more thirsty for new ways to see. But radical unlearning can "pull weeds and plant seeds," as Anjali Nath Upadhyay says, if we fight for its accessibility at every turn, creating free and low-barrier spaces and ways for people to enter conversations, fighting for access to information and critical thought on the frontlines of oppression.

Creating these spaces is urgent: We can't build the worlds we need if our visions and knowledge and skills are mired in harmful ideology. Unlearning is not a performance or a superficial pursuit of better persona or point of view; it is a necessity.

I am concerned that capitalists are ahead of the rest of us in this regard—they have people unlearning in order to be better managers and better managed, to integrate new technologies and to accept new realities of the capitalists' shaping. They have people letting go of knowledges that are ancient and needed in favor of newly learned survival skills that keep the capitalist economy running. Heck, they have machines doing the learning and the unlearning, simulating the logic of human beings through artificial intelligence. This nonradical unlearning—corporate unlearning—is accessible at many turns in life, often in the form of pro-paganda that persuades us to be better participants in structures that do not ultimately benefit us and teaches us not to trust our intuition or listen to our lived knowledge.

To this end, accessibility cannot be the opposite of rigor. Making something accessible is not the same as making it easy. On the contrary, we need accessible pedagogies of unlearning that can keep up with the rigor of the powerful. Of course, these pedagogies and practices exist and have existed around the world. Some of them have names in En-glish—pedagogy of the oppressed, theater of the oppressed, popular ed-ucation, politicized somatics—but many of them do not. And our human imaginations and cultures can absolutely outpace technology, not least because we are creative, strange, and surreal. Where computers can only solve problems, people in groups can experiment, hallucinate, and play. We can push outside the borders of rational thought, and that is where radical unlearning is uniquely formidable. The visionary and playful and love-based aspects of radical unlearning can't be reproduced outside of their context in communities and relationships, which means they can't be reproduced by machines. We will always have a leg up on the conditioning and propaganda produced by capitalists, and it can also be much more fun to swim in these waters than trudge through their muck.

Accessible unlearning helps ground us in shared visions. I dream about clean water for all; abundant healing rituals; high-tech medical resources and medication freely available; streets that are sanitary and full of laughter; kitchens full of healthy food; seed saving; no-cost spaces for protection, grief, and care; collective banks for art and fashion to be freely shared; interconnected game-playing and learning that facilitates multilingual communication; children who get to be barefoot in woods and creeks with no broken glass or oil slicks; healthy bodies walking, biking, wheeling, running; sharing rides on buses and trains; a billion deep breaths where the air is clean. I have a vision of nothing but trees and water, of human societies without war where the rituals focus on love and dreaming, a vision of conflict that is generative and unarmed, a vision of disarming ourselves.

Who can afford such naivete? Let's think of it another way: Who can afford not to dream of such a thing? Are you so close to utopia that there's no point in even trying? Are you sure that your life hasn't been made possible by someone else's wild dreams in the past? What do you desire? If you closed your eyes and let yourself truly dream, what would your yearning point you toward?

INTERLUDE: CHILDREN'S MINDS, ADULTS' LIMITS, AND UNLEARNING AS A DISRUPTIVE PIVOT

Jesa Rae is known around Durham as "Teacher Jesa" because of her work with very small children and kids' liberation. Jesa is my best friend—the person I've been growing alongside since we met and came out as queer together in eighth and ninth grade in Michigan, the person who supported me through my gender transition(s) and politicization(s) and moves across and around the country, and the reason I live in North Carolina (I followed her here). She's a brilliant thinker, and her passion is thinking and developing cultural space in collaboration with young children. She believes in the wisdom, curiosity, and emergent brilliance of two-, three-, and four-year-olds and fights doggedly for adults to recognize and liberate this brilliance, rather than teaching kids to control and limit their minds.

From Jesa and the kids she convenes, I have learned that many of the things we end up needing to "unlearn" in adulthood are not a problem for young children. Binary thinking, for example: this is something that has to be taught to them, but if they are introduced to nonbinary concepts, their fluidity with it is impressive (just ask the kids at Jesa's school about "they/them" pronouns . . .). They are similarly capable and wise and open in the areas of imagination, empathy, connection and interdependence with the natural world, and resistance to exploitive forms of power. I remember visiting Jesa's forest school (named "the Love Pod School" by the children) and trying to explain why my friend was in prison, and the logic of the prison guards, to a group of five- and six-year-olds. Having never encountered the logic of restricting and hurting someone as a so-called social good, they were baffled.

Jesa believes in kids' liberation and supporting kids' culture, and she is exploring an idea in her academic work that she calls "pedagogy of the unknown"—a practice of recognizing and valuing the unknown as an important component in learning. I have transcribed just a few excerpts of our conversations.

LEWIS: I've been thinking a lot about these liberal ideas of sort of "nudging" people to think how you want them to or act how you want them to, and also liberal education teaching a rigid way of thinking about oppression and race and so on. I don't really think that is unlearning; that's just replacing one rigid set of ideas with another. But I am having a hard time defining what's different with radical unlearning. What do you think is happening during the process of unlearning? Like, how is it different than just changing your mind to a new set of rigid beliefs? What is it that we're exploring here that is more conscious and critical?

JESA: There's something about the process or the action that's happening during the change and after. It's a different kind of change than change from a binary perspective, like where you go from one thing to the other—right or wrong, adopting the correct political view or whatever. That is just trying to get you to come to my side, buy the thing, change your behavior, to do this finite thing that I want. Then, when you do the thing that I want, it's done. Now you are in that location and you stay in that location. All that's doing is moving the line.

My interest is in the liminal space of the line—it's not about which side of the line are you on, but how are you engaging with the boundary crossing? If you're really engaging with it, the atomizing of the line, the space of the in-between, that's an ongoing engagement and an ongoing dialectical change. It's that deep curiosity and openness and extended discomfort. So the location is more ambiguous.

That seems to be a different process. From an education standpoint, if I as a teacher am trying to encourage knowledge construction from the location of the liminal space, that's an ongoing dialogue that's gonna require discomfort, and require all of us in the dialogue to not really be at a static location when we're done. Whereas if I'm trying to get a group of kids to "do the right thing," I can know when we are there. It's a certain amount of manipulation that is done in media, in psychology, in education.

LEWIS: But don't we still have an agenda, don't you have an agenda in what you want kids to learn?

JESA: I do believe in a society that's anti-racist, I do have an ethical agenda. But I don't feel that convincing young kids to, like, make recycling signs is what that's about. And that is what it's about in school. That's what many of the activists that we love do. But unlearning is that ongoing, relational, ambiguous location. And the thing about that is it's vulnerable for everybody. If a psychologist or a public health official or a journalist is working in that way, they can't locate themselves in a static location. You have to break down the power dynamic. There has to be a totally different power dynamic. So the unlearning is a different dialectical shape. That's deeply threatening to our social structures and much more connected to ecology. It's a much more planetary type of relation, and it doesn't really work with hegemony.

LEWIS: Hegemony is the ultimate "nudge."

JESA: It is, the ultimate nudge. It's spatial in my mind. . . . I was writing about the queer liminal space and imagining that dividing line that creates the binary as more of a river. I think a river is an incomplete metaphor, but I was thinking a river because it is a dividing line but it's also a space that's in constant movement in every direction, rising and falling and moving. It's not as if you draw a line. That's how a lot of borders are made, though. . . . In my mind it's as if I was going to put a right and a wrong next to each other, why I think about the river is that it's not a wishy-washy type of ambiguity, it's not "nothing is right or wrong or nothing is this or that"—it's strong. To be in that in-between is to be in an intangible, engaged, dialogic space. Like, when we talk about gender, it's not just you're either male or female or you are directly in between. But for people who have only seen deep heteronormative cisgender perspective, there are just those choices. Once you pull that apart, it's basically infinite. Not indecisive—but all of those possibilities can't be predetermined. It's a different way of looking at differentiation. I'm not sure what the language is for that.

LEWIS: It's a feeling. It's like poetry—it comes from a feeling place, and we can recognize it but it's hard to explain.

JESA: That's our life's work. How to say it. Part of it is because we're working with this language—English—that is this way for a reason. That's part of why poetry, why art can break down those binaries. Part of the obstacle here is how to deal with the language. Any medium can be used creatively enough to represent what you need it to.

LEWIS: In the high-modern era, there are all these people who are talking about poetry and the language of poetry. e. e. cummings, James Baldwin, Muriel Rukeyser, Aimé Césaire, the Surrealists . . . they're all saying poetry is what we need to make meaning. I think they are resisting the kind of linear, definitive, described realities of modernism and industrialism and saying that the way you resist it is actually by living in a way that's more like poetry—not meaningless, but more abstract. Can you say that thing again that you said to me before about unlearning being a disruption?

JESA: I said it's a conscious, disruptive, embodied pivot that transforms the learning that comes after.

LEWIS: I love that definition, that's so helpful. Because it's still all about learning, but learning in the wake of a disruptive change that doesn't allow you to learn the same way as before.

JESA: And the two are really in relationship because a lot of those repatternings are learnings, but the reason why you're doing a repatterning, a new practice, is because of that event that happened, that disruption. What is happening inside that disruption is actually so huge, even if it's just this little moment in someone's life. I'm not saying unlearning has to happen in one

particular discrete moment, but a lot of what you talk about
is these events. And the way you are describing it is not really
this linear cumulative thing, it doesn't have to be a particular
type of event, in terms of it happening in this one physical
way. You are getting at what's happening inside of it, what's the
chemical reaction? In terms of theories of learning it's an exciting way to have that conversation, because it's sort of shifting
the focus and loosening it up.

My interest is a lot in chaos and the unknown, so of course
I'm like, "Oooh, yeah, this is really cool." A disruptive pivot
suggests elements of chaos, suggests it's this letting go, this unknown, this "I don't know." That "I don't know" is so important.

I've been seeing it a lot, teaching college students versus
preschool. Preschool is a whole lot of learning. From my perspective, I could still be challenged on this, but not a whole lot
of unlearning. College is a whole lot of nothing, with—if you're
doing a good job—equal parts learning and unlearning. I'm
hoping that we're unlearning as much as we're learning here.
Otherwise, it's just doing the thing, just being polite, just using
the right pronouns, etc. But you're not actually *seeing* a thing
differently.

LEWIS: Definitely the way I'm thinking about unlearning is a collo-
quial concept, not a scientific one. There's not a clearly understood mechanism—it's phenomenological in that sense. It's
what people attest to as real. If you say you saw God, you saw
God, let's explore what that means. You say you unlearned, you
unlearned—let's explore.

JESA: That's why thinking of it as a pivot, thinking of it as a disruption is helpful. Because on the surface it seems like it's a
countering of learning, but you're also saying it's a somatic
experience . . . the pivot or the disruption is movement. That
movement could be so many different things, but we're studying the movement. That's what excites me about it so much.
The movement isn't something you can necessarily grab onto
and hold. As somebody who loves the unknown and chaos, it's

exciting to me, because those are parts of learning, but they're not in the same trajectory. Unlearning feels like it's akin to that, a movement. It almost diminishes it if you try to define it. If at the end of this book, people are like, "Now I've learned what unlearning is," you have failed. If they're like, "Oh, this is a different way to think about learning," or "When have I felt that feeling that was described in that book?," that's exciting.

1. What is the difference between closed-off and cult-like belief, and communities that facilitate and allow for ongoing unlearning?
2. What parts of your own beliefs or worldview are rigid? Why? What are you protecting and is it something you want to continue to protect?
3. What parts of your own life contain the conditions for unlearning? Where do you find love, cognitive dissonance, community, confrontation, questions, somatic practices, immersion in new environments, and accessible opportunities to learn and unlearn? How can you access more of these? How can you create more of these for others?
4. How do we create an accessible culture of unlearning? What are small ways to do this in your own community, family, or workplace?
5. What feelings come up when you are faced with something you know you need to unlearn? Where do you notice these feelings in your body?
6. What daily habits do you want to change or expand to facilitate unlearning?
7. Who are your unlearning inspirations?
8. What are your unlearning practices?

DESIRE, YEARNING, AND THE UNKNOWN

I used to believe that people don't *want* to change or be changed, that "you can't teach an old dog new tricks." For the first couple years of my studies of unlearning, as I read books and looked at articles on what changes people's minds, I accepted that interpretation even though it didn't resonate with my own lived experience, in which many people I knew had left behind their backgrounds and resisted dominant ideologies, often at great personal risk. Were the people I knew exceptional?

Over time, I started to wonder about the large percentages of people in each study about groupthink or not changing minds who *did* change, or went against the grain, and why so-called brain science wasn't more interested in how they worked. When so many people were capable of free thought, why were the ones who tended to conform held up as the more typical and predictable kind of people? Why weren't these studies questioning where people got their ideas about conformity and groupthink in the first place? As I spoke to more and more people about unlearning—not just the interviews in this book, but my family members, random people at the bar or on the street, friends in prison—"people are set in their ways" began to appear to me as more a statement of belief and a philosophy than a fact about the world. People unlearn all the time.

What about all the people who *want to* unlearn, for whom it is a desire, an urge, or even a necessity? What about all the people who are not set in our ways, for reasons of practicality or feelings we can't control, who can't reconcile our longings with the society we've been born into, and don't actually want to live like that? What about all the people, from my grandmother in the nursing home to Tashiena in the prison, who had unlearned not because the world demanded it or the people around them pressured them but because *they wished to?* And what are the implications of the assumption that we are incapable of transformation—what does such an assumption tell us about ourselves and each other? Whose power and cruelty are excused and justified, if inner change is impossible? Whose stories does that rigid narrative overlook?

In exploring what creates the conditions for radical unlearning, I have learned that we cannot simply think or argue our way out of the spells of habit and familiarity, powerful tonics for the human brain. But we can be jostled and forced and inclined out of them by love. By design, humans are meant to change in relationship with one another, in order to cooperate and learn and survive together. In fact, surviving solo—while a colonial fascination—is close to impossible. Our ability to unlearn is intertwined inextricably with our ability to experience connection, tenderness, and their limbic cousins, play and improvisation. This is why love, community, questions, and artistic engagement are all so important to creating conditions for unlearning.

But equally important are the conditions that stoke and sustain tension: these include confrontation, cognitive dissonance, immersion in challenging environments, and relationships that push us to wonder and doubt. To broaden our window of tolerance for these sometimes rankling experiences, somatic practices and centering in the body can also be key. And it is necessary in radical unlearning that we devote ourselves to the process, practicing and repeating much the way we devote ourselves when we learn an instrument or a language—practice itself can facilitate the unlearning as we systematically create and repeat new neural connections.

Finally, the material of unlearning—whether it is discussions, texts, stories, games, relationships, or frameworks—must be accessible. Many people are ready to unlearn but simply cannot access the information or connections that would facilitate this. State repression in its many forms tends to create the conditions for not unlearning, whether through incarceration, top-down education systems that train us into submission, or the daily grind of poverty and fear that entraps so many and then blames them for their own entrapment.

Unlearning is a cyclical process that exists within and responds to material conditions. Oppressive societies are quite effective at controlling and preventing the conditions for unlearning—teaching us, instead, to distrust and fear each other, to undervalue poetry and overvalue so-called rational thought, to disconnect from our embodied experience and intuition, and to accept our own and others' deprivation. It follows that another way to create conditions for unlearning is to directly challenge and change power relations. Lots of people don't explore unlearning simply because they fear the punishing consequences, especially in authoritarian or fascist societies or situations. In this way, unlearning is facilitated as much by confrontational interactions, protest, and pressure, as by patient and loving interactions between friends. Changing power relations can be necessary to unlearning, as unlearning can be necessary to changing power relations.

Unlearning sometimes happens in a cascade of events in a community or society, especially when this rethinking shakes the power structure to its core. There's safety in numbers, and unlearning in groups is much more efficient than studying in a room alone until you come to something. Such a collective cascade is what we often call a "movement"— women's liberation, for example, or the American Indian Movement, or the movements of the 1990s and 2000s for trans liberation were each based on a broad collective unlearning that might have felt sudden to bystanders, but was driven by a long-pent-up truth, finally being told in public.

There's one more driver behind unlearning that keeps arising, one that I'm unsure how to account for: few people seem to unlearn without, at some point, recognizing that they *want* to unlearn. How might you create conditions of desire, of yearning?

The people I spoke to and the stories I read gave this experience different names: magnetism, attraction, urge, longing, connection, and hunger were all mentioned as motivators or precursors to unlearning. For many queer and trans people, the element of desire in personal transformation is somewhat obvious: I think of Daniel Heath Justice unlearning his story about the awfulness of being gay when he saw a gay porn magazine and found it hot, or my own seventeen-year-old self chasing around and imitating the people I found appealing and attractive, who for some mysterious reason were all trans.

I started off this text by describing new synaptic connections and pathways as desire lines of the mind, maps of agency—desire was right there, this whole time. The directions we choose to map are shaped in community, but they can also emerge from an indefinable urge—something more like hunger, eroticism, or need. All the conditions for unlearning that I have explored can make that urge feel more possible to pursue: love softening and toughening us, cognitive dissonance giving us the itch to resolve, community giving us a place to safely explore, confrontation creating pressure. Questions and conversations can invite us into unlearning; somatics and practices can deepen and widen the path. Surrealism, poetry, and immersion can loosen the synapses, help us swim in confusion and surf juxtaposition, and expose desire lines we didn't know were there. But there remains the mystery of the desire itself.

"It's deeper than that. It's not even necessarily verbal or something that can be articulated," somatic coach and healer Eliana Rubin said of this ineffable force. "It's like something in you that gets moved and is almost magnetic. . . . There's something drawing me there."

In that state of magnetism, we are motivated to push through fear even when we can't explain it. Yashna Padamsee, also a leader in somatic transformation, pointed out that we usually have a strong intuitive sense of our desires when we're able to pause and pay attention: "We say these things all the time like, you know, I'm going to follow my heart. I'm going to trust my gut." Being stuck in the thinking brain and intellect can block, rather than facilitate unlearning, because it can keep us from connecting to these gut feelings or freely following curiosity where it leads.

One place where we know desire and longing can begin is in the experience of confinement and oppression. Black feminist Kai Barrow described unlearning as self-determination; another Black feminist, Denise Perry, described it as a move towards liberation: "That's scary in some ways, beautiful in others," she said. "I think about Harriet Tubman and having to do what she did, the risk of if I follow the sky, if I walk away from here, if I take the risk of bringing these folks with me . . . [she was] refusing to learn the nonsense of what she was in." For Harriet Tubman, she's suggesting, the unlearning was in the action of walking, the extreme risk-taking to cultivate literal, physical freedom. The underground railroad was a desire line.

How many oppressed people have yearned to follow new desire lines, inner and outer pathways out of entrapment, fear, and terror?

Desire is the part of the picture that I can't quite describe and don't exactly know how to generate, but that drives and transforms us. Desire is the voice in the forest, the underwater breathing, the unconscious dreaming that intimates another world. Poetry and rivers might be better sites for explaining this gravitational draw into the unknown—as my grandmother Sarah said, "We do not have adequate language to cover everything we need to say."

I have also been noticing yearning, desire tinged with mournfulness or a sense of impossibility. I yearn for strange spaces, for sailboats and underwater collectives, for Muppet capers on double-decker buses full of capricious blues musicians in oddball wigs. I yearn for the wordless expressions of my underwater surrealist character, Octocordion, and for children under siege to be free forever, and for the woods and waterways of my own childhood to be returned to their original caretakers and open to all who need them. Micha Kurz talked about yearning for reconnection to God as he lost his connection to the religious propaganda of his youth—his was a spiritual journey, driven by loss but also searching for what might heal him. Adrianne Black talked about much of the same in her journey both toward anti-racism and toward coming out as trans: she knew something was off, and she yearned for spaces and relationships where it would be safe to express her truth. These stories of yearning were also stories of loss and grief, beginnings that meant facing frightening precipices.

I come full circle, to the raw story of my grandmother Sarah, who could unlearn enough to love me but who could not quite let go of her own bigotry. She carried her fears of Blackness and transness to her deathbed, even though she desired something more in this life. I could feel that Sarah did not want to live with these fears, that these systems of belief were *in* her but not *of* her. As powerful and privileged as she was, I felt a striving for freedom in her, too. Near the end, I sensed that she looked forward to meeting God and what I'd call the "spirit world," maybe because she knew it would unite her with what she had lost of herself, passing through this world, this way. In a life full of painful paradoxes, there was something appealing about the precipice—whatever she believed about the hereafter.

I didn't think of her as someone who was in deep touch with her intuition and yearnings. This was my own quiet, intellectual upbringing: we had all been trained to listen to the rational, to ignore the heart and gut, to look to books for evidence or "proof." And, yet, I remember Sarah staring off into that spiritual abyss near the end of her life with undefined longing and unmistakable resonance.

One day as Raven and my cousin and I stood around her hospital bed watching her come back from the edge, Sarah told us in an uncharacteristic stammer that she couldn't explain or describe what she saw out there using words. But I could feel that she was witnessing something mystical, something in the beyond that made her want to stay open—to the ineffable, to those around her, maybe to death itself.

Later I held her hand—fluid wrinkled skin and warm wedding band, blue veins and the slowest breath, flickering eagle eyes under lids that had closed for good. Sarah kept breathing for days, and then weeks, moving through a cycle of letting go. Watching her continue to grapple, to love and say goodbye, I witnessed unspeakable magnetism, her curious reaching. I witnessed her sinking into abstraction, going below the real, and finding joy, rather than fear, on the path. She passed away and left me and my cousins and my brothers and Raven on this earth, still striving. Maybe what we can't unlearn in life, we can at least let go in death. Maybe dying becomes a desire line, the oldest and simplest possible path back into the freedom of the unknown.

ACKNOWLEDGMENTS

I am grateful to my community of unlearners, family, and friends for their enduring support of this project, particularly those who took the time to read chapters and give feedback: Sumayya Kassamali, Gabrielle Civil, Mia Henry, Danielle Purifoy, Sumi Dutta, Neena Pathak, Raven McCrory, Bruce Wallace, Tina Vasquez, and my brother Nick Wallace. The mysterious and talented artist Billy Dee did more than just read and reply to my work, as always: they dug deep into multiple chapters and sections and helped me be my better self at every stage. Jesa Rae, my forever confidante and partner in thought, pushed me on many fronts and let me turn on my recording device whenever she started saying smart stuff. My other brother, Clint Wallace, went above and beyond in his editorial support and saved me from a headache in the final hours of drafting. Eddie Gonzalez showed early interest in the idea and stuck with me through to some final-throes reading, giving generously of his time and creativity in the process. Janada Halbisen-Gibbs has been a guide and model for unlearning for almost my entire life, and first introduced me to some of the key ideas in psychology and somatics.

I have been lucky to create and learn the last few years alongside various brilliant friends and movement makers who happen to not be featured in this book, but could easily have been: Micah Bazant, Lei-Lani Dowell, Danette Wilkins, Kiki DeLovely, Roxana Bendezú, Steven Thrasher, Pooja Gehi, Sam Worley, Chelsea Higgs-Wise, Rae Garringer, Nadeen Bir, Andrea Ritchie, Mariame Kaba, and all the leaders and thinkers at Interrupting Criminalization, Press On, and Jewish Voice for

Peace (Triangle Chapter) and the extensive international community of the Ford Global Fellowship. In addition to my fellow Ford fellows who are featured in the text, I am thankful for learning and unlearning conversations with Nkosikhona Swaartbooi, Sely Martini, Daiene Mendes, Keamogetswe Seipato, Noah Mirembe Gabigogo, Waleed Abu Nada, Muzna Al-Masri, Juliana Lohar, Lulu Ning, Esteban Kelly, Hadeel Abdel Aziz, Adria Goodson, and all the thoughtful and curious friends I have made on that journey.

My agent, Tanya McKinnon, supported me to take this text from seed to sprout to flowering plant. A residency at the Camargo Foundation in Cassis, France, as well as my Ford Global Fellowship grant and incredible flexibility and love from Interrupting Criminalization, allowed me to finish this book peacefully, a gift and a privilege.

I am deeply grateful to each person I interviewed, whose contributions are described in the author's note. As I mentioned there, these interviews were not easy. Adrianne Black, in particular, spent so many hours with me and entrusted me with so much as she moved through her own tender journey in parallel. Yashna Maya Padamsee gave me careful and trusting feedback, stretching her own unlearning to help stretch mine. Catherine Edgerton offered intellectual stimulation and smart and challenging questions to the highest degree, and introduced me to both Surrealism and scuba diving. Mab Segrest, one of my first true teachers in unlearning, spent a long time with me for an interview that did not end up in here: you should read her books, starting with *Memoir of a Race Traitor*. Mr. Yaeger, the greatest teacher ever, deserves the world for what he has given his students. I also had meaningful and supportive conversations along the way with Katina Parker, Aljosie Harding, and Suzanne Pharr, and I looked to John Biewen as a model for sharing unlearning in public.

When things fell apart near the end of this writing process, Autumn Brown was there for me, big time, as were Micah Bazant and Skyler Sussman. Brooklyn Jeter supported my healing and transformation and cultivated peace around me as I crossed the finish line. Hooper and Nell inspired me and made me laugh. Frankie and Dogwood brought me daily joy.

I give thanks to my grandparents, particularly Sarah, and all my ancestors, for attempting, for existing, for allowing me a life and showing me that personal transformation and political engagement are possible and worthwhile. I give thanks to my parents, Bruce and Raven, for raising me to try.

NOTES

INTRODUCTION

1. Elizabeth Kolbert, "Why Facts Don't Change Our Minds," *New Yorker*, February 19, 2017, https://www.newyorker.com/magazine/2017/02/27/why-facts-dont -change-our-minds.

2. See, for example, Cass R. Sunstein and Richard H. Thaler, *Nudge: Improving Decisions About Health, Wealth, and Happiness* (New York: Penguin, 2009); and Adam Grant, *Think Again: The Power of Knowing What You Don't Know* (New York: Viking, 2021). This latter title explores both internal rethinking and external persuasion and draws on a wealth of contemporary scientific studies. A most excellent text on the obstacles to changing minds is Kathryn Schultz's *Being Wrong: Adventures in the Margin of Error* (New York: Ecco, 2010). Or simply google "books about persuasion" and you will find dozens, many focused on its uses in capitalism and pseudo-democracy.

3. A great book on the problem of arrogance on both the right and the left, which explores the problem without reducing it to a simple across-the-board critique, is Michael Patrick Lynch, *Know-It-All Society: Truth and Arrogance in Political Culture* (New York: Liveright, 2019).

4. Shawn Wilson, *Research Is Ceremony: Indigenous Research Methods* (Halifax: Fernwood, 2008), 127.

5. Leanne Betasamosake Simpson, *As We Have Always Done: Indigenous Freedom Through Radical Resistance* (Minneapolis: University of Minnesota Press, 2017).

CHAPTER 1: DESIRE LINES

1. See, for example, Anne Rooney, *Neuroscience: Unlocking the Mysteries of the Brain and Consciousness* (London: Arcturus, 2011), 222; and Thomas Lewis, Fari Amini, and Richard Lannon, *A General Theory of Love* (New York: Knopf Doubleday, 2007), preface, Kindle edition.

2. Moheb Costandi, *Neuroplasticity* (Cambridge, MA: MIT Press, 2016), 1.

3. See Maia Szalavitz, *Unbroken Brain: A Revolutionary New Way of Understanding Addiction* (New York: St. Martin's Press, 2016). This text theorizes drug addiction as a form of learning and debunks the idea of "your brain on drugs."

4. Costandi, *Neuroplasticity*, 145.

5. Costandi, *Neuroplasticity*, 2, 12; Rooney, *Neuroscience*, 79–80.

6. Costandi, *Neuroplasticity*, 49.

7. Costandi, *Neuroplasticity*, 50.

8. Norman Doidge, MD, *The Brain That Changes Itself: Stories of Personal Triumph from the Frontiers of Brain Science* (New York: Penguin, 2007), 54.

9. Doidge, *The Brain That Changes Itself*, 60.

10. Costandi, *Neuroplasticity*, 33.

11. Doidge, *The Brain That Changes Itself*, 65.

12. Costandi, *Neuroplasticity*, 14, 66.

13. Some scientists refer to this distinction as declarative versus non-declarative memory. See Rooney, *Neuroscience*, 223.

14. Lewis, Amini, and Lannon, *A General Theory of Love*, chapter 5, Kindle edition.

15. Most texts on neuroplasticity do not focus specifically on the idea of "unlearning" (unlearning is not a distinct concept or theory within neuroscience), but Doidge mentions this connection several times in his work. See, for example, Doidge, *The Brain That Changes Itself*, 60, 116.

16. Costandi, *Neuroplasticity*, 55, 147; Doidge, *The Brain That Changes Itself*, 65.

17. Costandi, *Neuroplasticity*, 88–89, 95–96; Doidge, *The Brain That Changes Itself*, 67.

18. Costandi, *Neuroplasticity*, 50.

19. Doidge, *The Brain That Changes Itself*, 112–14.

20. Lewis, Amini, and Lannon, *A General Theory of Love*, chapter 4, Kindle edition.

21. D. Purves, G. J. Augustine, D. Fitzpatrick et al., eds., *Neuroscience*, 2nd ed. (Sunderland, MA: Sinauer Associates, 2001).

22. Doidge, *The Brain That Changes Itself*, 68.

23. adrienne maree brown, *Emergent Strategy: Shaping Change, Changing Worlds* (Chico, CA: AK Press, 2017), 34.

CHAPTER 2: LOVE

1. Jennifer Dunning, "Torney's Insanity Defense Linked to Fact Slaying Victim Had No Gun," *New York Times*, November 29, 1977; Jennifer Dunning, "Officer Torsney Acquitted as Jury Rules Him Insane in Killing of Boy," *New York Times*, December 1, 1977.

2. In James Baldwin, *The Fire Next Time* (New York: Dell, 1963), 95.

3. Thomas Lewis, Fari Amini, and Richard Lannon, *A General Theory of Love* (New York: Knopf Doubleday, 2007), Kindle edition.

4. Lewis, Amini, and Lannon, *A General Theory of Love*, preface, Kindle edition.

5. Lewis, Amini, and Lannon, *A General Theory of Love*, chapter 3, Kindle edition.

6. Lewis, Amini, and Lannon, *A General Theory of Love*, chapter 3, Kindle edition.

7. Lewis, Amini, and Lannon, *A General Theory of Love*, chapter 4, Kindle edition; see also Norman Doidge, MD, *The Brain That Changes Itself: Stories of Personal Triumph from the Frontiers of Brain Science* (New York: Penguin, 2007), 119–20.

8. Doidge, *The Brain That Changes Itself*, 107.

9. Doidge, *The Brain That Changes Itself*, 116.

10. Doidge, *The Brain That Changes Itself*, 116.

11. Emily Cronkleton, "How Can You Tell If You're in Love?," *Medical News Today*, December 22, 2022, https://www.medicalnewstoday.com/articles/how-do-you -know-you-love-someone.

12. Doidge, *The Brain That Changes Itself*, 117.

13. Bruce D. Perry and Oprah Winfrey, *What Happened to You? Conversations on Trauma, Resilience, and Healing* (New York: Flatiron Books, 2021), 142–44.

14. See, for example, Perry and Winfrey, *What Happened to You?*, 282; Peter Levine, *In an Unspoken Voice: How the Body Releases Trauma and Restores Goodness* (Berkeley, CA: North Atlantic Books, 2010), 99–100.

15. Perry and Winfrey, *What Happened to You?*, 144.

CHAPTER 3: COGNITIVE DISSONANCE

1. Fayez Hammed, "A Brief History of the US-Israel 'Special Relationship,'" USC Dornsife, November 29, 2023, https://dornsife.use.edu/news/stories/brief -history-of-us-israel-relations; Jonathan Masters and Will Merrow, "U.S. Aid to Israel in Four Charts," Council on Foreign Relations, April 11, 2024, https:// www.cfr.org/article/us-aid-israel-four-charts.

2. "Israeli Settlers Raid Southern West Bank City of al-Khalil, Injure Palestinian," Tasnim News Agency, September 17, 2023, https://www.tasnimnews.com/en /news/2023/09/17/2957216/israeli-settlers-raid-southern-west-bank-city-of-al -khalil-injure-palestinian; see also "Al Khalil/Hebron—A Case Study for the Impact of Israeli Settlements on Palestinian Rights Under Occupation," United Nations: The Question of Palestine, https://www.un.org/unispal/al-khalil-hebron -a-case-study-for-the-impact-of-israeli-settlements-on-palestinian-rights-under -occupation-virtual-event/, accessed February 18, 2025.

3. Riyad Mansour, "Illegal Israeli Actions in the OPT/Settler Violence in Hebron— Letter from Palestine," addressed to the United Nations, December 5, 2008, https://www.un.org/unispal/document/auto-insert-184794/. Now Al-Khalil is home to about two hundred thousand Palestinians, according to "Occupied Hebron/Al-Khalil," Mapping the Apartheid, https://www.hebronapartheid.org /index.php?page=introduction, accessed February 18, 2025.

4. Robert A. Burton, *On Being Certain: Believing You Are Right Even When You're Not* (New York: St. Martin's Griffin, 2008), xiii.

5. Burton, *On Being Certain*, 51–52.

6. Burton, *On Being Certain*, 183.

7. Burton, *On Being Certain*, 101.

8. Carol Tavris and Elliot Aronson, *Mistakes Were Made (but Not by Me): Why We Justify Foolish Beliefs, Bad Decisions, and Hurtful Acts* (Orlando, FL: Harcourt, 2007), 16–17.

9. Tavris and Aronson, *Mistakes Were Made*, 27–28, 46–47.

10. Adam Grant, *Think Again: The Power of Knowing What You Don't Know* (New York: Viking, 2021), 165–69.

11. Tavris and Aronson, *Mistakes Were Made*, 28–35.

12. Ali Adam, "Palestinian Intifada: How Israel Orchestrated a Bloody Takeover," *Al Jazeera*, September 28, 2020, https://www.aljazeera.com/news/2020/9/28/palestinian-intifada-20-years-later-israeli-occupation-continues.

13. Associated Press, "Israel Has Right to Build in West Bank, Jerusalem, Huckabee Asserts," *Arkansas Democrat Gazette*, January 31, 2011, https://www.arkansasonline.com/news/2011/jan/31/israel-has-right-build-west-bank-jerusalem-huckabe/.

CHAPTER 4: COMMUNITY

1. Solomon E. Asch, "Opinions and Social Pressure," *Scientific American*, November 1955, 31–35. See also Cass R. Sunstein and Richard H. Thaler, *Nudge: Improving Decisions About Health, Wealth, and Happiness* (New York: Penguin, 2009), 56–57.

2. For a cogent critique of the "tribalism" assertions, see Dominic Packer and Jay Van Bevel, "The Myth of Tribalism: Beware of the False Notion That Group Solidarity Leads Inevitably to Conflict," *Atlantic*, January 3, 2022, https://www.theatlantic.com/ideas/archive/2022/01/tribalism-myth-group-solidarity-prejudice-conflict/621008/.

3. Shawn Wilson, *Research Is Ceremony: Indigenous Research Methods* (Halifax: Fernwood, 2008), 74.

4. Wilson, *Research Is Ceremony*, 127.

CHAPTER 5: CONFRONTATION

1. The Detroit metro area has been in the top five for various measures of racial segregation for decades. See, for example, City Observatory, "America's Least (and Most) Segregated Metro Areas: 2020," https://cityobservatory.org/most_segregated2020/, accessed December 24, 2024; Halley Potter, "School Segregation in U.S. Metro Areas," Century Foundation, May 17, 2022, https://tcf.org/content/report/school-segregation-in-u-s-metro-areas/, accessed December 24, 2024.

2. In James Baldwin, *The Fire Next Time*, 1st Vintage International ed. (New York: Vintage International, 1993), 43–44.

3. Toni Schmader, "Shame and Guilt: The Motivation for Self-Change," Social Identity Lab, University of British Columbia, https://socialidentitylab.psych.ubc.ca/research/shame-and-guilt/, accessed December 24, 2024; see also June Price Tangney and Ronda L. Dearing, *Shame and Guilt* (New York: Guilford Press, 2002), 63.

4. Tangney and Dearing, *Shame and Guilt*, 126–27.

5. Joaquín Selva, "Why Shame and Guilt Are Functional for Mental Health," Positive Psychology, January 22, 2018, https://positivepsychology.com/shame-guilt/, accessed December 24, 2024; see also Tangney and Dearing, *Shame and Guilt*, chapter 1.

6. See adrienne maree brown, *We Will Not Cancel Us, and Other Dreams of Transformative Justice* (Chico, CA: AK Press, 2020); Ngọc Loan Trần, "Calling IN: A Less Disposable Way of Holding Each Other Accountable," *BGD*, https://www

.bgdblog.org/2013/12/calling-less-disposable-way-holding-accountable/, accessed December 24, 2024.

7. Trần, "Calling IN."

8. brown, *We Will Not Cancel Us*, introduction.

9. Malkia Devich Cyril, *We Will Not Cancel Us*, afterword.

INTERLUDE: ON STORIES AND UNLEARNING

1. Daniel Heath Justice, *Our Fire Survives the Storm: A Cherokee Literary History* (Minneapolis: University of Minnesota Press, 2006), 46.

2. Justice, *Our Fire Survives the Storm*, 46.

CHAPTER 6: QUESTIONS

1. "NBA Moves North Carolina All-Star Game over 'Bathroom Bill,'" BBC News, July 22, 2016, https://www.bbc.com/news/world-us-canada-36863216; "HB2: North Carolina Facing College Sports Boycott over 'Bathroom Bill,'" BBC News, March 29, 2016, https://www.bbc.com/news/world-us-canada-39430043.

2. Down Home North Carolina, home page, https://downhomenc.org/, accessed January 3, 2024.

3. Down Home North Carolina, "Deep Canvassing: Building Bridges in a Divided Political Landscape," https://downhomenc.org/deep-canvass/, accessed December 24, 2024.

4. Bonnie Dobson interview, Deep Canvas Institute: Resources, https://deep canvass.org/research/, accessed December 24, 2024.

5. Leadership Lab, home page, https://leadership-lab.org/, accessed December 24, 2024.

6. David Broockman and Joshua Kalla, "Durably Reducing Transphobia: A Field Experiment on Door to Door Canvassing," *Science* 32, no. 6282 (April 8, 2016).

7. Brian Resnick, "How to Talk Someone out of Bigotry," *Vox*, January 29, 2020, https://www.vox.com/2020/1/29/21065620/broockman-kalla-deep-canvassing.

8. Resnik, "How to Talk Someone Out of Bigotry."

9. CRT Forward, home page, https://crtforward.law.ucla.edu/, accessed December 24, 2024.

10. ACLU, "Mapping Attacks on LGBTQ Rights in U.S. State Legislatures in 2023," https://www.aclu.org/legislative-attacks-on-lgbtq-rights-2023, accessed December 24, 2024.

CHAPTER 7: SOMATICS

1. "US Capitol Police Clash with Protesters Calling for Gaza War Ceasefire," *Al Jazeera*, November 16, 2023, https://www.aljazeera.com/news/2023/11/16/us -capitol-police-clash-with-protesters-calling-for-gaza-war-ceasefire.

2. Robert Trait, "Protesters Urging Gaza Ceasefire Accuse Washington Police of Violence," *The Guardian US*, November 16, 2023, https://www.theguardian.com /us-news/2023/nov/16/us-capitol-police-clash-protesters-demanding-ceasefire -israel-gaza.

3. Jan Schakowsky, "Schakowsky, Blumenthal Introduce New Bicameral Front-of-Package Food Labeling Legislation to Bolster Americans' Health," press release, https://schakowsky.house.gov/media/press-releases?page=8, accessed December 31, 2024.

4. Generative Somatics, "About Us," http://generativesomatics.org/about-us, accessed December 26, 2024.

5. Richard Strozzi-Heckler, "Generative Somatics/Strozzi Institute Living Lineage," https://static1.squarespace.com/static/5834a25503596e60dce93bb6/t/5fb5201 ce193ce1e00b926b9/1605705757015/gs_ilineage_info.pdf, accessed November 27, 2024.

6. Strozzi-Heckler, "Generative Somatics/Strozzi Institute Living Lineage."

7. Generative Somatics, "What Is a Politicized Somatics?" 2010 and 2014, https://generativesomatics.org/wp-content/uploads/2019/10/Copy-of-What-is-a-politicized-somatics.pdf, accessed November 27, 2024.

8. Prentis Hemphill, Patreon, https://www.patreon.com/prentishemphill/about?l=es, accessed November 27, 2024.

9. Staci K. Haines, *The Politics of Trauma: Somatics, Healing, and Social Justice* (Berkeley, CA: North Atlantic Books, 2019), 19.

10. Generative Somatics Podcast, "Trauma, Healing, and Collective Power," with adrienne maree brown, Spenta Kandawalla, Prentis Hemphill, and Staci K. Haines, https://soundcloud.com/generativesomatics/trauma-healing-collective-power, accessed November 27, 2024.

11. Haines, *The Politics of Trauma*, 257.

12. Eliana Rubin, *Taking the State out of the Body: A Guide to Embodied Resistance to Zionism* (Binghamton, NY: PM Press, 2024).

13. Bruce D. Perry and Oprah Winfrey, *What Happened to You? Conversations on Trauma, Resilience, and Healing* (New York: Flatiron Books, 2021).

14. Perry and Winfrey, *What Happened to You?*, 27.

15. Perry and Winfrey, *What Happened to You?*, 26.

16. Perry and Winfrey, *What Happened to You?*, 29.

17. Bessel Van Der Kolk, *The Body Keeps the Score: Brain, Mind, and Body in the Healing of Trauma* (New York: Penguin, 2015), 46–47, 63–65.

18. Perry and Winfrey, *What Happened to You?*, 142–44.

19. This idea as it applies to unlearning racism is explored extensively in Resmaa Menakem, *My Grandmother's Hands* (Las Vegas: Central Recovery Press, 2017).

CHAPTER 8: PRACTICE

1. Ng'ethe Maina and Staci K. Haines, "The Transformative Power of Practice," Strozzi Institute, https://strozziinstitute.org/the-transformative-power-of-practice/, accessed December 24, 2024.

2. Kelly Hayes and Mariame Kaba, "How Much Discomfort Is the Whole World Worth?" *Boston Review*, September 6, 2023, https://www.bostonreview.net/articles/how-much-discomfort-is-the-whole-world-worth/.

3. adrienne maree brown, *Pleasure Activism: The Politics of Feeling Good* (Chico, CA: AK Press, 2019), 269.

4. Thomas Lewis, Fari Amini, and Richard Lannon, *A General Theory of Love* (New York: Knopf Doubleday, 2007), chapter 6, Kindle edition.

5. Bruce D. Perry and Oprah Winfrey, *What Happened to You? Conversations on Trauma, Resilience, and Healing* (New York: Flatiron Books, 2021), 73.

6. BOLD, "What Is Bold?," https://www.boldorganizing.org/who-we-are#VISION, accessed December 24, 2024.

7. Roxy Manning, *How to Have Antiracist Conversations: Embracing Our Full Humanity to Challenge White Supremacy* (Oakland, CA: Berrett-Koehler, 2023).

8. Joanna Macy and Chris Johnston, *Active Hope: How to Face the Mess We're in Without Going Crazy* (Novato, CA: New World Library, 2022), 3.

CHAPTER 9: POETRY AND SURREALISM

1. *The Art of Tyree Guyton: A Thirty-Year Journey*, University of Michigan, https://umma.umich.edu/exhibitions/the-art-of-tyree-guyton-a-thirty-year-journey/, accessed December 24, 2024; Tyree Guyton: Detroit-based Artist, Tyree Guyton personal website, https://www.tyreeguyton.com/about, accessed December 24, 2024; Tyree Guyton, Heidelberg Project website, https://www.heidelberg.org/tyree-guyton, accessed December 24, 2024.

2. Dawn Ades, "Surrealism, but Not as You Know It," Tate Museum, https://www.tate.org.uk/tate-etc/issue-54-spring-2022/surrealism-not-you-know-it, accessed December 24, 2024.

3. Ian Gibson, *The Shameful Life of Salvador Dalí* (London: Faber & Faber, 1997), 387, 396–97.

4. Robin D. G. Kelley *Freedom Dreams: The Black Radical Imagination* (Boston: Beacon Press, 2002), 5.

5. D. Scot Miller, "A Conversation with Robin D. G. Kelley," SF Moma, May 30, 2017, https://openspace.sfmoma.org/2017/05/a-converstion-with-robin-d-g-kelley/.

6. Kelley, *Freedom Dreams*, 170.

7. Kelley, *Freedom Dreams*, 159–60.

8. Franklin Rosemont, "Surrealists on Whiteness," *Race Traitor* 9, *Special Issue: Surrealism: Revolution Against Whiteness* (Summer 1998): 5, https://files.libcom.org/files/Race%20Traitor%2009%20(1998%20Summer).pdf, accessed December 24, 2024.

9. Penelope Rosemont, *Surrealism: Inside the Magnetic Fields* (San Francisco: City Lights, 2019), 83.

10. The Surrealist Movement in the US, "For Tyree Guyton," *Race Traitor* 9 (Summer 1998): 120–21.

11. The Surrealist Movement in the US, "For Tyree Guyton," 121.

12. Rosemont, "Surrealists on Whiteness," 5.

13. adrienne maree brown, *Pleasure Activism: The Politics of Feeling Good* (Chico, CA: AK Press, 2019), 70.

14. Kai Barrow, Gallery of the Streets website, https://www.galleryofthestreets.org/, accessed December 24, 2024.

15. Amber Baylor, "Centering Women in Prisoners' Rights Litigation," *Michigan Journal of Law* 25, no. 2 (2018): 109–10.

16. Saidiya Hartman, *Lose Your Mother: A Journey Along the Atlantic Slave Route* (New York: Palgrave Macmillan, 2008).

17. Ronnie Burk, "Racist Cliches in the U.S.A.," *Race Traitor 9* (Summer 1998): 71.

18. Muriel Rukeyser, *The Life of Poetry*, 1st Paris Press ed. (Ashfield, MA: Paris Press, 1996), 26.

19. Rosemont, *Surrealism*, 170

20. Rukeyser, *The Life of Poetry*, 49.

CHAPTER 11: ACCESSIBILITY

1. Liberation Spring, https://liberationspring.com/#, accessed March 10, 2025.

2. Liberation Spring, https://liberationspring.com/#, accessed December 24, 2024.